Asian and Pacific Regional Cooperation

Also by Michael Haas

Approaches to the Study of Political Science, edited with Henry S. Kariel (1970)
International Systems: A Behavioral Approach, ed. (1974)
International Conflict (1974)
Basic Documents of Asian Regional Organizations, comp., vols. 1–4 (1974)
Politics and Prejudice in Contemporary Hawai'i, edited with Peter P. Resurrection (1976)
Basic Documents of Asian Regional Organizations, comp., vols. 5–7 (1979)
Fundamentals of Asian Regional Cooperation (1980)
Basic Data of Asian Regional Organizations (1985)
Korean Reunification: Alternative Pathways, ed. (1989), 1st ed.
The Pacific Way: Regional Cooperation in the South Pacific (1989)
The Asian Way to Peace: A Story of Regional Cooperation (1989)
Cambodia, Pol Pot, and the United States: The Faustian Pact (1991)
Genocide by Proxy: Cambodian Pawn on a Superpower Chessboard (1991)
Polity and Society: Philosophical Underpinnings of Social Science Paradigms (1992)
Institutional Racism: The Case of Hawai'i (1992)
Improving Human Rights, ed. (1994)
Deconstructing International Relations Theory, ed. (1997)
Racism, Sexism and Heterosexism, ed. (1997)
The Political Film Today, ed. (1998)
Multicultural Hawai'i: The Fabric of a Multiethnic Society, ed. (1998)
International Human Rights, ed. (1999)
The Singapore Puzzle, ed. (1999)
American Government in Turmoil, ed. (2000)
Discrimination, American Style, ed. (2000)
The Politics of Human Rights, ed. (2000)
Comparing Governments and Global Policies, ed. (2001)
Discrimination and Public Policy, ed. (2001)
Human Rights Imperiled, ed. (2001)
Choices: An American Government Reader, ed. (2001)
International Relations: Arena of Terror, ed. (2002)
International Human Rights in Jeopardy, ed. (2004)
International Human Rights: A Comprehensive Introduction (2008)
George W. Bush, War Criminal? The Bush Administration's Liability for 269 War Crimes (2009)
America's War Crimes Quagmire, From Bush to Obama (2010)
Looking for the Aloha Spirit: Promoting Ethnic Harmony (2010)
Barack Obama, The Aloha Zen President; How a Son of the 50th State May Revitalize America, Based on 12 Multicultural Principles (2011)
Modern Cambodia's Emergence from the Killing Fields: What Happened in the Critical Years? (2011)
Mr. Calm and Effective: Evaluating the Presidency of Barack Obama (2012)
Korean Reunification: Alternative Pathways, ed. (2012), 2nd ed.

Asian and Pacific Regional Cooperation

Turning Zones of Conflict into Arenas of Peace

Michael Haas

palgrave
macmillan

ASIAN AND PACIFIC REGIONAL COOPERATION

First published in 2013 by
PALGRAVE MACMILLAN®
in the United States—a division of St. Martin's Press LLC,
175 Fifth Avenue, New York, NY 10010.

Where this book is distributed in the UK, Europe and the rest of the world, this is by Palgrave Macmillan, a division of Macmillan Publishers Limited, registered in England, company number 785998, of Houndmills, Basingstoke, Hampshire RG21 6XS.

Palgrave Macmillan is the global academic imprint of the above companies and has companies and representatives throughout the world.

Palgrave® and Macmillan® are registered trademarks in the United States, the United Kingdom, Europe and other countries.

ISBN: 978–1–137–30439–1

Library of Congress Cataloging-in-Publication Data is available from the Library of Congress.

A catalogue record of the book is available from the British Library.

Design by Newgen Imaging Systems (P) Ltd., Chennai, India.

First edition: March 2013

10 9 8 7 6 5 4 3 2 1

Dedicated to the memory of seminal theorists
Karl W. Deutsch and Ernst B. Haas

Contents

Illustrations

Figures

Tables

Preface

My books *The Asian Way to Peace: A Story of Regional Cooperation* and *The Pacific Way: Regional Cooperation in the South Pacific* were published in 1989, just as the Cold War was coming to an end. The information about intergovernmental organizations in both publications was derived from interviews and documents collected during several field trips, beginning from 1971. The two books, definitive as of the date of publication, are still the only ones to provide detailed organization charts, membership rosters, and descriptions of programs of the full range of regional organizations in Asia and the Pacific.

However, many developments occurred by 2013. Some organizations changed their names to reflect wider membership. New organizations were born, and earlier ones folded. The need for an update became obvious. But an approach that focuses more on the meaning of regional cooperation than on organizational structures is needed now. Accordingly, I test whether the world pluralism of Karl W. Deutsch or the integration theory of Ernst B. Haas provides the best explanation for successful functional organizations and security communities in Asia and the Pacific.

Meanwhile, other authors have written extensively on regional cooperation in Asia and the Pacific. Most publications have focused on economic issues, and political scientists have written descriptively on various developments in the most highly publicized organizations, yet they have completely ignored important functional organizations. Although my previous publications were also descriptive and nontheoretical, in the present volume I apply the information that I have monitored for several decades to longstanding theoretical frameworks that have so far been dominated by scholars who have pushed their own ideological agendas with no desire to pay any attention to alternative approaches.

Lessons from regional cooperation in Asia and the Pacific need to be learned, not just in these regions but also elsewhere. Because theory is best advanced by testing hypotheses, one important objective herein is to identify testable propositions. With empirical evidence, one can determine which among the various ideologically-derived theories is worthy of support. Without such a critical test, allowing data to determine which theories are close to or distant from the facts, there can be no scientific progress.

Having to catch up with a quarter century of developments without the benefit of a multicountry research trip, I made inquiries by email to get up-to-date information. Accordingly, I wish to express my profound gratitude for information supplied by Hollie Ainslie (Australian Department of Infrastructure and Transport), Romulo N. Aroncon, Jr. (Asian and Pacific Coconut Community), Fred Christopher (Pacific Islands Telecommunication Association), Davaasuren Chultemjamts (Statistical Institute for Asia and the Pacific), Derek Ferrar (East-West Center), John Gresson (Reef Shipping Ltd.), Lisa Harvey (Civil Aviation Safety Authority, Australia), Capt. John Hogan (Secretariat of Pacific Community), LeRoy Hollenbeck (UN Asian and Pacific Centre for Agricultural Engineering and Machinery), Elisa W. Johnston (East-West Center), Surkafa F. Katafono (International Labour Organisation, Suva), Harry Lund (Pacific Islands Chiefs of Police Secretariat), Adrienne Mak and Maureen Mecozzi (AVRDC-World Vegetable Center), Eddie Marahare (Pacific Islands Forum Fisheries Agency), Esther Morrel (South Pacific Tourism Organisation), Pranee Phumbangpa (Asia-Pacific Telecommunity), Professor Peter Pollard (re the Southeast Asia Tin Research and Development Centre), Paul Prouse (New Zealand Civil Aviation Authority), Rachel Tan (Association of Asia Pacific Performing Arts Centres), Naoko Tsuruta (Asian Productivity Organization), Seiuli Alvin W. Tuala (General Manager, Pacific Aviation Safety Office), John van der Heyden (Pacific Island Chiefs of Police), Stuart Valentine (Secretariat of the Pacific Community), Ms. Vasuhi (Asia-Pacific Institute for Broadcasting Development), Kesaia Filsoni (Forum Secretariat), and Dr. Sebastiao Dias Ximenes (Ombudsman or Provedor for Human Rights and Justice, Timor-Leste).

I also wish to thank the press of the University of the South Pacific for permission to extract a portion of my essay "Comparing Regional Cooperation in Asia and the Pacific," which was published in 1986 as a chapter in a collection of conference papers entitled *Toward a World of Peace: People Create Alternatives* and co-edited by Jeanette P. Maas and Robert A. C. Stewart. The analysis in Chapter 7 herein is partly an update from that essay, which primarily tests the security community theory of political scientist Karl W. Deutsch, under whom I studied at Yale University. Although we were acquainted, I am not related to Ernst Haas.

I also wish to commend Yoran Z. Haftel, whose research with a similar focus is extraordinary. Not only did I have a very useful conversation with him prior to finalizing the text herein, but he was also kind enough to send me a final copy of the text of his *Regional Economic Institutions and Conflict Mitigation: Design, Implementation, and the Promise of Peace*, which was published in 2012.

Although I contemplated an update of my earlier publications on the subject some 15 years ago, when developments in Asia and the Pacific were in flux, for various reasons I focused my attention elsewhere. Today, I am happy that I waited for inchoate developments to come to fuller fruition, permitting more solid, substantive, and theoretical contributions. Whether my efforts are worthy of applause I leave to perspicacious readers of the present volume.

MICHAEL HAAS
Los Angeles

Abbreviations

AALCC	Asian African Legal Consultative Committee
AALCO	Asian African Legal Consultative Organization
AARDO	Afro-Asian Rural Development Organization
AARRO	Afro-Asian Rural Reconstruction Organization
ACC	Asian Coconut Community
ACU	Asian Clearing Union
ACW	ASEAN Committee on Women
ADB	Asian Development Bank
ADMM	ASEAN Defense Ministers Meeting
AEC	ASEAN Economic Community
AEM	ASEAN Economic Ministers
AEMM	ASEAN Education Ministers Meeting
AFMM	ASEAN Finance Ministers Meeting
AFTA	ASEAN Free Trade Area
AHMM	ASEAN Health Ministers Meeting
AIBD	Asia-Pacific Institute for Broadcasting Development
AIPA	ASEAN Inter-Parliamentary Assembly
AIPO	ASEAN Inter-Parliamentary Organization
AJC	Asian Judicial Conference
ALAWMM	ASEAN Law Ministers Meeting
ALCC	Asian Legal Consultative Committee
ALMM	ASEAN Labor Ministers Meeting
AMAF	ASEAN Ministerial Meeting on Agriculture and Forestry
AMBDC	Ministerial Meeting on ASEAN Mekong Basin Development Cooperation
AMCA	ASEAN Ministers Responsible for Culture and Arts
AMDA	Anglo-Malayan Defence Agreement
AMDA	Anglo-Malaysian Defence Agreement
AMEM	ASEAN Ministers on Energy Meeting
AMF	Asian Monetary Fund

AMM	ASEAN Ministerial Meeting
AMMDM	ASEAN Ministerial Meeting on Disaster Management
AMME	ASEAN Ministerial Meeting on Environment
AMMin	ASEAN Ministerial Meeting on Minerals
AMMST	ASEAN Ministers Meeting on Science and Technology
AMMSWD	ASEAN Ministerial Meeting for Social Welfare and Development
AMMY	ASEAN Ministerial Meeting on Youth
AMMTC	ASEAN Ministerial Meeting on Transnational Crime
AMRDPE	ASEAN Ministers Meeting on Rural Development and Poverty Elimination
AMRI	ASEAN Ministers Responsible for Information
AMRO	ASEAN+3 Macroeconomic Office
ANRPC	Association of Natural Rubber Producing Countries
ANZUS	Australia, New Zealand, and the United States
AOPU	Asian-Oceanic Postal Union
APCC	Asian and Pacific Coconut Community
APCC	Asian-Pacific Cultural Center
APDC	Asian-Pacific Development Center
APEC	Asia-Pacific Economic Cooperation
APF	Asia Pacific Forum of National Human Rights Institutions
APIL	Association of Pacific Island Legislatures
APMCS	Asian and Pacific Maritime Cooperation Scheme
APO	Asian Productivity Organization
APPF	Asia Pacific Parliamentary Forum
APPU	Asian-Pacific Parliamentarians' Union
APPU	Asian-Pacific Postal Union
APSC	ASEAN Political-Security Community
APT	Asia-Pacific Telecommunity
APTA	Asia-Pacific Trade Agreement
APU	Asian Parliamentarians' Union
ARF	ASEAN Regional Forum
ARTF	Asian Rice Trade Fund
ASA	Association of Southeast Asia
ASC	ASEAN Sociocultural Community
ASCA	Association for Science Cooperation in Asia
ASEAN	Association of South-East Asian Nations
ASEANAPOL	Meeting of the Chiefs of National Police of the ASEAN Countries

ASEM	ASEAN European Meeting
Asian Re	Asian Reinsurance Corporation
ASPAC	Asian and Pacific Council
ATM	ASEAN Transport Ministers Meeting
ATPC	Association of Tin Producing Countries
AUSMIN	Australia-U.S. Ministerial Meeting
AVRDC	Asian Vegetable Research and Development Center
CAC	Central Asian Commonwealth
CAEC	Central Asian Economic Cooperation
CAEU	Central Asian Economic Union
CALM	Conference of Asian Labor Ministers
CAPLM	Conference of Asian and Pacific Labor Ministers
CCAMLR	Commission for the Conservation of Antarctic Marine Living Resources
CCOP	Committee for Co-ordination of Joint Prospecting in Asian Offshore Areas
CCOP/SOPAC	Committee for Co-ordination of Joint Prospecting for Mineral Resources in South Pacific Offshore Areas
CCPASWPR	Conference of Commissioners of Police of Australasia and the South West Pacific Region
CCSBT	Commission for the Conservation of Southern Bluefish Tuna
CENTO	Central Treaty Organization
CEPT	Common Effective Preferential Tariff
CHARM	Customs Heads of Administration Regional Meeting
CIRDAP	Centre for Integrated Rural Development for Asia and the Pacific
CM	Cooperative Mechanism
COORDCOM	Coordinating Committee of Southeast Asian Senior Officials on Transport and Communications
COP to AATHP	Conference of the Parties to the ASEAN Agreement on Transboundary Haze Pollution
C-Plan	Colombo Plan for Co-operative Economic Development in Asia
C-Plan	Colombo Plan for Cooperative Economic and Social Development in Asia and the Pacific
CROP	Council of Regional Organisations in the Pacific
CSTO	Collective Security Treaty Organization

CULSOCEN	Cultural and Social Center for the Asian and Pacific Region
DGCA	Conference of Directors General of Civil Aviation, Asia and Pacific Regions
EAEC	East Asian Economic Caucus
EAEC	Eurasian Economic Community
EAEG	East Asia Economic Group
EALAF	East Asia-Latin America Forum
EAS	East Asia Summit
ECAFE	UN Economic Commission for Asia and the Far East
ECO	Economic Cooperation Organization
ECOCEN	Economic Cooperation Center for the Asian and Pacific Region
ECSC	European Coal and Steel Community
EMEAP	Executives' Meeting of East Asia Pacific Central Banks
EPG	Eminent Persons Group
ESCAP	UN Economic and Social Commission for Asia and the Pacific
EU	European Union
EurAsEC	Eurasian Economic Community
EWC	Center for Cultural and Technology Interchange Between East and West
EWC	Center for Cultural Interchange Between East and West
FAMM	Forum Aviation Ministers Meeting
FAO	Food and Agriculture Organization of the United Nations
FCMM	Forum Communications Ministers Meeting
FEALAC	Forum for East Asia-Latin America Cooperation
FEER	Far Eastern Economic Review
FEMM	Forum Economic Ministers Meeting
FEMM	Forum Education Ministers Meeting
FEMM	Forum Energy Ministers Meeting
FFA	South Pacific Forum Fisheries Agency
FFAMM	Forum Foreign Affairs Ministers Meeting
FFMM	Forum Finance Ministers Meeting
FFTC	Food and Fertilizer Technology Center for the Asian and Pacific Region
FPDA	Five Power Defence Arrangements
FTMM	Forum Trade Ministers Meeting

GATT	General Agreement on Tariffs and Trade
GCJPC	Government Consultation among Jute Producing Countries
IATTC	Inter-American Tropical Tuna Commission
ICC	International Criminal Court
ICFDTTP/ED	Intergovernmental Consultative Forum of Developing Tropical Timber Producing/Exporting Countries
ICJ	International Court of Justice
IFMC	Indochinese Foreign Ministers Conference
IGCC	Southeast Asia Regional Organization for Inter-Governmental Cooperation and Coordination in Family and Population Planning in Southeast Asia
IGO	intergovernmental Organization
ILO	International Labour Organisation
IMC	Interim Mekong Committee
INRO	International Natural Rubber Organization
Interpol	International Criminal Police Organization
IOR-ARC	Indian Ocean Rim Association for Regional Cooperation
IOTC	Indian Ocean Tuna Commission
IPC	International Pepper Community
ITLOS	International Tribunal for the Law of the Sea
ITRO	International Tripartite Rubber Organization
ITTO	International Tropical Timber Organization
ITU	International Telecommunications Union
JCC	Joint Commercial Commission
JSS	Cook Islands/Niue/New Zealand Joint Shipping Service
M-ATM	ASEAN Tourism Ministers Meeting
MEDSEA	Ministerial Conference for the Economic Development of Southeast Asia
METO	Middle East Treaty Organization
MRC	Mekong River Commission
MSG	Melanesian Spearhead Group
NAFTA	North American Free Trade Agreement
NAM	Non-Aligned Movement
NATO	North Atlantic Treaty Organization
NPO	national productivity center
OCAC	Organization of Central Asian Cooperation
OCO	Oceania Customs Organisation

OECD	Organization for Economic Cooperation and Development
OPEC	Organization of Petroleum Exporting Countries
PACER	Pacific Agreement on Closer Economic Relations
PACOM	Pacific-Asian Congress of Municipalities
PASO	Pacific Aviation Safety Office
PBDC	Pacific Basin Development Council
PC	Pacific Community
PC	Pepper Community
PCIJ	Permanent Court of International Justice
PECC	Pacific Economic Cooperation Council
PEMM	Pacific Island Energy Policy and Pacific Energy Ministers Meeting
PFD	Post-Forum Dialogue
PFL	Pacific Forum Line
PIAC	Pacific Islands Aviation Council
PIC	Pacific Islands Conference
PICP	Pacific Islands Chiefs of Police
PICTA	Pacific Island Countries Trade Agreement
PIDB	Pacific Islands Development Bank
PIF	Pacific Islands Forum
PIFFA	Pacific Islands Forum Fisheries Agency
PILMC	Pacific Islands Labour Ministers Conference
PILOM	Pacific Islands Law Officers' Meeting
PILON	Pacific Islands Law Officers' Network
PIPA	Pacific Islands Producers' Association
PITA	Pacific Islands Telecommunications Association
PITAA	Pacific Island Tax Administrators Association
PITDC	Pacific Islands Tourism Development Council
PITIC	Pacific Islands Trade and Investment Commission
PJC	Pacific Judicial Conference
PLG	Polynesian Leaders Group
PMC	Post Ministerial Conference
PREP	Pacific Regional Environmental Programme
RCD	Regional Cooperation for Development
RCGS	Regional Consultative Group on Silk
RCT	Regional Committee on Trade
RIHED	Regional Institute of Higher Education and Development
SAARC	South Asian Association for Regional Cooperation
SCO	Shanghai Cooperation Organization

SEACEN	South East Asian Central Banks Group
SEAFDEC	Southeast Asian Fisheries Development Center
SEAMCED	Ministerial Conference for the Economic Development of Southeast Asia
SEAMEO	Southeast Asian Ministers of Education Organization
SEANZA	Central Banks of Southeast Asia, Australia and New Zealand
SEAPCENTRE	Southeast Asian Promotion Centre for Trade, Investment and Tourism
SEATAC	Southeast Asian Agency for Regional Transport and Communications Development
SEATO	South-East Asia Treaty Organization
SEATRADC	Southeast Asian Tin Research and Development Centre
SGATAR	Study Group on Asian Tax Administration and Research
SIS	Smaller Island States Summit
SOPAC	Pacific Islands Applied Geoscience Commission
SPARTECA	South Pacific Regional Trade and Economic Co-operation Agreement
SPATC	South Pacific Air Transport Council
SPBEA	South Pacific Board for Educational Assessment
SPC	Secretariat of the Pacific Community
SPC	South Pacific Commission
SPCPC	South Pacific Chiefs of Police Conference
SPEC	South Pacific Bureau for Economic Co-operation
SPECTEL	South Pacific Regional Meeting on Telecommunications
SPF	Secretariat of the Pacific Islands Forum
SPF	South Pacific Forum
SPHS	South Pacific Health Service
SPJC	South Pacific Judicial Conference
SPLMC	South Pacific Labour Ministers Conference
SPOCC	South Pacific Organisations Coordinating Committee
SPRCAC	South Pacific Regional Civil Aviation Council
SPREP	Secretariat of the Pacific Regional Environmental Programme
SPREP	South Pacific Regional Environmental Programme
SPRSC	South Pacific Regional Shipping Council
SPTC	South Pacific Trade Commission
SPTO	South Pacific Tourism Organisation
SwPD	Southwest Pacific Dialogue

TC	Tripartite Council
TCCC	Taxation and Customs Cooperation Conference
TCSP	Tourism Council of the South Pacific
TIFA	Trade and Investment Framework Agreement
TELMIN	ASEAN Telecommunications and IT Ministers Meeting
TTPI	Trust Territory of the Pacific Islands
UK	United Kingdom of Great Britain and Northern Ireland
UN	United Nations
UNCTAD	UN Conference on Trade and Development
UNESCO	UN Educational, Scientific and Cultural Organization
UNMOGIP	UN Military Observer Group in India and Pakistan
UPU	Universal Postal Union
US	United States
USA	United States of America
USP	University of the South Pacific
USSR	Union of Soviet Socialist Republics
WCPFC	Western and Central Pacific Fisheries Commission
WTO	World Trade Organization
ZOPFAN	Zone of Peace, Freedom and Neutrality

Part I

Theories

After World War II, there was a belief that Europe could not abide yet another world war. Yet the division between the communist Eastern Europe and capitalist Western Europe meant that both were armed to the teeth, even rattling nuclear weapons as modern-day sabers.

Responses to the challenge differed. Division into two superpowers was the immediate reaction, but that kept the world in an uneasy suspense over who would prevail and where. A second response was reliance on the United Nations (UN) to mediate or at least to mitigate divisions, but the UN was divided between the Eastern and Western blocs of countries, and a third bloc of nonaligned states wanted attention directed toward them. Some envisioned a "United States of Europe," but that meant dismantling sovereign states that had spent centuries guarding their borders from attack. A less ambitious plan was to bring about some economic and social unity through regional organizations without political unification.

A flood of academic writing developed to promote regional organizations in Europe. Leaders in Africa, the Americas, Asia, the Middle East, and the South Pacific found reasons to develop regional institutions as well. One of the reasons is that Chapter VIII of the UN Charter serves to integrate regional organizations into the world's global polity. Very recently, one scholar has maintained that Chapter VIII permits regional intergovernmental bodies to act on security matters when the UN's Security Council is deadlocked, provided that the Security Council is officially notified (Slaughter 2012). Thus, an analysis of how regional organizations handle interstate conflicts is vital to the maintenance of global peace and security today. Accordingly, this volume seeks to determine how regional organizations in Asia and the Pacific have turned zones of conflict into arenas of peace over the past five decades.

Chapter 1 in this section of the book summarizes several theoretical approaches. Chapter 2 applies cultural elements, sometimes left out of discussions by theorists who focus on Europe, to regional cooperation in Asia and the Pacific.

1

International and Regional Cooperation

Arenas of Peace

World peace has been a goal for millennia. The continents of the Americas, Africa, Asia, and Europe are so vast that the most practical way to bring incessant warfare to an end would be to hope that small arenas of peace will be established and grow in size.

In a quantitative analysis, my study found that the most peaceful eras in world history have been unipolar—dominated by a single country (M.Haas 1970), though, of course, those dominated were usually unhappy. A multipolar world, according to the data, is the least peaceful. The level of conflict in a bipolar world, such as the Cold War division between Soviet and Western spheres of influence, falls between the unipolar and multipolar worlds.

World War II engulfed almost every corner of the globe. Afterward, bipolar Europe remained at relative peace. Asia was home to the most international conflicts, involving China, India-Pakistan, Indonesia, Korea, Vietnam, and various border conflicts. Yet, except for the ongoing war in Afghanistan and recent flare-ups on the Korean peninsula, Asia has enjoyed an almost continuous period of peace for the last two decades.

Although the island states of the Pacific remained calm since the battles of World War II, internal conflicts have recently erupted in Fiji, Papua, Papua New Guinea, and the Solomon Islands. In all four cases, the conflicts have not spilled over to other countries.

There are several reasons why the zone of conflict in Asia has become an arena of peace similar to that in the Pacific. One of the most important is the rise of friendly relations among countries of both regions, as developed through intergovernmental cooperative arrangements. The present volume seeks to explain how and even why this has occurred.

The Rise of International Cooperation

There was a time when empires in the Americas (the Aztecs and the Incas), Asia (China and India), Europe (Rome), and the Middle East (Egypt and Persia) arose when one state could impose its domain over previously independent states. Dynastic rulers in China and India succeeded in creating unified empires where once there were warring states. Both efforts to unify Asia, which date back to 2,500 years ago, constitute major achievements in international statecraft (Bozeman 1960:Ch4; Grousset 1953; Spear 1960).

When no such dominance was possible within a geographic region, interimperial conflict prevailed. Rulers were considered "sovereigns" who could not be challenged. Cooperation among hegemony-seeking empires was not the norm.

With the rise of technological advances in warfare, prosperous countries acquired the means to resist imperial ambitions on the basis of various defense systems. One result in Europe was the Peace of Westphalia of 1648, an agreement to stop endless wars by accepting nation-states rather than rulers as sovereign, while ignoring whether their rulers required subjects to be Catholic or Protestant. Thus, the current states system developed when European countries and empires tired of endless warfare, decided to recognize states as the legitimate units of an international society, and promised not to interfere in the affairs of other countries. In other words, European powers sought an arena of peace.

But the most advanced European states then extended imperial control overseas to engulf the non-European world, stressing global rather than regional ambitions in a scramble for colonies that trampled on the sovereignty of non-European peoples. In time, those colonized resisted, starting in the Americas, whereupon Europe began to accept governments of the new states into the states system.

Proposals to unite warring European states into peacemaking arrangements appeared from the Middle Ages to the nineteenth century,

conflict → great-power intervention → peace

Figure 1.1 Congress of Vienna model.

such as those of philosophers Dante, Immanuel Kant, and the duc de Sully. They consisted of pious plans for intergovernmental organizations (IGOs) of states to resolve conflicts short of war. After the Napoleonic Wars, the major powers met at the Congress of Vienna in 1815 to reestablish the Westphalian acceptance of individual states within defined borders and an agreement to enforce that order with force after multilateral consultation among the great powers. The major powers, thus, took responsibility for assuring peace in Europe (see Figure 1.1). But the Vienna system of multistate cooperation broke down quickly because of conflict among the major powers.

Simón de Bolívar's concept of a federation of South American states led to a conference at Panamá in 1826. His objective was to promote the solidarity of the newly independent states of South America. The legacy of his effort is an array of cooperative, regional international organizations in Latin America, beginning with the Pan American Union of 1890, which set an example for other regions.

The calamity of World War I persuaded countries to establish a League of Nations in order to avoid future wars. But the United States refused to join the League, and colonized people were excluded because they lacked sovereignty.

After World War II, the United Nations emerged as an organization with nearly universal membership, committed to ending colonialism and thereby achieving universality. In 1949, the Council of Europe was formed, bringing Western European countries together, though countries in Eastern Europe did not join until the Cold War ended.

When large numbers of new states in Africa and Asia became independent, regional organizations of states formed in those regions. The island nations of the South Pacific are the latest to form regional bodies. The most, notable is the South Pacific Forum (SPF) in 1971, which changed its name to Pacific Islands Forum (the Forum) in 2000 as island states in the North Pacific joined the organization, emerging from the UN trusteeship system administered as a "strategic trust" by the United States.

Nowadays, the international arena consists of three main elements—individual countries organized as states, the United Nations and other

IGOs, and such nongovernmental organizations (NGOs) as Amnesty International that try to influence both states and IGOs. Some IGOs and NGOs have been universal in membership, but others have been specific to certain regions. Very few have been biregional or transregional.

What regional organizations have shared in common is the view that the League and the United Nations have encompassed too many countries for consensus to develop on matters of intimate importance among states within various geographic regions. For some countries, unwelcome domination by Western countries in the UN was reason enough to form separate regional bodies. Conflict was globalized during the Cold War, so some regions sought to uncouple themselves from East-West entanglements in order to establish an arena of peace.

When I embarked on a study of regional organizations in Asia during 1971 on behalf of the Carnegie Endowment for International Peace and the UN Institute for Training and Research, one view at the UN New York headquarters was that regional organizations were disrupting the need to build a world community. The term "regionalism" was used, as if the formation of regional bodies was some form of ideological dissent from the universalism of the UN. After I submitted my report, published several years later (M.Haas 1979), the UN shifted perspective, realizing that regional organizations were building a regional spirit that was a precondition for the development of a true world community. Indeed, as my report had recommended, the UN began to provide assistance to regional organizations, and symbiosis between regional and universal organizations became the goal and the reality.

Asia was transformed from a zone of war into an arena of peace, thanks particularly to the Association of South-East Asian Nations (ASEAN).[1] The Pacific islands region was fortunate to be at peace after World War II, and regional cooperation has ensured that the Pacific has not become a zone of interstate conflict.

Approaches to the Study of International Cooperation

Scholarship on regional international organizations initially consisted of accounts of the basic structure and purposes of regional arrangements, largely without overt theoretical considerations (M.Haas 1971:Part E). Descriptive accounts of particular organizations prevailed.

conflict → IGOs → peace

Figure 1.2 International organization model.

When I wrote such an essay about the Asian Development Bank (ADB) (M.Haas 1974a) without employing a theoretical approach, the editor of a scholarly journal agreed to publish my work as a representative of an old-fashioned genre that needed to be respected, though the call for more theoretical research was increasing (M.Haas 1974b).

Pervading academic writing on international organizations for several decades was the view that nation-states are, at best, passé. Whether to promise greater security or to urge countries to seek peace, some scholars of international relations propounded the view that nations should abandon nationalism and band together for the human race to survive. Regional and universal organizations are often seen as realistic stepping stones toward a unified and peaceful world (see Figure 1.2).

Integration Theory

In *The Uniting of Europe* (1958), Ernst Haas saw the formation of the European Coal and Steel Community (ECSC) as a possible first step toward a world that might ultimately abolish the nation-state (cf. E. Haas 1974). In what is known as **integration theory**, Haas and others began to analyze how regional institutions might proceed toward the objective of political union (see Figure 1.3). ECSC, they argued, would begin to do so by having economic powers over governments, that is, by forming supranational regional entities.

The goal of ultimate **political integration** was presumed to be achievable through **economic integration**, that is, the abolition of trade barriers by such arrangements as customs unions, common markets, and free trade agreements. National sovereignty on economic matters was to be surrendered to a supranational authority. Consistent with their vision, there was a progression from ECSC to the European Economic Community and then to the European Community and

conflict → regional organizations → regional integration → peace

Figure 1.3 International integration model.

finally to the European Union (EU). The goal of economic integration was advanced thereby. So persuasive was integration theory that the same perspective was applied to regional efforts outside Europe (E.Haas 1961; E.Haas and Schmitter 1964; E. Haas 1975; Nye 1971; cf. Schmitter 2005). Visionaries saw the process ultimately as a global effort that would bring about a peaceful world.

Political integration was assumed to result as states increasingly surrendered slivers of sovereignty. Yet political integration of sovereign states was not achieved. By the mid-1970s, Ernst Haas (1976) questioned whether a focus on political integration should continue. Soon, integration theory was all but abandoned.

After all, how could a disunited world of sovereign states ever bring about a peaceful globe? Unpacking the assumptions of integration theorists and others, there are two main **strategies**—working within the existing nation-state system or transcending nation-states to establish a new type of international polity. The **methods** of achieving greater unity have stressed either military means, political negotiations, or socioeconomic penetration. Thus, there are at least six ways in which the world might become an arena of peace (see Table 1.1).

The **hegemonism** of a Rome and the **imperialism** of a Great Britain are inhumane and overly bloody pathways toward world unification. World War II proved that hegemonic methods are obsolete. The vulnerability of colonized peoples to be conquered by new hegemons also suggested that imperialism should be eliminated. Therefore, those in the quest for world peace considered four alternative approaches:

1. **Federalists** believe that separate political states must be unified. The federalist approach envisions the formal transfer of political authority to regional or global institutions and is a direct, constitutional attack on national sovereignty. The unification of the

Table 1.1 Forms of international cooperation

Strategy	*Methods of Cooperation*		
	Military	*Political*	*Socioeconomic*
transcend nation-states	hegemonism	federalism	world pluralism
work within the existing nation-state system	imperialism	intergovernmentalism	functionalism

13 American colonies, into a confederation and later a federation, is seen as the paradigm most appropriate at the international level, since peace might be maintained if a global authority had a monopoly on the use of force. Federalists espouse two tactical methods. **Compact federalists** urge world leaders to agree to a unified federal world through the "high politics" of diplomacy and international conferences to write a world constitution (Streit 1943; Hutchins 1948). **Functional federalists** would take one policy arena at a time, seeking to build up a federal supranational authority to deal with each issue-area, from agricultural policy to water policy, that is, on matters of "low politics" (Etzioni 1965; Friedrich 1968). Either way, the result would be a supranational entity with power over all previous states.

Within Asia, a federal approach hardly seems realistic. The only example is the unification of sultanates under the Union of Malaya (1946), later the Federation of Malaya (1948), and still later the Federation of Malaysia (1963). In the latter case, Indonesia mobilized troops, characterizing the formation of Malaysia as an act of neocolonialism. The Philippines even severed diplomatic ties with Malaysia when the latter added Sabah as a federal state. In addition, two years later, Singapore was expelled from the Federation. Brunei decided not to join Malaysia, remaining under British rule, and regained self-rule on January 1, 1984. Although Singapore formed a common market with Malaysia after the two parted company, within two years the common market was dissolved.

Leaders of North and South Korea, seeking unification, have proposed confederation or federation over the years. But no such arrangement is possible until the Korean War ends with a peace treaty and the United States withdraws its military forces (M.Haas 2012).

2. **Intergovernmentalists** respect the sovereignty of nation-states but expect that few supranational powers will ever be conferred on a central body. At best, they envision a confederation. Such IGOs as the United Nations allow countries to join and make global decisions together. But compliance with decisions made by IGOs is voluntary. The agenda for intergovernmentalists, therefore, is to build an overwhelming international political consensus around the view that states should concede some sovereignty to have joint decisions enforced by a body that they trust (cf. Hoffmann 1965; Moravscik 1991; Garrett and Tsebelis 1996; Grieco 1993; Mearsheimer 1994/1995:5; Tsebelis and Garrett 2001). A related approach is baptized the "empirical system

approach" (Cantori and Spiegel 1973). Intergovernmentalism is often based on "realism," an approach drawing on the ideological perspective of Hans Morgenthau (1948).

Thus, the United Nations acts as an intergovernmental entity when members make decisions that lead to concrete actions, such as allocating contributions to units of the organization or having peacekeepers wear blue helmets while keeping the peace in conflict zones. Acceptance of a common currency, the Euro within the European Union, is an example of a supranational confederation. The World Trade Organization (WTO) has set up an enforcement mechanism in which countries are supposed to take sanctions against any country found to be violating the rules, but the imposition of sanctions is up to individual states. In all three cases, intergovernmental authority over nation-states could collapse if the UN, the EU, or the WTO made foolish decisions that were out of sync with a significant part of the world. The United States, for example, refuses to accept the supranational jurisdiction of the International Criminal Court (ICC), thus limiting that body's full potential.

Those who favor the intergovernmental approach over the federal as more realistic believe that leaders of states will only surrender slivers of sovereignty. Sliver by sliver, but not irrevocably, an intergovernmental world polity might ultimately become confederal or federal, but intergovernmentalists doubt that governments will ever give up their sovereignty permanently (cf. Grieco 1993; Mearsheimer 1994/1995). Some intergovernmentalists concede that IGOs can contribute to world peace, but only to a conditional, limited extent (Glaser 1994/1995; Jervis 1999). Some try to prove their point by engaging in broad quantitative analyses that ignore case studies and thereby miss the reality (cf. Singer and Wallace 1970; Domke 1988; Gartzke, Li, and Boehmer 2001).

IGOs can operate formally or informally. Informal IGOs consist of regularized **conferences** of leaders with some authority in their countries to discuss matters of international significance. The leaders may vary from police chiefs to cabinet members to heads of the countries. Meetings of heads of government are known as "summit conferences." Coordination of informal IGOs is usually done by the country hosting the conference. Committees of the conference may report to the plenary sessions of conferences. Elsewhere, I have referred to such informal IGOs as **conferocracies** (M.Haas 1989a:Ch12).

Formal IGOs are intergovernmental **institutions** with permanent structures. Minimally, a formal IGO will have a Secretariat located in one of the member countries. Some IGOs also set up study centers, whether alongside the host country of the Secretariat or in other member countries.

3. **World pluralism**, in contrast, assumes that the term "nation-state" is an oxymoron, since few states have only one national group within their borders. The fundamental causes of war for the pluralists lie within domestic conditions of states (Fisher 1969), so efforts should be undertaken to weaken loyalty to states and strengthen bonds that transcend states. Pluralists agree with federalists that it is important to deal with issues of power politics whenever possible, but pluralists seek an expansion of cooperation into many issues and tasks, avoiding any direct confrontation wherein states would be forced to transfer what they regard as their precious sovereignty to an international body. Pluralists hope that patterns of interaction will make peace an imperative by establishing a community spirit on a regional and ultimately a global basis.

Pluralists focus on **regionalization**, the growth of integrated clusters of states within the global polity, and **globalization**, the building of a world community. Proponents of globalization hope that regional clusters will develop into interregional arrangements and then merge or that pluralism will extend worldwide. There are four types of pluralists, depending on the form of regionalization or globalization—social, cultural, security, and transactional. All four agree that unifying IGOs emerge from regionalized patterns of interaction.

For **social pluralists**, increased social interaction is the precondition for more intense political cooperation. Karl Deutsch, a Prague-born German fluent in Czech and German, constructed an argument to counter Adolf Hitler's claim that Germany should rule over areas where Germans lived in Czechoslovakia. From his experience, Sudetenlanders and others of German origin in Czechoslovakia interacted with Czechs more than across the border with Germans. Observing the growth of regional institutions in Europe after 1945, he argued that governments collaborate closely together only after peoples have developed regionalized social communication patterns. In support of his approach, he pointed to numerous illustrations of the rise of nationalism in Europe, such as the process by which smaller German and Italian states merged into larger states (Deutsch 1953,

1954). Thus, social pluralists expect that informal communications across borders, such as telephone calls, promote an increased desire within nations to develop better relations with neighboring countries. As states become more mutually responsive through greater contact across their borders, more pressure will build to perceive such ties as fraternal to the point when unification will seem practical and desirable. Later, Deutsch and associates (1957) broadened the approach beyond social pluralism (see Chapter 7 below).

In contrast, **cultural pluralism** believes that common traditions and cultural values underpin increases in social communication. Although former adversaries may achieve a pluralistic détente, such a step will be short-lived unless both nations see their common characteristics, traditions, and values as more salient and rooted in a regionalized fraternal bond among the peoples (cf. Downs, Rocke, and Barsoom 1996; Solidum 1974). One scholar refers to cultural pluralism as "culturalism" (Emmerson 2006:11).

IGOs composed of democratic states have the advantage of a common political culture, but so do IGOs formed among likeminded authoritarian governments. When countries are transitioning from authoritarian to democratic regimes, however, cultural affinities are often blurred. Some researchers have found that transitional democracies are more likely to engage in interstate conflict than either democracies or autocracies (Mansfield and Snyder 1995, 2002).

Within Asia, cultural pluralism was cultivated by the governments of Indonesia and Malaysia in the period after their confrontation in 1962–1966. In both countries, the Malay race is predominant, and the Malay language was unified into a single tongue. Cross-border travel for a period of up to one week was soon undertaken without a visa. Later, the same visa-free travel was adopted among all other members of Association of South-East Asian Nations (ASEAN). Indeed, the goal of ASEAN has been to break down artificial barriers between the countries of Southeast Asia by stressing common cultural characteristics. The same cultural emphasis pervades South Pacific regional organizations headquartered in Island countries. Chapter 2 in this volume provides more details on how cultural pluralism works in both regions.

Of course, the merger of social with cultural pluralism can be characterized as **sociocultural pluralism**. In addition, the focus on styles of governance, in particular democracy and good governance (accountable government), can be labeled **sociopolitical pluralism**.

For **security pluralists**, countries are likely to cooperate if they band together in the face of common enemies (Waltz 1979; Wallander and Keohane 1999:30–32; Fortna 2004:31; Lake 1997:53–55). Military alliances cement ties, regionalizing security, especially when a severe military threat is viewed as imminent or probable. However, when the danger lessens, the alliance will be viewed as less urgent, and the desire to maintain unity will peter out. In addition, alliances often have strong and weak members, producing tensions of the sort that eventually destroyed the South-East Asia Treaty Organization (SEATO). Alliances against threats mean that counter-alliances may exist, so the formation of alliances could provoke wars. Military pacts are temporary détentes at best. An Orwellian world of countries stuck inside alliances cannot easily evolve into an arena of peace.

For **transactional pluralists**, such as nineteenth-century philosopher Richard Cobden (1835), economic integration in the form of increased trade is the key to expanding cooperation between nations. For Norman Angell (1910) and others (Crescenti 2005; Polachek 1980), lucrative trade discourages interstate conflict that might disrupt economies. Thus, governments will seek to promote and protect trade with other countries in order to advance the prosperity of the people. Lowering trade barriers, the argument goes, will lead to a more peaceful world. Some argue that democracies never go to war with one another because they preserve free markets and thereby create trade patterns so vast that war becomes unprofitable and thereby unthinkable (Gartzke 1998). Others contend that IGOs promoting world trade serve to advance world peace thereby, though some argue that the IGOs must have institutional elements that provide platforms of diplomatic dialog toward that end (e.g., Haftel 2012). Transactional pluralists, in other words, favor economic regionalization as a stepping stone toward a peaceful world with universal economic globalization.

However, Johan Galtung (1973) has thrown cold water on transactional pluralism in his analysis of the movement toward a European Common Market. He argues that greed and profits, not idealism, motivate those trying to unify Europe economically. He has warned that transactional pluralism may stoke competition that might backfire when some countries fail to maintain comparative advantage in what they produce.

All four types of pluralists hope that regionalization and globalization will inexorably lead to world peace, serving as preconditions for institutional arrangements. For pluralists, informal patterns of interstate association and interaction cry out for regularization through international bodies. After IGOs are formed, the experience of cooperation within institutions will serve as an impetus for even more regionalized ties among member countries. Although regionalization may be irrelevant if leaders of states set up IGOs solely for expedient reasons, the goal of conflict resolution may be strengthened on balance when organizations build on the pluralism of regionalization (Mansfield, Pevehouse, and Bierce 1999/2000; Russett, Oneal, and Davis 1998).

4. **Functionalism** envisages a process in which institutions are created on a rational basis first, and pluralistic communities of experts from many countries then develop close associations and friendships. The functionalist scenario is one in which international cooperation will grow more rapidly and will be more irreversibly effective if the scope of initial concern is confined to low-priority sectors of public policy where grants of sovereignty to an intergovernmental body are relatively inconsequential in their impact upon sovereignty (Mitrany 1943). Functionalists believe that federal and confederal solutions have failed because they require cooperation exclusively at levels of "high politics" wherein states must surrender their sovereignty and sacrifice vital interests. There are four variants of functionalism—classical functionalism, neofunctionalism, multifunctionalism, and institutional functionalism.

Classical functionalists advocate IGOs in such areas as international postal traffic in which questions about power politics are unlikely to be raised. Functional organizations can be formed with ease because they will not threaten any state, while providing assistance in matters of a technical nature. As functionally specific organizations grow, according to functionalists, a web of activities and agencies will be sewn across the globe. Success in one functional area will then "spill around" to other areas. For example, cooperation in the arts within a region of the world will inevitably enhance the need for regional cooperation in matters of education. As functional bodies multiply, what was once perceived as a matter of high politics can be depoliticized in practice, since technical experts will do a better job of handling international problems than politicians. While legal sovereignty will continue to reside in nation-states, effective responsibility in each issue-area would be assumed increasingly by the technical bodies. Peace will come in pieces (cf. Nye 1971), for at some indefinite time in the future, the experts will favor integrating all the piecemeal linkages into a single, standardized framework—the new, unified world polity. Unlike federalism and pluralism, functionalism assigns a minor role to state leaders. Technical experts, without even perceiving that their decisions are politicizable, will find solutions to problems of human welfare in a process of task self-determination. The loyalties of the ordinary citizens, hence, will in due course shift away from nation-states toward the overlay of international agencies. Sovereignty will wither away from states, leading to the establishment of a true world community.

Neofunctionalism contends that functionalists are naïve because no regional or international organization can grow or derive adequate funding without strong political backing from top government leaders. IGOs among experts in social and economic issue-areas may serve as a prelude to the ultimate formation of organizations within politically sensitive matters—but only when leaders of member countries pay attention to what they are doing (E.Haas 1964; E.Haas and Schmitter 1966; Nye 1971; Schmitter 1971). Neofunctionalists predict that success in less controversial areas, particularly in economic matters, will "spill over" into political matters when leaders recognize that the risk of potential "spillback" cannot be tolerated. Gains secured through economic cooperation, for example, must be cemented by support from powerful domestic interests to prevent an erosion of support in the future. Neofunctionalists see folly in separating technical matters from politics. By making political capital out of the success of functional cooperation, the speed of growth in international organizations and the movement toward a unified commonwealth will be greatly accelerated, according to the neofunctionalists. Unlike federalists, neofunctionalists pay little attention to legalistic or constitutional implications of any particular success, for in time charters and treaties, always perceived as makeshift, can be revised and strengthened. As a new international bureaucracy arises to administer functional organizations, the public in member countries will place increasing trust in the good sense and objectivity of international civil servants as harbingers of world peace. So the argument goes among scholars who have sought to generalize from the case study of the growth of the European Economic Community into the European Union. Nevertheless, neofunctionalists maintain that the scope of such intergovernmental bodies will initially be restricted to the original issue-areas. Political support is needed for expansion beyond the original activities and tasks in that issue-area before moving forward to other issue-areas. Ernst Haas (1976), indeed, reported that European organizations formed to advance economic goals consistently resisted efforts to increase the scope to political matters, so his eagerness for a "United States of Europe" was frustrated, and he later abandoned his integration "pre-theory" approach.

Multifunctionalism is a third variant, more ambitious in expectations than functionalism or neofunctionalism. Multifunctionalists believe that few organizations in single issue-areas will ever expand beyond the limited design of founding members. Similar to neofunctionalists, multifunctionalists anticipate that IGOs will take on new tasks and new members only when political will is strong. In addition, as more issues and tasks are adopted by an organization, there will be more of value for member countries old and new (Hurrell 2001; Martin 1994).

The League of Nations was formed with a limited assignment, preventing war, but developed some subsidiary bodies relating to refugees and other matters. Meanwhile, the Permanent Court of International Justice (PCIJ), the International Labour Organisation (ILO), and other international bodies remained outside the framework of the League. The UN, from inception, was multifunctional, and the ILO became one of several "Specialized Agencies of the United Nations."

Within Asia and the Pacific, ASEAN and the Forum started modestly, but today are multifunctional. (Chapter 5 of the present volume explains how.) Multifunctional organizations that bring together government leaders have the potential to resolve interstate or even intrastate conflicts, as the UN has done so. Chapter 6 identifies wherein ASEAN and the Forum have asserted conflict-resolution capabilities. At the same time, political unification is not the ultimate goal of multifunctionalism.

A fourth form of functionalism may be identified as **institutional functionalism**. The basic premise is that the design of an IGO is critical in achieving results. Yoran Haftel (2012), for example, finds that regional economic organizations with formal Secretariats are more successful than those without, and he finds that frequent top-level leader interactions within an organizational context improve the chances for results.

The earliest institutional functionalist was Johan Galtung (1973:Ch2), who argued that the creation of functional organizations has a definite sequence, rather than a gradual spillover (neofunctionalism) or spillaround (classical functionalism). His "staircase" theory was that organizations that broaden membership inevitably must respond to new members by deepening tasks that define the IGO, including the adoption of new issue-areas. New issue-areas, in turn, will attract new members. This zigzag resembles a staircase of gradually increasing organizational goals and membership size. Thus, staircase functionalism is realistic about organizational growth: New countries will not be admitted to membership until all problems among existing members are ironed out within the various issue-areas. New members are likely to press for a deepening in scope, which in turn might produce spillback if an inadequate consensus existed among previous members. The staircase pathway, thus, suggests how neofunctionalist task expansion comes about empirically. Staircase functionalism can also be used to describe how single-issue IGOs become multifunctional.

In classical functionalism, there is no hurry to politicize, whereas in neofunctionalism and multifunctionalism, the quest to expand tasks requires approval from political leaders. According to staircase functionalism, a new member country of an organization must be prepared to accept things as they are initially, but the newest countries are expected to want attention to be directed to new issue-areas that will most benefit them. Galtung describes the upward-moving escalator in his analysis of the growth of the original European Economic Community, both in issue-areas and membership. Thus today, to achieve true multifunctionality, the European Union must gain acceptance of a more comprehensive treaty that would transform the scope of the organization.

Institutional functionalism has become popular among those who look at the procedural elements of regional organizations (Acharya and Johnson 2007; Aggarwal and Koo 2008; Bearce and Omori 2005; Breitmeir, Underdal, and Young 2011; Fortna 2004; Haftel 2007, 2010; Koremenos, Lipson, and Snidal 2001; Moravscik 1994; Tsebelis and Garrett 2007). They seek to identify key elements that can optimally make IGOs more productive.

Research Agenda

The six major approaches to world peace are familiar to many students of international and regional cooperation. However, thus far they have been espoused ideologically, that is, believed fervently without any attempt to test them empirically with any rigor. Realist, neoliberalist, and constructivist scholars, similarly, follow an ideology, and eschew critical proposition testing, that is, research designs that pit predictions of one theory against another. Following up on the superb quantitative efforts of Yoran Haftel (2007, 2012), later chapters of the present volume bring the various lofty ideas into the realm of empirical analysis.

Of the six major approaches to world peace, history proves that the use of military means has failed to bring peace because no continuously peaceful unipolar system has ever prevailed for long. Dominant states, whether hegemons or empires, have always maintained armies to suppress revolts from peoples who disliked being governed by elites in far off lands. Federalism has been tried in some countries with success, but world federalism is unlikely until states get tired of maintaining their sovereignty, and that day has not yet arrived.

Thus, several approaches appear to compete for acceptance as passageways for peace—intergovernmentalism, four types of pluralism, and four types of functionalism. As ideologically driven approaches, the debate could go on indefinitely. But the time has come to end such wrangling and to test alternative approaches empirically, using case study data and statistics.[2]

One hypothesis, for example, is that increased pluralism is a precondition for growth in the membership and scope of intergovernmental, supranational, and functional organizations. Proponents of confederation and functionalism maintain the opposite hypothesis. But which type of pluralism and which functional pathway?

An interesting example of empirical research has recently been offered by economists Won-Ho Kim, Heungchong Kim, and Jehoon Park (2011), who use the term "integration" to mean "regionalization."[3] What interests them is the extent of commonality in six subregions—ASEAN, East Asia, the European Union, Mercosur, North American Free Trade Agreement (NAFTA), and Northeast Asia.[4] Their analysis bears scrutiny.

Across three time periods, they compute quantitative measures of regionalization that are closely related to the four types of pluralism identified above. They then determine which forms of regionalization are helpful and which provide barriers to advancing regionalization.

Perhaps their most startling finding is that economic (financial) integration is unrelated to institutional integration, contradicting observers

Table 1.2 Regionalization in six subregions

Subregion	*Types of Regionalization*			
	Sociocultural	*Political-Security*	*Institutional*	*Financial*
East Asia	X			
N.E Asia	X			
NAFTA	X	X		X
Mercosur	X	X	X	
ASEAN	X	X	X	
EU	X	X	X	X

Key: X means that the characteristic is present.

who believe that greater regional economic interdependence leads to regional institutions or the reverse (cf. Deutsch et al. 1957; E.Haas 1964). Conventional wisdom has been that greater economic interdependence through increased trade, especially after the end of the Cold War and the formation of the WTO, has had a profound impact on regional IGOs focused on economic goals (cf. Kahler 2000).

The three economists report that East Asia and Northeast Asia have the lowest levels of regionalization on all four measures, whereas the EU has the highest levels of regionalization. ASEAN, Mercosur, and NAFTA fall in between (see Table 1.2). More revealingly, the study also can be interpreted to determine which types of pluralism best predict the establishment of other forms of pluralism. Although a crude test of alternative theories, their findings appear to support cultural pluralism as the precondition to all other forms of pluralism. Security pluralism is necessary before either institutional (social pluralism) or financial (transactional pluralism) regionalization. The pattern is almost a perfect Guttman scale.

Beyond Integration Theory to Cooperation Theory

Before examining Asian and Pacific regional organizations, there should be clarity that the term "integration" has a very special meaning in Asia and the Pacific—and with a decidedly pejorative connotation. Indeed, the term evokes images of imperial domination by Western powers or hegemonic subordination to dynastic rulers of China and India in the period before Western control. The imperial powers took control of domestic economics and politics, whereas China allowed local political autonomy so long as economic tribute was paid to dynastic authorities. In the 1920s, the Japanese conception of the Greater East Asia Co-Prosperity Sphere constituted another scheme of economic integration, one by which Tokyo wanted to end Western imperial control in the region. But implementation of Japan's goal by military force from the 1930s was entirely distasteful. Asians, now and then, have not wanted to trade one form of external domination with another and have been cautious about adopting integration proposals lest the scheme provide disproportionate benefits to some countries.

Hence, the notion of **regional integration** is resisted in Asia and the Pacific as are dependency and exploitation in other parts of the developing world. In an analysis of 42 African international organizations, Louis Sohn (1971–1972) found that the goal of regional institutions is to preserve rather than erode sovereignty by shielding member countries from outside influences (cf. Acharya and Johnson 2007:262; Hansen 1969). In the mid-1970s, Ernst Haas (1975) wrote that political integration theory had become "obsolescent" for Western Europe, as economic goals had become paramount over political integration, and his judgment has indeed been vindicated.

Regional cooperation, in contrast, has positive connotations in Asia and the Pacific, implying that likeminded countries will get together to develop means by which they can jointly promote peace and prosperity. Intergovernmental cooperation has been effectively practiced in functional regional organizations (see Figure 1.4).

Regimes and Global Governance

As a result of the disenchantment with political integration theory, a new form of scholarship emerged. The focus shifted from international and regional organizations to international and regional **regimes**. Many former integration theorists looked at arenas for international cooperation first, similar to functionalists, and then located the forms of cooperation working within each issue-area to assess their effectiveness. The journal *International Organization* introduced the new focus in the Summer 1974 issue. Subsequently, special issues followed

conflict → regional organizations → cooperation → peace

Figure 1.4 Regional cooperation model.

with essays on oceans (Spring 1977) and on food (Summer 1978). In some cases the form of cooperation was organizational, whether regional or international, but regime analysis also involved searching for informal methods of cooperation. However, regime analysis preferred careful description and assessment of effectiveness within international regimes. Theorizing was largely abandoned.

Looking back over the past decades, regime analysis has survived as a major approach in analyzing international cooperation. A recent article about the effectiveness of international environmental regimes (Breitmeir, Underdal, and Young 2011) seeks correlations of various degrees of success in achieving regime objectives.

Regime analysis easily leads from the study of regional communities to the international community as a whole through an even newer focus—**global governance**, that is, an assessment of how effectively diverse issue-areas are being handled on a global basis. Although the present volume could be said to apply global governance theory to the study of regional regimes, the more profound question posed herein is how zones of conflict have transformed into arenas of peace through the actions of regional IGOs in Asia and the Pacific.

Outline of the Book

Research on regional organizations as progenitors of peace needs further study. Rather than static accounts of regimes, the present book seeks to determine whether regional organizations in Asia and the Pacific have dynamically advanced the goal of peace. Accordingly, the book will answer which forms of cooperation have worked best.

Since 1971, I personally visited several regional organizations in Asia and the Pacific on many occasions. By "Asia," I mean a region including the countries from Iran in the east to the countries bordering the Pacific Ocean. By the "Pacific," I primarily mean the island countries in the middle of the Pacific as well as Australia and New Zealand.

To determine how a zone of conflict could become transformed into an arena of peace, several research designs are incorporated herein. First of all, I propose that the fundamental basis for all such cooperative efforts is cultural (M.Haas 1989a,1989b). Both the forms and scope of cooperation, in my judgment, depend on shared norms and values. I discovered during my travels that a common cultural thread in Asia and the Pacific differs fundamentally from European culture. I have presented that formulation in several publications (esp. M.Haas 1989a, 1989b) and summarize my findings in the following chapter, identifying the Asian Way and Pacific Way as forms of regionalized cultural pluralism.

A second approach is to study the formation of regional organizations in terms of their progenitors. Various powers have sought to shape Asia and the Pacific in a peaceful direction by founding regional organizations, but most such attempts have failed because they have not taken cultural regionalization into account.

Part II, then, examines whether cultural pluralism accounts for the burgeoning of IGOs in Asia and the Pacific. Chapters 3 and 4 identify waves of cooperation, that is, successful and unsuccessful attempts to provide leadership in building a regional community. Both chapters demonstrate that success in forming regional organizations has emerged whenever common cultural affinities underlie the spirit of the organizations.

Chapter 5 presents a third approach, identifying the most transformative organizations in Asia and the Pacific, that is, the IGOs with the greatest potential for creating an arena of peace from a zone of conflict. One is clearly the UN Economic and Social Commission for Asia and the Pacific (ESCAP). However, ESCAP avoids political issues and thus is incapable of managing political conflicts. That leaves two organizations that are at the center of regional developments. Evidence is presented to prove that ASEAN, in which no country has sought to play a dominant role, has maneuvered itself into a central position within Asia. Similarly, the Forum is central to peacemaking within the island states of the Pacific. In both cases, cultural bonds account for the formation of various organizations, and the bonds became even closer after governments interacted within the new bodies.

Part III identifies two more approaches. The fourth approach is to examine the role of political-security IGOs in resolving actual conflicts within each subregion. Chapter 6 examines how ASEAN and the Forum have provided leadership in resolving regional conflicts, whereas other subregions—Central Asia, East Asia, and South Asia—have not yet fully developed capabilities for regional conflict resolution.

The fifth approach, found in the final chapter herein, is to use quantitative measures to determine why ASEAN and the Forum have excelled while other organizations have either maintained themselves at comfortable levels of operation or failed. The measures operationalize all four types of regionalization and all four variants of functionalism. The aim is to determine whether any factors identified in the various theoretical formulations explain the relative success of regional organizations in Asia and the Pacific.

2

The Asian Way and the Pacific Way

The Role of Culture in International Cooperation

As countries in Asia and the Pacific became independent after World War II, there was a surge in various forms of regional cooperation. By the 1990s, there were about 50 intergovernmental organizations in Asia and 25 in the Pacific region. Within 20 years, those figures had nearly doubled for both regions. One explanation for the increase is that they shared common values rooted in historical experiences and common approaches linked to cultural affinity.

For anthropologists, **culture** is a set of norms developed by a group of humans that defines their way of living from generation to generation. In international studies, culture is usually viewed as an "operational code" guiding behavior (Anand 1981).

When persons from similar countries try to cooperate, their cultural backgrounds make communication smoother, even if policy differences are sharp, because all countries observe certain basic rules of conduct with which they are familiar. Cooperation between those of dissimilar cultures can occur, but communication will be difficult because sometimes those of one culture may maladroitly assume commonality or will imperialistically try to impose their norms on those of the other culture.

The imperial ambitions of European countries, thus, involved not only imposing dominance by military means but also an effort at cultural imperialism—trying to force subject peoples into abandoning their own culture. When Christian missionaries from Europe arrived as colonists, they were often resisted because they wanted subject peoples to abandon norms that had been developed over centuries. A culture clash resulted, and the seeds of anticolonialism were planted. Within Asia, the culture clash was particularly sharp, and wars of independence were sometimes bloody. The quest for independence in India, Indonesia, and Vietnam, in other words, was not only based on a desire to achieve state sovereignty but also was a mission to reestablish cultural norms.

Development of the Asian Way

Attempts to unify Asia date back some 2,500 years to a period of hierarchically organized state relations. As early as ca. 1500–1100 BCE, the Shang dynasty of China established a pattern of imperial control over nearby mainland Asian territories, requiring tribute. If rulers failed to pay tribute, their countries were attacked and vanquished until compliant rulers were installed. Peace in East Asia prevailed in this manner until the early nineteenth century. By the fourth century BCE, meanwhile, centralized rule was established in India, but Muslim armies destroyed the Indic empire in a struggle from the eighth to the sixteenth century, and then Britain entered to establish hegemony. Meanwhile, Southeast Asians in the Srivijaya kingdom resisted both Chinese and Indian encroachment. The defeat of hegemonic ambitions of the Khmer Empire in mainland Southeast Asia meant that Cambodia became a buffer between the stronger Thais and the Vietnamese.

The peoples of the Pacific region developed largely in isolation on small islands, but trade involving Europe and Asia developed as explorers developed cash crops. War, by no means absent in Asia, was uncommon in the Pacific. But the greed to control trade from Asia grew with the rise of capitalism in Western Europe, resulting in imperialism as a means to stabilize trade. Lacking strong military forces due to a long era of peace in the region, the West easily prevailed.

The traditional cultures associated with Buddhism, Confucianism, Hinduism, and Islam provided Asia with a complex set of norms of international relations in which peace was considered normal (M.Haas 2008:Ch2). The incursion of the West not only introduced disruptive war into the region but also interrupted normal contact and trade among the peoples, confining them within strict boundaries.

Soon after World War II, as British military power withdrew from South Asia, India and Pakistan were at odds with each other. Civil war broke out in Korea. Vietnam sought independence from France, as did Indonesia from the Netherlands. Later, Indonesia was unhappy when Malaysia was formed from territories that Jakarta considered part of its archipelago. Indeed, more wars were being fought in Asia than anywhere else in the world. Threats of war also meant that new states emerged with strong military ministries, making democratic rule difficult. Prosperity resulting from investment was elusive because the region was perceived as unstable.

A peacekeeping organ, the UN Military Observer Group in India and Pakistan (UNMOGIP), was set up in 1948. The UN Security Council also authorized a military force in Korea from 1950 to 1953. No similar organ was formed elsewhere in Asia. There was no need to do so in the South Pacific when Britain granted independence much later to peaceful island states. The UN had offices for technical assistance in many countries of the Asian and Pacific region but was largely irrelevant to regional politics.

The desire for prosperity and stability persisted, so a transformation of the region was needed—from a zone of war into an arena of peace. Western powers, believing that they knew best, established forums of military cooperation, the most notable of which was a treaty adopted in 1954 among two Southeast Asian countries (the Philippines and Thailand), three Western powers (Britain, France, United States), two Pacific countries (Australia and New Zealand), and one South Asian nation (Pakistan)—the Southeast Asia Collective Defense Treaty. In 1955, the Council of the treaty countries set up the South-East Asia Treaty Organization (SEATO) to contain presumed threats from China and North Vietnam.

Asian countries disliked being forced to take sides in the Cold War. Some preferred to replace alignments dividing the region with the concept of a nonaligned Asia if not a nonaligned world outside the East-West conflict. As a result, they sought to cooperate together to build a new community.

But political independence was not associated with a total pullout of Western influence. Corporations with head offices in the former metropolitan countries remained in the region, exerting a strong influence over the governments.

Asian and Pacific countries were considered "underdeveloped." Under the guise of advancing them to the state of "developing" countries, Western powers persuaded countries in the region to accept foreign economic assistance. But the aid conceived by the West was carefully calculated to improve prosperity for Western corporations, with a meager trickle-down for countries of the region. The political reason for aid was to persuade them to prefer a capitalist development model to a socialist one.

In a word, the region was experiencing "neocolonialism," with prosperity achieved only by the few local capitalists who facilitated investment and by government officials who accepted aid after demanding bribes. From 1947, the United Nations Economic Commission for Asia and the Far East (ECAFE), known as the "economic parliament of Asia," doled out some of the aid, but primarily on Western terms, as the West was the source of the funds.

Impatient Westerners within ECAFE, meanwhile, encountered the more relaxed diplomacy to which Asian countries are accustomed. The tradition of sharp disputation in the West clashed with the Asian need to show respect to others. Postcolonial Asian leaders were trying to unlearn Western practices in order to appeal for support from their own citizens. The culture clash sharpened during the 1950s, when Western countries wanted proposals in ECAFE to be put to a vote. Some Asian countries were then confronted with the choice of voting for Western proposals to curry favor in the distribution of aid while alienating other Asian countries that voted against the proposals for various reasons.

Inasmuch as China, Japan, and Thailand never entirely lost their independence to colonial powers, one might presume that they would side with fellow Asians in resisting Western influence. But China was isolated diplomatically. Japan, having waged war in Asia, was in no position to exert leadership. Thailand's longtime foreign minister, Thanat Khoman, played an important role in SEATO and was thus collaborating with Western countries, though he played a critical role later on.

Then U Nyun, a Burmese UN official first appointed to ECAFE in 1951, became its executive director in 1959. During the 1950s, he observed the tensions between Asian and Western delegates as a problem to be solved. Burma had joined the Non-Aligned Movement (NAM) and had a policy of avoiding entanglement with Western trade, experimenting to develop an autarkic economy. Economists in Asian countries had ideas about how best to develop their own economies but were trapped by the neocolonial direction of foreign aid. U Nyun opposed neocolonialism, but he could not convince outside sources of investment to pay more attention to proposals for investment coming from Asian countries themselves.

U Nyun's strategy, then, was to articulate something that he called the "Asian Way," a set of norms observed by Asian delegates. He specifically asked Western countries to stop dominating discussions about aid priorities in ECAFE forums and to respect the norms of what he called the "Asian Way." He was not asserting an anthropologically devised set of principles but rather an operational code of conduct within meetings of ECAFE, in 1975 the Economic Commission for Asia and the Far East (ESCAP). His conception caught on with other Asian delegates, who already observed the same Asian Way norms in non-ECAFE regional forums.

Two levels and six principles appear to constitute the Asian Way. The first level consists of general beliefs and orientations toward human and international relations. The second level consists of practices and procedures followed in concrete situations.

Elsewhere, I have developed the principles of the Asian Way in more detail (M.Haas 1974; M.Haas 1989a:Ch1). Yet some scholars have misquoted my formulation as a statement of the "ASEAN Way" in their discussions of the Association of South-East Asian Nations (e.g., Bellamy 2004:94). The very same scholars have also ignored the role of U Nyun, the UN offices in Bangkok, and the proliferation of technical organizations that could not have been formed, in my opinion, without prior acceptance of the principles of the Asian Way.

U Nyun coined the term "Asian Way" in distinct opposition to the way ECAFE had been operating, when non-Asian members dominated discussions in the annual Commission meeting to the chagrin of Asian countries. Nevertheless, U Nyun was able to secure agreement on Asian Way principles through unanimous adoption of the Lahore Convention of 1951, which stated,

> [T]he time has come when clearer recognition should be given to the principle that member countries belonging to the region should make their own decisions in the Commission on their own economic problems...In pursuance of this principle the member countries of the Commission not in the region would be willing, as a general rule,

> to refrain from using their votes in opposition to economic proposals predominantly concerning the region which had the support of a majority of the countries of the region.

A summary of the six principles of the Asian Way should clarify how the Asian Way transcends ASEAN and even Southeast Asia:

Asian solutions to Asian problems. Following a slogan popularized by Japan in the 1920s, Asian diplomats tend to see Western models and solutions to problems as inappropriate. They want to solve problems in their own way rather than by relying on Western models about paths to economic development and means for dealing with international conflicts. The principle may be identified in the Lahore Convention of 1951, as adopted by ECAFE, which asked Western delegates to "refrain from using their votes in opposition to economic proposals predominantly concerning the region which had the support of a majority of the countries of the region."

Equality of cultures. As Thanat Khoman once said, the Asian Way comprises a "spirit of tolerance and partnership" that contrasts sharply with the "concept of domination and subjection" that typified imperialist powers in dealing with Asians. International relations should not be likened to fights, games, or debates (cf. Rapoport 1960) but instead to informal conversations in which each party is accorded equal status. In Confucianism, for example, there is no acceptance of the Western concept of "reason of state," the view that states are not bound by norms applicable to individuals. Instead of Westerners' penchant for rational and impersonal calculations prior to agreements, Asians first develop personal relationships with one another to reach a level of mutual trust, whereupon agreement becomes possible. According to the Indonesian concept of *mushawarah*, discussions take place between friends on the same side of the negotiating table rather than between adversaries on opposite sides.

The equality principle is manifest in at least three ways: (1) Asians are reluctant to join or form organizations that are likely to be dominated by a big country, including even China, India, or Japan. (2) Asians accept the Confucian principle that big countries should exercise restraint in dealing with weaker states, while small states look up to larger states as big brothers. (3) When envoys from other countries appear to contradict positions laid down by leaders in their own country, they accept such unproductive meetings as "exchanges of views."

Consensus decision-making. Power plays, trade-offs, and deals that produce temporary compromises and modi vivendi in Anglo-European bargaining are eschewed by the Asian Way, which seeks unanimity. A decision is the outcome of consensus, a flexible accommodation of different views that is built gradually. After initial views are stated, there is an effort to find areas of agreement, however minute. Barack Obama, who grew up in an environment where Asian-Pacific norms are prevalent, refers to such a process as finding "common ground" (M.Haas 2011a). The Pilipino term *pakikisama*, which lays emphasis on observing convivial interpersonal relations, illustrates well why there is a search for unanimous consensus built from the ground up. *Mufakat*, to use an Arabic-derived Malay term, refers to the process of building consensus through discussion rather than confrontation or the majority voting that Westerners demanded before adoption of the Lahore Convention.

Asian Way decision-making proceeds without a count of votes. Deliberations are informal in tone, conducted initially in private and with no formal records of proceedings until a public session is held. Malaysia's onetime Prime Minister Tun Abdul Razak once contrasted Asian "sport-shirt diplomacy" with the formality of Western "business-suit diplomacy." Conflict that might result in loss of face can thereby be softened, so that a joint responsibility for progress can emerge from respectful discussions. Decisions are based more on "give" rather than Western "give-and-take." Coercive tactics are not allowed. If friction is anticipated at a meeting, the meeting is postponed. If one country holds out from a consensus, no decision is made, and informal communications take place outside of formal meetings to enable the country holding back to find a way to go along. One of the best examples is how the Cambodian peace process developed among Asian countries, primarily at the behest of Indonesian diplomacy (M.Haas 2011b:Ch3). A majority never has the right to shame the minority, since everyone is entitled to the dignity of holding their own views. Otherwise, conflict might worsen.

Informal incrementalism. Asians recognize that shared goals, such as a common market in the region, can be best achieved through small steps rather than the Western penchant to draw up grand blueprints or timetables. A famous Chinese proverb says that a thousand-mile journey begins with a single step. Care is undertaken to ensure that there is solid backing in principle before taking concrete action.

Incrementalism in the West often involves setting up an institution or charter with a specific purpose. In contrast, Asians avoid formalizing steps toward a goal, preferring to nurse progress along noninstitutionally. When organizations are set up, Asians do not tie them to elaborate constitutional specifications.

Asian nonlegalistic incrementalism results from the fact that governments have often sought popular support without the benefit of strong political parties, pluralistic interest groups, and an informed citizenry. In such circumstances, leaders must engage in a complex process of consultation at local levels, determining whether the inarticulate might react negatively if certain actions were taken. For example, objections to proposed increases in busfare do not occur while the proposals are debated; they occur, sometimes violently, on the day when fares go up. As ESCAP's twenty-fifth annual report in 1975 states,

> Priorities...are determined by the needs of the countries and their willingness to participate. A project will be successful only when there is general understanding of its nature and a conviction of its worth. As the United Nations has no power of sovereignty, this means working at it, but often also proceeding slowly until a better understanding is developed[.]

Inherent limitations of any government in a developing country, thus, warrant caution and modesty.

Primacy of politics over administration. Matters of implementation are separated from consideration of principles. The Asian Way expects policymaking to first focus on broad goals without discussions about technical problems of execution. ASEAN, for example, developed the concept of "neutralization of Southeast Asia" as an ideal goal. How the goal was to be achieved was a matter of less importance in discussions on its adoption. Whereas some Western observers ridiculed ASEAN for adopting a goal that might be hard to carry out (Cf. Leifer 1973), ASEAN diplomats used the neutralization notion as a framework to guide decisions. Implementation of broad decisions within Asia is often left to lower-level bureaucrats who are not supposed to throttle progress by bringing up feasibility issues. Thus, Asian leaders will not allow a lack of immediate resources to weaken their political resolve. Management in Asian organizations is macrolevel rather than microlevel. The staff is selected carefully, consisting of persons with appropriate administrative or technical expertise. The Western preference for only making decisions that can be quickly translated into action is not part of the Asian Way. Decisions are made in principle. If a goal is infeasible today, that may not be a problem tomorrow.

Pan-Asian spirit. The final principle is that Asians should support one another. After centuries of colonial divisions, Asian countries want to catch up with the West while avoiding internecine conflict. The Asian Way is not aimed at any state or even at the West but instead is based on such concepts as what Filipinos call *bayanihan*—community spirit. If one person in a barrio loses a roof due to a hurricane, for example, others will join in rebuilding the roof along with the owner. Collective interdependence and responsibility for one another contrast with the Western mind-your-own-business mentality that leads adults to abandon their parents in their old age. Impersonality in human relations is contrary to the Asian Way. Western traders promoted competition between Asian countries, so the Asian Way looks for ways to enable former competitors to increase their trade together through joint arrangements. Rivalries between states would limit all, so one goal of cooperative regional efforts is to find ways to prosper simultaneously by sharing technological advances, for example, in the production of silk and other commodities.

One concrete example of Pan-Asianism is the general agreement to accept existing borders yet allow free traffic in border regions where there may be a blurring of national identities. Colonial powers, after all, drew boundaries arbitrarily. What is important is not where the line is drawn but whether countries on both sides of a border can provide peace and prosperity to all. Successful regional cooperation would otherwise be impossible.

The ASEAN Way

Principles of the Asian Way could easily have been recast as the "Southeast Asian Way" in light of prominent Malay and Tagalog terms in the definitions provided above. But U Nyun sought to describe a broader geographic focus, since ECAFE's membership included East Asia and South Asia, where Asian Way principles are somewhat less firmly embedded in the cultures. Even within Southeast Asia, sharp-tongued Singaporean diplomats have not always followed respectful Asian Way norms (Deck 1999; M.Haas 2011b:30).[1] Nevertheless, within a decade of its existence, Malaysia's Prime Minister Datuk Hussein Onn referred to the "ASEAN Spirit" as ASEAN's "greatest achievement" (van den Kroef 1978a:144).

An ASEAN Way, a set of common practices developed at meetings among Southeast Asians, could only exist after the organization was formed in 1967. For one observant scholar (Bellamy (2004:95), the ASEAN Way embodies three principles: (1) decision making by consultation and consensus, (2) a commitment to use peaceful rather than military methods for conflict resolution, and (3) the practice of steering clear of any discussion of the internal affairs of sovereign member countries. But while the first principle comes from the Asian Way concept, the second is unremarkable, and the third is a Westphalian principle. Moreover, the latter principle no longer applied in the late 1990s, when ASEAN imposed conditions on admission to membership by undemocratic Burma and Cambodia.

Not mentioned in Bellamy's threefold characterization of the "ASEAN Way" is ASEAN informality, exemplified by karaoke-singing diplomats in sports shirts, faithful to the Asian Way principles of informal incrementalism and the Pan-Asian spirit. And ASEAN also practices the other Asian Way principles ignored in the threefold formulation. In other words, repeated references by some scholars to the "ASEAN Way" have not really captured the "ASEAN Spirit" to which Hussein Onn referred.

The ASEAN Charter, adopted in 2007, formally states several principles of the ASEAN Way, some of which had long been implicit. These include

- centrality of ASEAN in regional cooperation;
- respect for territorial integrity, sovereignty, non-interference, and respect for national identities;
- peaceful settlement of disputes through dialogue and consultation;
- renunciation of aggression;
- affirming international law with regard to human rights, social justice, and multilateral trade; and
- friendly external relations.

The primacy of normative concerns is so important for ASEAN that economic and security matters are perceived to be of secondary importance (cf. Acharya and Johnson 2007:262). Some scholars referring to the "ASEAN Way" inexplicably show ignorance of the important struggle by U Nyun within ECAFE which laid the foundation for Asian Way principles that inform the ASEAN Way.

Development of the Pacific Way

Principles of the Pacific Way are almost identical to those of the Asian Way. But they developed in a different manner. Aside from a common colonial background, which mostly ended in the 1970s, the situation in the South Pacific was different in many respects. Economic exploitation was minimal. After the bloody battles of World War II, there was no war or threat of war. Some peoples of the South Pacific came originally from the Indonesian archipelago, but that was many centuries ago.

The one common thread in the South Pacific is delayed independence. In 1948, the first major regional organization was formed—the South Pacific Commission (SPC). Headquartered in French New Caledonia, membership consisted initially of Western powers. In 1965, Samoa became the first South Pacific state accepted for membership, having been admitted as a sovereign state after New Zealand granted it independence in 1962. The experience of Samoa and later South Pacific countries within SPC was similar to that of Asian countries within ECAFE.

In 1974, ECAFE was renamed the Economic and Social Commission for Asia and the Pacific (ESCAP), thereby according some recognition to South Pacific island states. By then Samoa (1963), Nauru (1971), and Tonga (1971) had joined ECAFE, even before their admission to SPC.

Fiji became independent in 1971 and was admitted to SPC membership the same year. Fiji's longtime Prime Minister Ratu Sir Kamisese Mara immediately became aware of the fact that six Western powers presumed to set the agenda within SPC for four independent countries and more than a dozen colonies, as after the Session, SPC's annual plenary meeting of external powers, there was a triennial South Pacific Conference so that colonial non-SPEC members of the region were accorded the privilege of commenting on SPC programming.

Even before independence, Mara (1977) began to give a series of public speeches about the "Pacific Way," based in part on the view of Ratu Lala Sakuna, who had struggled for Fijian independence until his death in 1958. In 1965, Mara startled fellow indigenous leaders as well as Western powers at one of those triennial meetings by proposing that SPC's work program should be formulated by the island states first, with later comments by Western powers. His proposal, similar to that of the Lahore Convention of 1951, bore fruit when in 1973 the South Pacific Conference became the plenary body, to be held annually thereafter. The Session was then abolished.

Mara used the phrase "Pacific Way" in 1970 in an address to the UN General Assembly. What he had in mind was similar to the Asian Way, another politically motivated concept. Pacific islanders wanted to honor social practices that they had enjoyed before Western intrusion as the basis for their diplomatic interactions. The principal political agenda was to advance the interests of the region through a united front vis-à-vis external powers. Whereas Asian countries benefited from UN and Western aid, Pacific island countries could not survive without that assistance.

Accordingly, Mara founded the South Pacific Forum (SPF) in 1971 as an intergovernmental body that would admit only sovereign states in the region. Australia and New Zealand were the only Western states allowed to join SPF. After all, they were in the region and felt responsibility toward the Pacific Island states. France, still maintaining colonies in the region, was excluded.

The principles of the Pacific Way parallel those of the Asian Way, but with subtle differences (see Table 2.1). The wording is different, but the concepts are almost the same.

Pacific solutions to Pacific problems. Unlike Asian countries, the unique problem of island states is how to survive as independent states with extremely limited resources. Countries with only bananas, coconuts, and fish for exports would need extensive aid to enjoy the status of modern states. For example, many residents of Tuvalu,

Table 2.1 Comparing the Asian Way with the Pacific Way

Asian Way Principles	*Pacific Way Principles*
Asian solutions to Asian problems	Pacific solutions to Pacific problems
equality of cultures	equality of cultures
consensus decision-making	unanimous compromise
informal incrementalism	optimistic incrementalism
primacy of politics over administration	primacy of political goals
Pan-Asian spirit	Pan-Pacific spirit

Source: Haas (1989a, 1989b).

which is sinking into the Pacific Ocean due to global warming, have moved away and are living on interest from a trust account in a bank, mainly supplied by aid donors Australia and New Zealand. Aid projects, thus, have to take more extreme conditions into account. The problems are unusual, so the solutions must recognize realities in the Pacific.

Equality of cultures. According to Tekoti Rotan of the Fiji Nuclear Test Veterans Association, the spirit of the Pacific Way is "that dialog and discussion in an atmosphere of tolerance and goodwill offers the best prospects for the settlement of...differences" (Crocombe 1976:15). Meetings of Pacific Islanders, long isolated from one another, are viewed in part as adventures in learning how similar the attitudes and customs of the participants are. National dress is often worn, reminding outsiders and one another that Islanders take pride in their cultures. Business suits are almost unknown. The term "brother" is applied widely to imply an ideology of mutual help, common origins, and thus common interests. In Hawai'i, the term *'ohana* is often used to refer to the sense of community in which an extended family is broadly defined. As Ratu Sakuna once said, "Strive for the things that unite rather than those that divide" (Inder 1987:27). Although Australia and New Zealand could have been awarded observer status rather than member status in many Pacific island regional bodies, they are welcomed as "big brothers." Hostility toward former colonial powers is noticeably absent in Pacific Island organizations.

Unanimous compromise. As coined by Sir Albert Henry, onetime prime minister of the Cook Islands, "unanimous compromise" means that "nobody gets left out" (Crocombe 1976:20). Discussion often begins with modest comments by island-nation representatives, who may seek outside assistance but feel too humble to make special pleas. Frank discussions often follow without causing resentment. When Westerners offer appropriate aid, Pacific leaders show profuse gratitude rather than exhibiting a sense of accomplishment that justice previously denied has been rectified. Warm interpersonal relations build the mood for consensus.

Optimistic incrementalism. Whereas Asians and Westerners are often regarded as "too serious," Professor Asesela Ravuvu of the University of the South Pacific has characterized Pacific islanders as following "the ad hoc way" (Crocombe 1976:34). The tendency not to plan, to let the future take care of itself, is in sharp contrast to Western planning and implementation. Their patience and cheerful regard for the inevitability of amelioration becomes a self-fulfilling prophecy, encouraging outsiders to be even more generous and helpful. Of course, the amounts required for aid projects are minuscule compared to those in Asia.

Primacy of political goals. Political will prevails over practical considerations of administrative feasibility, as in Asia. Economic considerations are secondary to political goals. In 1956, France began atmospheric nuclear weapons tests in the South Pacific, resulting in protests and the possibility that France would stop funding aid projects through the SPC. Australia and New Zealand then took Paris to the International Court of Justice (ICJ) on behalf of the region. As a result, the World Court condemned France in 1973, and France stopped atmospheric nuclear tests in 1974 but aid continued.

Pan-Pacific spirit. Collective priorities prevail over national self-interest in the region. Discussion in regional bodies is held to determine common needs with an understanding that squabbling should be avoided. According to Maori Kiki, who agitated for Papua New Guinea's independence, joint responsibility and sharing of wealth characterize Pacific islanders (Crocombe 1976:24). Village leaders tend to share their resources with commoners, including meals and other necessities. Satellite communications, for example, were negotiated in 1988 on a group basis for the region rather than only being provided to the larger states with the most wealth. Ground stations were supplied to even the smallest country, Niue, with a current population of about 1,400.

As Pacific Community cultural adviser Elise Huffer (2011) has noted, the Forum continually stresses cultural elements. Member countries agree that they would achieve very little as an organization without the strong cultural principles that bind them together.

Conclusion

Sociobiologist Edward O. Wilson (2012) reports that the only species to have survived for millennia are those which develop social modes of existence. He refers to ants and bees, which maintain a division of labor, as well as humans. He believes that humans who maintain integrated, peaceful forms of existence are more likely to survive than those who are loosely connected. The primary basis for interlinked human groups, holding individuals harmoniously together, is a sense of common culture, which in turn spawns complex social interaction networks, dense transactional systems, international organizations, and security communities.

The cultural basis for regional cooperation in Asia and the Pacific determines the forms and content of that cooperation, as will be clear in the descriptive accounts in the next chapters. Unlike some visionaries in Europe, the countries of Asia and the Pacific have had no interest in political integration, but they are eager for closer economic cooperation to achieve greater prosperity.

Cultural pluralism has been a precondition for the development of regional organizations. When countries began to interact within organizational frameworks, they developed a new sense of cultural affinity by practicing principles of the Asian Way and Pacific Way (see Figure 2.1). In my two books on Asian and Pacific regional cooperation, I identify specific decisions by some 100 IGOs based on those principles (M. Haas 1989a,1989b).

Among the four types of regionalization, economic and social communication patterns do not explain the rise of regional cooperation in Asia and the Pacific, since countries in both regions were isolated from one another in the colonial era and, thus, never developed cross-border or regional social communication ties that eased or prompted the transition to institutionalized arrangements. Security regionalization through SEATO was divisive. The fourth type of regionalization, cultural pluralism, thus emerges as the dominant explanation for regional cooperation within Asia and the Pacific.

Nevertheless, cultural affinity among countries in the region has not always led to increased political cooperation after the formation of new technical intergovernmental bodies. When countries establish

Asian cultures → Asian organizations → Asian Way

Southeast Asian cultures →ASEAN → ASEAN Way

Pacific cultures → Pacific organizations→ Pacific Way

Pacific cultures → Forum → Forum Way

Figure 2.1 Cultural pluralism as the foundation for international cooperation.

new politically oriented organizations, they pledge themselves to abide by political principles, such as alignment or nonalignment. Within Asia, ASEAN has developed new norms. Within the Pacific, the Forum has played a similar role.

In conclusion, cultural pluralism is vindicated as a legitimate approach for studying organizational behavior. Within Europe, the cultural context has been capitalism for the European Union along with human rights for the Council of Europe. Insofar as cultural norms can be identified in other regions around the world, the cultural theory of international cooperation presented herein can be used to predict success in increased activities, membership, and scope.

Part II

Dynamics

Countries in Asia and the Pacific are the latest to embark on regional intergovernmental cooperation. The Americas led the parade with the Pan American Union before World War I and the Organization of American States after World War II.

Europe after 1945 was divided into two regions, one forcibly incorporated into the Warsaw Treaty Organization, the other bound together with a variety of cultural, economic, military, political, and technical organizations that culminated in the European Union.

Outside of the Americas and Europe, the League of Arab States was launched in 1945, and the Organization of African Unity began in 1963. In both cases, a proliferation of regional institutions followed.

By 1971, the South Pacific Forum, later renamed Pacific Islands Forum, emerged to bring together annual summit conferences of leaders of newly independent island nations. No region-wide organization has been forged by Asian countries. Instead of a comprehensive regional political forum, Asia has several subregional bodies instead.

Chapters 3 and 4 trace distinct waves of regional cooperation in Asia and the Pacific, mostly but not entirely chronologically, to demonstrate which waves have been more productive than others. All the organizations listed are intergovernmental: Their members are governments, consisting of at least three countries, and their participants consist of either ministerial-level officials or heads of government. They vary from loosely organized (rotating annual ministerial-level conferences) to centrally organized (with Secretariats) structures.

Chapter 5 identifies organizations that have been pivotal in enabling the regions to come together so that zones of conflict might become arenas of peace.

3

Waves of Asian Regional Cooperation

Over the years, regional cooperation in Asia[1] has flourished since the first intergovernmental body in the region was established in 1947—the United Nations Economic Commission for Asia and the Far East (ECAFE), known since 1974 as the Economic and Social Commission for Asia and the Pacific (ESCAP). Thus far, Asian countries have hosted some 100 non-UN regional organizations. As the region is so vast, they have tended to be subregional.[2] They have been formed in waves; that is, an organization has been formed as a model that has been followed by similar organizations. But many waves have ended because of a fundamental flaw in their leadership, so Asian regional cooperation has gone through a learning experience. None have developed supranational capabilities, and the confederal approach has not worked within the region.

A major reason for focusing on waves is to detect whether pluralist influences have operated in what Deutsch and associates (1957:38) have referred to as a "core area." Asia is a region so extensive, and countries are connected by water more than by land, that social pluralism (social communication patterns) could not explain why regional institutions emerged. Security pluralism is inapplicable, too, as Asian countries were divided by the Cold War. Transactional pluralism also cannot explain the growth of Asian regional organizations, as the densest transactional linkages were with former imperial powers. Increased trade has been a goal, not a precondition. In other words, only cultural pluralism can explain why the climate has existed for a profusion of regional bodies in Asia.

If **classical functional** theory is correct, the success of regional institutions should not depend upon matters of "high politics" and would stick to technical issue-areas that provide a contagion for parallel bodies in other issue-areas. Experts are supposed to make the organizations work because they tend to ignore vital interests of particular countries and instead focus on the welfare of the region or subregion as a whole. **Neofunctionalists** expect that organizational stability and growth emerges when political leaders give their blessing to organizations, even though they may not develop supranational capabilities. **Multifunctionalists** expect that political leaders alone have the power to expand the scope of successful organizations into many new issue-areas. **Institutional functionalists** try to identify procedural and structural elements that predispose an IGO to favorable outcomes. Thus, the present chapter provides a qualitative test of which theory best explains organizational developments in Asia.

External Leadership

In the first wave, the period from the mid-1940s to the mid-1950s, external powers tried to create regional institutions:

- **Colombo Plan for Co-operative Economic Development in Asia** (1951)
- **South-East Asia Treaty Organization** (1955)
- **Middle East Treaty Organization** (1955)
- **Central Banks of Southeast Asia, Australia and New Zealand** (1956)
- **Anglo-Malayan Defence Agreement** (1957).

The **Colombo Plan for Co-operative Economic Development in Asia** (C-Plan) began as a British initiative at a meeting of the Commonwealth in 1950, when countries in Asia were asked to present five-year economic development plans for possible funding, similar to the Marshall Plan for Europe. The organization was officially launched and named at the 1951 conference where the plans were presented, but a large amount of aid could hardly be provided by Britain, which was still recovering from the devastation of World War II. In 1997, the name changed to the **Colombo Plan for Cooperative Economic and Social Development in Asia and the Pacific**. C-Plan became an arena for Third World countries to shop for aid from First World country representatives.

John Foster Dulles, President Dwight Eisenhower's secretary of state, pursued a policy of containment by establishing a ring of alliances around the Soviet Union. One of his ideas was the **South-East Asia Treaty Organization** (SEATO), which was set up in 1955 as a Cold War pact aimed at providing protection to Cambodia, Laos, and South Vietnam from aggression by China and North Vietnam. Only Pakistan (from South Asia), and the Philippines and Thailand (from Southeast Asia) were its Asian members. When SEATO failed to support Pakistan in the Bangladesh War of 1971, Pakistan withdrew. Six years later, Bangkok pulled the plug on the organization.

A second initiative bore fruit as the **Middle East Treaty Organization** (METO) in 1955, with Britain, Iran, Iraq, Pakistan, and Turkey as members; the United States was an Associate Member. In 1959, when Iraq withdrew, the headquarters moved from Baghdad to Ankara, and the organization was renamed **Central Treaty Organization** (CENTO). In 1979, the organization was dissolved after the fall of the Shah of Iran.

Britain also formed the **Central Banks of Southeast Asia, Australia and New Zealand** (SEANZA) in 1956 and the **Anglo-Malayan Defence Agreement** (AMDA) in 1957. Three South Asian countries (Ceylon, India, and Pakistan) were members of the initial five-member SEANZA, which later expanded to nearly all Southeast Asian countries. The AMDA agreement, set up for a country that refused to join SEATO, was renamed the **Anglo-Malaysian Defence Agreement** in 1965, and Australia, Britain, and New Zealand were members of the new AMDA. In 1971, AMDA was superseded by a set of bilateral agreements known as the **Five Power Defence Arrangements** (FPDA), adding Singapore, which had separated from Malaysia in 1965, as the fifth member.

Meanwhile, the United States established bilateral military relations with Japan, the Philippines, the Republic of China, and the Republic of Korea in the 1950s. Thus, the Commander in Chief, Pacific Command, at Pearl Harbor became the de facto head of a pseudo-international organization that continues to the present. The Soviet Union followed suit by establishing bilateral security relations in the 1950s with China, the Democratic People's Republic of Korea, and Mongolia, though the alliance with China became moribund by the end of the decade, and the collapse of the Soviet Union ensured that the other arrangements would wither.

Regional cooperation promoted by external powers placed Asian countries in roles of dependence. Regional powers wanted to construct their own edifice of cooperation—and did so instead.

Leadership by India

In the second wave of regional cooperation, during the last half of the 1950s, India tried to cultivate an Asian political forum. The non-governmental Asian Relations Organisation, set up at New Delhi in 1947 as a "think tank" for larger efforts, sired the Colombo Powers Conferences of 1954 and 1955 and the Conference of Nonaligned Nations at Bandung in 1955, which soon evolved into the Non-Aligned Movement (NAM) that extended far beyond Asia and the Pacific. Subsequently, India initiated efforts on behalf of three organizations:

- **Asian Legal Consultative Agreement** (1956)
- **Afro-Asian Rural Reconstruction Organization** (1962)
- **Indian Ocean Rim Association for Regional Cooperation** (1995).

Although India sponsored the intergovernmental **Asian Legal Consultative Committee** (ALCC) in 1956 as an innovative Asian organization, with New Delhi as the headquarters, interest from countries within NAM countries served to broaden the scope, resulting in a change of name to **Asian African Legal Consultative Committee** (AALCC) by 1958. In 2001, the organization was retitled again—**Asian African Legal Consultative Organization** (AALCO).

In 1962, the **Afro-Asian Rural Reconstruction Organization** (AARRO), a similar effort headquartered in New Delhi, gained membership outside the region. But India then decided to give more priority to NAM than to developing more regional cooperation bodies within Asia, and resources to both organizations did not keep up with increasing membership. (The IGO was renamed the **Afro-Asian Rural Development Organization** (AARDO) in 2000.)

After proposing an Indian Ocean organization for many years, Indian leadership resulted in the formation of the **Indian Ocean Rim Association for Regional Cooperation** (IOR-ARC), which includes African and Asian countries as well as aligned Australia, thus breaking from the NAM mold. The aim of the organization, as launched in 1995, is to promote economic cooperation and trade among countries bordering on the Indian Ocean. Six of the eighteen members are from the Asia-Pacific region, the rest are from Africa and the Arabian peninsula, so the organization is only marginally Asian in scope. The Secretariat is located in Cyber City, Ebène, Mauritius.

Organizations Inspired by UN Organizations

In the early 1960s, four regional technical bodies emerged. All were initiated by UN agencies:

- **Committee for Coordination of Investigations of the Lower Mekong Basin** (1957)
- **Conference of Directors General of Civil Aviation, Asia and Pacific Regions** (1961)
- **Asian-Oceanic Postal Union** (1962)
- **Conference of Asian Labor Ministers** (1966).

ECAFE started the process by recommending the formation of the Mekong Committee (formally, the **Committee for Coordination of Investigations of the Lower Mekong Basin**) in 1957 (cf. Wightman 1963).[3] Although three Indochinese countries and Thailand formally endorsed water resource management projects for the Mekong, most funds and upper management personnel were provided from sources outside the member countries. In the 1960s, when Cambodia became embroiled in conflict, internally and externally, the successor **Interim Mekong Committee** kept the organization on hold. After peace came to Cambodia in 1991, the Mekong Committee reconstituted itself in 1995 as an independent, intergovernmental body, the **Mekong River Commission** (MRC). By then, ECAFE had become ESCAP (The name change occurred in 1974).

The International Civil Aviation Organization, a UN Specialized Agency was eager to coordinate air traffic in the region. In 1961, the Philippine Director of Aviation, accordingly, convened the first of several meetings now known as the **Conference of Directors General of Civil Aviation, Asia and Pacific Regions** (DGCA).

Similarly, the Universal Postal Union (UPU), a UN Specialized Agency encouraged the formation of regional postal unions. As a result, the **Asian-Oceanic Postal Union** (AOPU) began in 1962. AOPU was renamed the **Asian-Pacific Postal Union** (APPU) in 1981, thereby according recognition to South Pacific independent states as new members.

In 1966, the **Conference of Asian Labor Ministers** (CALM) began with the blessing of the International Labour Organisation (ILO), another UN Specialized Agency. In 1973, after some Pacific island countries joined, the name changed to **Conference of Asian and Pacific Labor Ministers** (CAPLM) in 1976. The organization has no central secretariat but has been assisted by ILO's regional office in Bangkok.

Japanese Leadership

During the 1920s, Japan tried to persuade Asian peoples to agree to a Greater East Asia Co-Prosperity Sphere that would liberate them from colonial control. But Japan's aggression to forcibly create a common economic community was unwelcome. After World War II, the Japanese economic recovery was remarkably quick, and Japanese investors went to newly independent Asian countries to establish subsidiary companies. Corporation executives suggested that the Japanese government should assist the region by providing finances and technical assistance, and several organizations emerged:

- **Asian Productivity Organization** (1961)
- **Asian Development Bank** (1965)
- **Asian Parliamentarians' Union** (1965)
- **Ministerial Conference for the Economic Development of Southeast Asia** (1966)
- **Southeast Asian Fisheries Development Center** (1967)
- **Southeast Asian Agency for Regional Transport and Communications Development** (1971)
- **Southeast Asia Regional Organization for Inter-Governmental Cooperation and Coordination in Family and Population Planning in Southeast Asia** (1971)
- **Study Group on Asian Tax Administration and Research** (1971)
- **Southeast Asian Promotion Centre for Trade, Investment and Tourism** (1972)
- **Asia Pacific Parliamentary Forum** (1993).

The first IGO sponsored by Japan, the **Asian Productivity Organization** (APO), was launched in 1961 as an umbrella for national productivity centers (NPOs). Although Japan had originally hoped to form APO as a nongovernmental body, NPOs in several countries were governmental entities, so Tokyo had no alternative but to launch an intergovernmental body.

The high point of Japan's initiatives came in 1965, when the agreement to form the Asian Development Bank (ADB) was signed. Japanese have continuously headed the bank.

Members of Japan's Diet formed the Asian Parliamentarians' Union (APU) with opposite numbers in noncommunist Asian legislatures during 1965. The primary aim was to bypass foreign ministries in order to comment on political developments in the region. The press saw the organization more as a legislators' club, but several countries withdrew to maintain a more neutral stance toward Cold War conflicts after the Republic of China (Taiwan) was replaced at the UN by the People's Republic of China in 1971. Accordingly, Taiwan attempted to set up diplomatic missions in the South Pacific, so APU began admitting Pacific Island states, even Guam, as new members. The result was a retitling of the organization to **Asian-Pacific Parliamentarians' Union** (APPU) in 1980. The organization, in turn, established two subsidiary bodies, each with their own offices—the Asian-Pacific Cultural Center (APCC) and the Asian-Pacific Development Center (APDC). Neither became independent organizations, and they eventually closed their doors.

In 1966, Japan sponsored a series of meetings known as the **Ministerial Conference for the Economic Development of Southeast Asia** (SEAMCED), wherein countries of Southeast Asia were encouraged to propose regional bodies that would be financed by Japan. Tokyo's promotion of organizations focused on Southeast Asia was rather awkward, however. When Southeast Asians were asked to propose new organizations, their ideas were not always accepted by Japan in SEAMCED, so in many cases they passively listened to proposals from Tokyo and then reacted. SEAMCED, also known as MEDSEA, gave birth to five technical organizations, largely composed of Southeast Asian countries.

SEAMCED's first creation was the **Southeast Asian Fisheries Development Center** (SEAFDEC). Thereafter, Japan assisted in the formation of the **Southeast Asian Agency for Regional Transport**

and Communications Development (SEATAC), the **Southeast Asia Regional Organization for Inter-Governmental Cooperation and Coordination in Family and Population Planning in Southeast Asia** (known by the acronym IGCC), the **Study Group on Asian Tax Administration and Research** (SGATAR), and the **Southeast Asian Promotion Centre for Trade, Investment and Tourism** (SEAPCENTRE). But Japan was unwilling to support the five bodies indefinitely, and the United States did not pick up the tab (cf. Grieco 1999). The final meeting of SEAMCED was held in 1975. SEAPCENTRE closed in 1978, IGCC in 1982, but the rest still exist.

In 1993, former Prime Minister Yasuhiro Nakasone sponsored the inaugural meeting of the **Asia Pacific Parliamentary Forum** (APPF) as an outgrowth of the Asia-Pacific Economic Cooperation (APEC) forum (discussed below). One unstated aim was to supersede Asian-Pacific Parliamentarians' Union, which retains the Republic of China as a member and continues to function. APPF host countries provide the secretariat for each session. Seeking to parallel APEC with regard to political and security matters, legislators at APPF have taken strong political stands, such as urging North Korea to comply with International Atomic Energy Agency safeguards.

Japan, in short, has had self-centered motives for forming IGOs. Tokyo's leadership has usually been out of sync with wider regional concerns.

Korean-Sponsored Organizations

After formation of APU by parliamentarians, the foreign ministers of the very same countries were brought together by South Korea to form the **Asian and Pacific Council** (ASPAC), yet another anti-communist forum. The principal aim was to build a coalition of countries to prevent the People's Republic of China from displacing the Taiwanese government in the China seat at the United Nations. ASPAC also decided to spawn regional international organizations in nonpolitical issue-areas as a way to enhance its respectability. Accordingly, Seoul was responsible for six new bodies:

- **Asian and Pacific Council** (1966)
- **Cultural and Social Center for the Asian and Pacific Region** (1968)

- **Economic Cooperation Center for the Asian and Pacific Region** (1970)
- **Food and Fertilizer Technology Center for the Asian and Pacific Region** (1970)
- **Asian and Pacific Maritime Cooperation Scheme** (1971)
- **Registry of Scientific and Technical Services for the Asian and Pacific Region** (1971).

The **Cultural and Social Center for the Asian and Pacific Region** (CULSOCEN) and the **Food and Fertilizer Technology Center for the Asian and Pacific Region** (FFTC) are the only organizations that survived beyond the 1970s, though CULSOCEN ceased to exist sometime in the 1990s. The **Asian and Pacific Maritime Cooperation Scheme** (APMCS) operated for only a year. The **Registry of Scientific and Technical Services for the Asian and Pacific Region** completed its rolodex in three years and shut down. The **Economic Cooperation Center for the Asian and Pacific Region** (ECOCEN) closed down in 1974, when Indochina was undergoing profound change and ASPAC had become an anti-communist relic.

During its existence, the anti-communist rhetoric in ASPAC meetings rankled neutral Indonesia. Malaysia, in turn, did not want to antagonize neighboring Indonesia. No country offered to host ASPAC after 1972. Malaysia withdrew from FFTC in 1972 and from CULSOCEN in 1973. Korean leadership, pushing an anti-communist agenda, was not on the same page with Southeast Asian countries.

Southeast Asian Leadership

Many Southeast Asian countries wanted to form their own subregional bodies, independent of donor countries. They wanted to formulate their own policies first and to secure resources later, either inside Southeast Asia or through joint requests to the developed countries, operating as a bloc of countries. The result was a proliferation of new regional bodies:

- **Association of Southeast Asia** (1951)
- **Asian Judicial Conference** (1963)
- **Southeast Asian Ministers of Education Organization** (1965)
- **South East Asian Central Banks Group** (1966)

- **Association of South-East Asian Nations** (1967)
- **Association of Natural Rubber Producing Countries** (1970)
- **Southeast Asian Agency for Regional Transport and Communications Development** (1971)
- **Tripartite Council** (1971)
- **Association for Science Cooperation in Asia** (1972)
- **ASEAN Inter-Parliamentary Organization** (1975)
- **Meeting of the Chiefs of National Police of the ASEAN Countries** (1981)
- **Association of Tin-Producing Countries** (1983)
- **Executives' Meeting of East Asia and Pacific Central Banks** (1991)
- **ASEAN-Europe Meeting** (1996)
- **International Tripartite Rubber Organization** (2001)
- **ASEAN Regional Forum** (2004)
- **East Asia Summit** (2005)
- **Asian Monetary Fund** (2010).

In 1961, Malaya, the Philippines, and Thailand had agreed to form the Association of Southeast Asia (ASA). Although the three countries started the organization with some initial political goals in mind, they formally pledged cooperation only on technical matters. But a territorial dispute between Malaya and the Philippines soon arose over Britain's proposal to include Sabah in an expanded Malaysia. Britain also mooted the idea of including Sarawak in Malaysia, whence Indonesia objected strenuously, urging that Southeast Asia should be united, not divided.

The Philippines secured vague agreement for a proposed confederation under the hybrid name Maphilindo (to include Malaya, the Philippines, and Indonesia) in 1963 to stop the formation of Malaysia, but the organization was stillborn. Border disputes continued instead, though diplomacy by Foreign Minister Thanat Khoman within the ASA framework prevented a further deterioration between Malaysia and the Philippines (Gordon 1966:185), and a change of regimes in Indonesia brought moderating influences to Jakarta.

In 1963, meanwhile, the Philippines sponsored an initial conference of what became known as the **Asian Judicial Conference** (AJC). The body, consisting of meetings of chief justices of independent countries in Asia, continued until 1973. Attendance included some South Asian countries, so the organization does not really fit as a purely Southeast Asian organization, though AJC existed because of Southeast Asian leadership.

The United States, eager to encourage organizations to complement SEATO, cautiously indicated that funding would be available if Southeast Asian countries formed their own organizations but refrained from establishing a body to duplicate SEAMCED. Washington promised to finance new bodies but would not join them. The first such organization came in 1965 with the formation of the **Southeast Asian Ministers of Education Organization** (SEAMEO). SEAMEO, in turn, sponsored regional centers within every member country to improve primary, secondary, and even tertiary institutions by offering sabbatical locations for curriculum development specialists and educators in a wide variety of fields of study ranging from archaeology to language study.[4] When American funding dried up after 1975, European countries filled the gap.

At the instigation of the Malaysian Central Bank, the **South East Asian Central Banks Group** (SEACEN) was formed in 1967 to provide training courses not offered by SEANZA. In the same year, Malaysia spearheaded the **Coordinating Committee of Southeast Asian Senior Officials on Transport and Communications** (COORDCOM). When Japan offered to fund prefeasibility studies for new projects, COORDCOM was superseded by the **Southeast Asian Agency for Transport and Communications Development** (SEATAC) in 1971.

In the mid-1960s, Indonesia took center stage in Southeast Asia, having coped with the earlier anticolonial struggle and flirtation under its first president, Sukarno, with a nonalignment that tolerated a large domestic Communist Party. General Suharto, who led a coup in 1965 and became president in 1967, inherited a military confrontation with Malaysia. His appointment of Foreign Minister Adam Malik was part of a plan to extricate Southeast Asia from Western neocolonialism. Malik then spearheaded the formation in 1967 of the **Association of South-East Asian Nations** (ASEAN) among Indonesia, Malaysia, the Philippines, Singapore, and Thailand. ASEAN then superseded ASA.

In 1971, Malik persuaded his five colleagues in ASEAN to agree to the concept of the neutralization of Southeast Asia from the Cold War, thus rejecting any form of security cooperation (cf. Jorgensen-Dahl 1982:114–115; Leifer 1989:69). Noncommunist governments of Cambodia, Laos, and Vietnam were allowed to attend ASEAN as

Observers, but they stopped attending when Communist revolutions to power in 1975 (although all three returned not long after the Cambodian peace agreement of 1991). Burma (Myanmar), which initially rejected membership, joined in 1997.

ASEAN began as a meeting of foreign ministers with little interest in economic matters (cf. Haftel 2010). In 1976, one year after Hanoi's victory in that country's civil war, heads of state met in the first **ASEAN Summit** to formalize the organization, establish a Secretariat at Jakarta, and encourage new directions. In 1977, annual meetings of **ASEAN Economic Ministers** (AEM) began, seeking to promote intraregional trade and similar matters. ASEAN's annual meeting of foreign ministers then became the **ASEAN Ministerial Meeting** (AMM). Other ministerial bodies have also been established (see Chapter 5 below). Those with an economic focus were reorganized as the **ASEAN Economic Community** (AEC), with AEM as one among several ministerial bodies.

In 1979, ASEAN decided to organize an annual **Post Ministerial Conference** (PMC) with foreign aid donor countries, including at first Australia, Canada, the European Community, Japan, New Zealand, and the United States. The initial aim was to coordinate economic aid to the region, but other issues soon crept into the discussions.

ASEAN countries, in turn, have inspired and spawned many organizations. When the Cambodian conflict was resolved in 1991 and the Philippines refused to allow American military bases to remain in the country after 1992, ASEAN countries were concerned that the United States might withdraw from the region, leaving China as the unchecked regional superpower. Accordingly, Southeast Asian countries organized the **ASEAN Regional Forum** (ARF) in 1994 to bring together defense ministers from East Asia, Southeast Asia, and the United States. Papua New Guinea, Russia, South Asian countries, the European Union, and even North Korea joined later. ARF meets immediately after annual ASEAN foreign minister meetings.

ASEAN was also the linchpin in the formation of the **Asian-Europe Meeting** (ASEM) in 1996. The aim is to facilitate economic assistance and coordinate foreign policies of the countries involved. Strictly speaking, therefore, ASEM is not an Asian regional organization, but it is listed here because the ASEAN Secretariat in Jakarta serves as ASEM's coordinating body. ASEM was the first biregional body to emerge from Asia.

In 1970, thanks to Malaysian leadership, the **Association of Natural Rubber Producing Countries** (ANRPC) was formed. The organization seemed particularly appropriate during the era when commodity communities, notably the Organization of Petroleum Exporting Countries (OPEC), were gaining favor.

Despite Japanese interest in sponsoring an organization that would maintain safe passage from pirates in the Straits of Malacca and Singapore, the three littoral states of Indonesia, Malaysia, and Singapore formed the **Tripartite Council** (TC) in 1971, excluding Japan. After an oil spill by a Japanese ship in 1973, Tokyo continued to apply pressure to enter the cooperative relationship. The result in 2009 was the establishment of the **Cooperative Mechanism** (CM) among the littoral states as well as among countries that account for traffic in the narrow waterway, including a Cooperation Forum for policy discussion.

In 1972, the Philippines organized the **Association for Science Cooperation in Asia** (ASCA) with wide membership throughout Asia. The aim was to provide a forum for scientific cooperation. Today, there is no evidence that ASCA still exists.

In 1975, Southeast Asian legislators formed the **ASEAN Inter-Parliamentary Organization** (AIPO) and in 2007 renamed the body the **ASEAN Inter-Parliamentary Assembly** (AIPA). Similarly, police chiefs in the region also organized regular meetings, which were formalized in 1981 as the **Meeting of the Chiefs of National Police of the ASEAN Countries** (ASEANAPOL). The latter organization grew out of an informal caucus within the International Police Organization (Interpol). Neither AIPA nor ASEANAPOL are officially linked to ASEAN.

In 1980, ANRPC's three major rubber-exporting countries joined hands with rubber-importing countries to establish the **International Natural Rubber Organization** (INRO) to stabilize prices. Both ANRPC and INRO were set up in Kuala Lumpur, Malaysia. But, in 1999, the three major exporters (Indonesia, Malaysia, and Sri Lanka) withdrew from INRO on the basis of an ANRPC decision to cut production in order to prop up falling prices of natural rubber. INRO then collapsed, and in 2001, the **International Tripartite Rubber Organization** (ITRO) was formed, also in Kuala Lumpur, with only Indonesia, Malaysia, and Thailand as members.

Indonesia, Malaysia, and Thailand are also major tin-producing countries. After evaluating precursors in the colonial era and studies by UN organizations, they decided to form the **Association of Tin Producing Countries** (ATPC) in 1983. Although they hoped to stabilize the falling price of tin, there have fluctuations ever since, most recently upward.

In 1990, Malaysian Prime Minister Mahathir Mohamad proposed an East Asian caucus before meetings of the newly formed APEC conference. But he demurred when objections came from many quarters. In 1997, during the Asian economic crisis, he got his wish with the establishment of an informal **East Asian Economic Caucus** (EAEC) after the annual ASEAN meeting, bringing foreign ministers from China, Japan, and South Korea to discuss economic concerns with ASEAN countries. Meetings of EAEC, known colloquially as the "ASEAN+3 Forum," continued until 2005, when an **East Asia Summit** (EAS) of government heads convened for the first time, also after the ASEAN meeting. Those initially attending also included India, Australia, and New Zealand. In 2010, Russia and the United States attended as full members.

In 1991, an **Executives' Meeting of East Asia Pacific Central Banks** (EMEAP) was held to complement SEACEN. During the Asian financial crisis of the mid-1990s, there was considerable dissatisfaction with the role of the International Monetary Fund. Accordingly, in 1996, the Bank of Japan invited central bank governors under the EMEAP framework to a meeting in Tokyo to discuss options. Rather than a Yen bloc, an Asian Dollar, or an Asian monetary fund, the bankers decided to allocate more resources to anticipate and correct problems through study groups. Singapore's central bank, then, intervened to save the Thai currency. In 2003, the group set up an Asian Bond Fund that invests in a basket of US dollar-denominated bonds by Asian sovereign and quasi-sovereign issuers to assist Indonesia, Malaysia, the Philippines, and Thailand.

But during the worldwide financial crisis of 2007–2008, the proposal for a monetary fund resurfaced. In 2010, EMEAP finance ministers signed an agreement that allocates a swap currency fund of US$120 billion. A country with a dollar shortage can get support within a week after making the request, if approved by two-thirds of member states. EMEAP also agreed at last to establish the **Asian Monetary Fund** (AMF), and the **ASEAN+3 Macroeconomic Research Office** (AMRO) became AMF's Secretariat in Singapore. With only a US$120 billion fund, consisting of foreign exchange reserves pooled by member countries, AMRO now serves as the regional lender of last resort.

Southeast Asia has developed more IGOs than any other subregion. It should be no coincidence: Southeast Asians practice the Asian Way more than other Asian subregions.

Taiwan-Sponsored Organizations

At one time, the UN recognized the Republic of China on Taiwan as the sole representative of China. Two regional organizations emerged from that era but collapsed after Taiwan lost representation in the UN:

- **Asian Vegetable Research and Development Center** (1971)
- **Taxation and Customs Cooperation Conference** (1972).

After careful planning, the **Asian Vegetable Research and Development Center** (AVRDC) was launched at Tainan in 1971, the year coincidentally when Taiwan was unseated in the UN. Inspired by the nongovernmental International Rice Research Institute, whose executive officer moved to administer AVRDC, the organization launched efforts to develop strains of healthy vegetables that could withstand extreme weather conditions in Asia. In 1982, AVRDC expanded operations to Africa, transforming the scope of the organization. In 2008, accordingly, the organization became a nongovernmental entity under the working name AVRDC—The World Vegetable Center.

In 1972, the Republic of China invited three other countries to a meeting of what became the **Taxation and Customs Cooperation Conference** (TCCC). Although the headquarters was later located in the Philippines, in 1975 one member (South Vietnam) ceased to exist, and the People's Republic of China forced the other two members to withdraw, as Beijing does not abide a "two China" policy. TCCC then folded.

More UN-Sponsored Organizations

The UN headquarters in New York developed an attitude of rivalry at first as new regional organizations throughout the world appeared to compete with or duplicate programs of its various bodies. In the mid-1970s, there was a shift in perspective toward the idea that the UN could play a constructive role by supporting regional efforts (Andemicael 1979). The concept of a New International Economic Order was dawning with the view that less developed countries should join forces to gain control of their economies and charge developed countries more to purchase their primary products. More than a dozen organizations emerged:

- **Asian Coconut Community** (1969)
- **Regional Institute for Higher Education and Development** (1971)
- **Pepper Community** (1972)
- **Asian Clearing Union** (1974)
- **Asian Rice Trade Fund** (1974)
- **The Bangkok Agreement** (1975)
- **Asia-Pacific Institute for Broadcasting Development** (1977)
- **Centre for Integrated Rural Development for Asia and the Pacific** (1978)
- **Southeast Asian Tin Research and Development Centre** (1978)
- **Asian Reinsurance Corporation** (1979)
- **Asia-Pacific Telecommunity** (1979)
- **Government Consultation among Jute Producing Countries** (1979)
- **Intergovernmental Consultative Forum of Developing Tropical Timber Producing/Exporting Countries** (1982)
- **Regional Consultative Group on Silk** (1982)
- **Association of Tin Producing Countries** (1983)
- **Commission for the Conservation of South Bluefish Tuna** (1994)
- **Indian Ocean Tuna Commission** (1996).

ECAFE not only forged the agreement for the **Asian Coconut Community** (ACC) in 1969 but also provided the temporary secretariat. In 1971, ACC set up its headquarters in Jakarta and in 1975 became the **Asian and Pacific Coconut Community** (APCC) after accepting representation from South Pacific coconut-producing countries. Proposals for APCC to become an international body have been mooted, but thus far the only response has been to hold international conferences of coconut-producing countries from time to time.

A second commodity organization, the **Pepper Community** (PC) was launched in 1972 in a similar manner, with three Asian member countries. But when Brazil was accepted for membership, the organization became the **International Pepper Community** (IPC), no longer a strictly regional organization.

ECAFE also set up an **Asian Rice Trade Fund** (ARTF) in 1974 to balance the supply of rice between years of bad and good harvests. But the organization never got to the implementation stage, and no meetings of the plenary body have been held since 1977.

In 1971, the **Regional Institute of Higher Education and Development** (RIHED) emerged from an assessment by the UN Educational, Scientific and Cultural Organization (UNESCO) of the need to transform colonial-era colleges and universities into modern institutions of higher learning. Due to objections from the Philippines, which believed that its colleges and universities were up to date, SEAMEO rejected the idea of RIHED as a regional center. Instead, RIHED was constituted as an independent intergovernmental body. But in 1985, external funding dried up, and RIHED closed down. Then SEAMEO reconsidered its earlier rejection of the organization, and RIHED became one of its regional centers in 1993.

Among ECAFE's ideas about increasing economic integration or interdependence within Asia, the **Asian Clearing Union** (ACU) emerged in 1974. The concept was that countries in Asia could not count on immediate convertibility of their domestic currencies in intraregional trade, so at great expense they relied on the US dollar instead. ACU was set up to provide convertibility in local currencies, but only attracted India and eight countries adjacent to the South Asian subcontinent rather than all of Asia.

In 1975, ECAFE sponsored the **Agreement on Trade Negotiations among Developing Member Countries of the Economic and Social Commission for Asia and the Pacific**, otherwise known as the Bangkok Agreement, which established a framework for preferential tariff reductions among five countries (Bangladesh, India, South Korea, Laos, and Sri Lanka). Scattered across three subregions, the agreement languished until China joined in 2001. The name was changed in 2005 to **Asia-Pacific Trade Agreement** (APTA) to signal the beginning of four new rounds of trade concessions. Laos, however, has not participated in APTA. ESCAP continues to provide coordination.

In 1977, UNESCO laid the groundwork for the **Asia-Pacific Institute for Broadcasting Development** (AIBD) in 1977. The organization's headquarters is in Kuala Lumpur.

In 1978, the Food and Agriculture Organization of the UN (FAO) was instrumental in the formation of the **Centre for Integrated Rural Development for Asia and the Pacific** (CIRDAP). The organization was an obvious rival to AARRO, which then became moribund until revitalized.

In 1978, the **Southeast Asia Tin Research and Development Centre** (SEATRADC) became the fourth commodity community developed by ESCAP, and the **Government Consultation among Jute Producing Countries** (GCJPC) emerged in 1979 as the fifth. The Jute organization, however, collapsed in 2000, when India withdrew. SEATRADC shut down in 1994, but ATPC, formed by three Southeast Asian countries in 1983, as noted above, continues to operate.

ESCAP and the UN Conference on Trade and Development (UNCTAD) were also concerned that Asian insurance companies lost money because they relied on American and European sources to underwrite insurance policies. Asia did not have sufficient reserve capital. Accordingly, the **Asian Reinsurance Corporation** (Asian Re) was established in 1979, with a headquarters in Bangkok.

The International Telecommunications Union (ITU), a UN Specialized Agency, paved the way for the **Asia-Pacific Telecommunity** (APT) in 1979. The scope extends to radio, television, as well as telecommunications.

Two more commodity efforts by ESCAP emerged in 1982—the **Regional Consultative Group on Silk** (RCGS) and the **Intergovernmental Consultative Forum of Developing Tropical Timber Producing/Exporting Countries** (ICFDTTP/EC). However, the **International Tropical Timber Organization** (ITTO) superseded the timber forum in 1983. With many members outside Asia, ITTO is not an Asian-Pacific regional body, strictly defined.

After many years of discussion within FAO, the UN Fish Stocks Agreement was signed in 1995. The agreement provides the framework for regional efforts to mitigate overfishing. Two involve Asia. The first, the **Commission for the Conservation of Southern Bluefish Tuna** (CCSBT), began in 1994. The **Indian Ocean Tuna Commission** (IOTC) followed in 1996. Similar bodies are identified in the following chapter on Pacific regional organizations.

Central Asian Organizations

The dissolution of the Union of Soviet Socialist Republics (USSR) in 1991 meant independence for seven countries in Central Asia, known as the "stans." Gone was the security of an economic union and a mutual security arrangement. Building on a framework previously established in Iran, the result was seven new international organizations:

- **Regional Cooperation for Development** (1964)
- **Economic Cooperation Organization** (1985)
- **Central Asian Commonwealth** (1991)
- **Eurasian Economic Community** (2000)
- **Shanghai Cooperation Organization** (2001)
- **Collective Security Treaty Organization** (2002)
- **Organization of Central Asian Countries** (2002).

In 1964, Iran constructed an economic cooperation organization with Pakistan and Turkey known as **Regional Cooperation for Development** (RCD). When the Shah of Iran was toppled in 1979, RCD was abolished.

Then, in 1985, Iran revived the RCD framework as the **Economic Cooperation Organization** (ECO). In 1992, the body admitted as members six of the "stan" countries of Central Asia; Azerbaijan, Pakistan, and Turkey also belong to it. In 1995, when an agreement to establish an **ECO Trade and Development Bank** was signed, Uzbekistan was admitted to membership. However, implementation was deferred until 2005, when the treaty was ratified by the three original ECO members. In 2009, ECO countries agreed in principle to form a Trade Promotion Organization, but implementation has stalled.

In 1991, meanwhile, a **Central Asian Commonwealth** (CAC) was formed by Kazakhstan, Kyrgyzstan, Tajikistan, Turkmenistan, and Uzbekistan. CAC was renamed **Central Asian Economic Union** (CAEU) in 1994, though Tajikistan and Turkmenistan dropped out. In 1998, the group was renamed **Central Asian Economic Cooperation** (CAEC) when Tajikistan rejoined. In 2002, CAEC was renamed **Organization of Central Asian Cooperation** (OCAC).

Republics of the USSR enjoyed an economic union, but when the Soviet Union broke up, some Central Asian countries wanted to continue the close relationship. The result in 2000 was formation of the **Eurasian Economic Community** (EurAsEC or EAEC) with some Central Asian countries. The split between OCAC and EAEC ended in 2006, when the former merged into the latter.

In 1992, Russia sponsored a collective security treaty—the Commonwealth of Independent States Security Treaty—with several

Central Asian and European countries. No treaty organization was then established, however.

In 1994, concerned about the possible spread of Taliban extremism from Afghanistan, Kazakhstan President Nursultan Nazarbayev proposed a Central Asian Union to include Kazakhstan, Kyrgyzstan, and Uzbekistan. Short of foreign exchange for economic development, he also proposed a Central Asian Bank for Cooperation and Development, but the ideas never came to fruition.

In 1995, concerned about Russia's sponsorship of a collective security treaty involving countries on its border, China saw an opportunity to befriend Central Asian countries that formerly had been part of the once-hostile Soviet Union. In its first multilateral initiative, Beijing formed a grouping called the **Shanghai Five** with Kazakhstan, Kyrgyzstan, Tajikistan, and Russia as a mutual security grouping that served initially to coordinate reduction of troops on the China-Russia border (Bailes et al. 2007). When Uzbekistan joined the five in 2001, the grouping was renamed the **Shanghai Cooperation Organization** (SCO). Today, through SCO, China and Russia cooperate in matters of jihadism and terrorism. Although SCO members have signed an investment and trade agreement, implementation has not been forthcoming.

Partly in response to the expansion of the North Atlantic Treaty Organization (NATO) to Eastern Europe, in 2002 Russia formalized the mutual security treaty adopted in 1992 as the **Collective Security Treaty Organization** (CSTO). Initial members were Armenia, Belarus, Kazakhstan, Kyrgyzstan, Russia, and Tajikistan. Uzbekistan joined in 2006. The Secretariat of the biregional organization is in Moscow. Although CSTO holds peacekeeping exercises, they mostly involve Russian forces.

In spring 2008, the European Union launched an Eastern Partnership to attract participation by European countries formerly in the Soviet Union. Later that year, Russia in response offered EurAsEC countries membership in a customs union. The result is the **EurAsEC Customs Union Commission**.

Unlike Southeast Asia, regional organizations in Central Asia are a patchwork. Countries have joined and resigned from the organizations from time to time, and some rivalry between China and Russia pervades the framework. Iran's efforts to escape from international isolation add to the mix.

Copycat Organizations

The success of ASEAN spurred efforts to follow the same models. Two new organizations arose:

- **Conference of Foreign Ministers of Kampuchea, Laos, and Vietnam** (1980)
- **South Asian Association for Regional Cooperation** (1983).

In 1980, ASEAN was the model for an organization formally known as the **Conference of Foreign Ministers of Kampuchea, Laos, and Vietnam**. Vietnam had removed the Khmer Rouge from Cambodia by 1979 and sought to interlink the economies of the three countries as well as to provide a foreign policy forum. Sometimes referred to as the Indochinese Foreign Ministers Conference (IFMC), the economic aspect was not successful. IFMC folded when the foreign policy objective changed in 1988 to enhance the Cambodian peace process, which resulted in conferences and a peace agreement in 1991. Later, the Indochinese countries were eventually admitted to ASEAN.

In South Asia, the undisputed superpower is India, which has often annoyed neighboring countries in matters of trade. Bangladesh, accordingly, took the leadership in forming the **South Asian Association for Regional Cooperation** (SAARC) in 1983, which quickly grew along the lines of ASEAN, including adoption of a South Asian Free Trade Area Agreement in 1993 that remains unimplemented. SAARC remains hostage to the conflict between India and Pakistan (Dash 2008).

Post–Cold War Organizations

The dissolution of the Soviet Union and the end of the Cold War created ripple effects throughout the region. So did negotiations to form the World Trade Organization, which began operation in 1995. Four new organizations emerged:

- **Asia-Pacific Economic Cooperation** (1989)
- **Asia Pacific Forum of National Human Rights Institutions** (1996)
- **Forum for East Asia-Latin America Cooperation** (2001)
- **Southwest Pacific Dialogue** (2002).

While Europe was embarking on trade integration through the European Union, Australia, Canada, and the United States conceived of a forum that would bring about discussion that might lead to the removal of trade barriers in the Pacific. Canadian Prime Minister Kim Campbell, for example, expressed a desire to expand the North American Free Trade Agreement (NAFTA) beyond the Americas to the Pacific Rim (FEER 1993). ASEAN was initially opposed to having external powers dictate the terms of cooperation but agreed to participate in **Asia Pacific Economic Cooperation** (APEC) conferences when promised that they would operate informally rather than into binding agreements.

Since 1989, APEC has focused on trade liberalization, business cooperation, and economic and technical cooperation. The visibility of the organization was assured because conferences involve not only finance and trade ministers but also heads of governments. APEC members include Southeast Asian, East Asian, and South American countries bordering on the Pacific, along with Australia, New Zealand, and Papua New Guinea. APEC is biregional and therefore not an Asian regional organization in the pure sense. The potential for making important decisions, such as an APEC free trade area, has resulted in mass protests in the streets during annual meetings. In addition, APEC's inaction in the Asian financial crisis of 1997/1998 spurred countries of the region to consider a body of their own. Accordingly, with ASEAN leadership, EAS emerged in 2005 and AMF in 2010, as described above.

In 1996, four national human rights bodies (Australia, India, Indonesia, and New Zealand) met in Darwin, Australia, believing that matters of human rights had been left out of regional organizations. They decided to form the **Asia Pacific Forum of National Human Rights Institutions** (APF), with headquarters in Sydney. Today, 15 such bodies are members of this organization, including some in Western Asia (Jordan, the Palestinian State, and Qatar). Three country institutions are Associate Members. To become a full member, a national human rights body must conform to the Paris Principles, guidelines developed at a UN conference in Paris during 1991 to establish minimum standards for national human rights bodies. The organization holds meetings to determine priorities for the region. A major objective is to encourage other countries, particularly Myanmar, to set up national human rights institutions.

Not be outdone, ASEAN set up an Intergovernmental Commission on Human Rights in 2009. A consultative body to ASEAN, all ten ASEAN member countries participate.

For decades, government leaders in Asia had little contact with those on the Pacific Coast of Central and South America. APEC changed that. In 1999, a formal link was established between 15 Asian countries and 18 Latin American countries by an organization at first called the East Asia-Latin America Forum. In 2001, the biregional organization was renamed the **Forum for East Asia-Latin America Cooperation** (FEALAC) (cf. Spyros 2011).

Although Timor-Leste (East Timor) declared independence in 1975, Indonesia claimed and occupied the territory. A bitter struggle ensued, and the country's independence was recognized in 2002. Since ASEAN deferred to Indonesia's claim over the territory for many years, contrary to UN resolutions, Timor-Leste sought membership in both ASEAN and the Pacific Islands Forum. But ASEAN would not allow the country to have dual membership, so Timor-Leste has applied for ASEAN membership while being accorded Observer status in the Forum.

To provide a platform for the new country to interact with neighbors on all sides, Jakarta hosted a **Southwest Pacific Dialogue** (SwPD) in 2002 that includes Australia, Indonesia, the Philippines, Papua New Guinea, New Zealand, and Timor-Leste. Foreign ministers of the six countries meet annually, sometimes at UN headquarters in New York. The grouping sponsors scholarships, security information, training, and other forms of cooperation.

Testing Theories of Functionalism

Functionalist theory expects the formation of technical organizations to precede those focused on political and security issues; low politics linkages are expected to proliferate before organizations arise in matters of high politics. Neofunctionalists predict the opposite. Staircase functionalism predicts that technical bodies will indeed precede political IGOs, which in turn will spur more technical IGOS. The evidence presented above permits a critical test of all three theories within the various subregional waves (see Table 3.1).

Evidence for functionalism applies only to organizations led by India. The Korean case alone supports neofunctionalism. The two Taiwan-led organizations were dead ends, supporting none of the three theories. Staircase functionalism applies to the other four waves. In other words, there is a mixed result.

Table 3.1 Evidence for theories of functionalism in Asia

Leadership	*Technical IGOs Formed before Political IGOs*	*First Political IGO*	*Technical IGOs Formed after Political IGOs*
External	1	SEATO	1
Indian	2	IOR-ARC	0
Japanese	2	APU	6
Korean	0	ASPAC	5
Southeast Asia	4	ASEAN	5
Taiwan	2	none	0
Central Asia	2	SCO	1

However, multifunctionalism has been crucial in the transformation of ASEAN from a Southeast Asian organization to a keystone institution for all of Asia. The formation of ASEAN and the Forum, as discussed in the following chapter, suggests that a single multifunctional IGO can best bring peace to a region, whereas other forms of functionalism merely explain the waxing and waning of organizations.

Conclusion

The present chapter has reviewed many types of regional bodies.[5] Some are organizations with Secretariat offices. Some are rotating conferences of ministerial officials. Most are functional bodies that do not engage in "high politics."

The mere existence of an organization attests to some consensus within founding countries. Consistent with functionalism, most Asian organizations stick to their original purposes, hoping to attract new members without becoming politicized.

The Southeast Asian Ministers of Education Organization is an outstanding example of deepening activities within a single issue-area. The reason for increased activities has been external aid, not an increase in political commitment. From a half dozen regional centers in the beginning, SEAMEO now has about two dozen, partly because new members joined but mainly because financial commitments have mushroomed.

Only a few Asian organizations have become multifunctional. ASEAN has grown far beyond the original conception of the organization. SAARC, similarly, is multifunctional in scope, with many administrative divisions and functional bodies under a single umbrella. Neither Central Asia nor East Asia has developed a keystone institution.

As explained in Chapter 5 below, ASEAN is the most pivotal organization for Asia.

Many years ago, I had a discussion with Ernst Haas about Asian regional organizations. He expressed the judgment that they had not accomplished much. As compared with the economic integration taking place in Europe, he was right at that time. Proposals for a free trade area in Southeast Asia, then only adopted in principle, nevertheless have come into fruition very recently.

But he misjudged the main reason for Asian regional organizations—to build a web of functional interconnections so that war would be perceived as fratricide. While Western Europe had a united front with the Soviet Union, Asia was divided. The growth in regional organizations in Asia has served a much greater purpose than financial gain: With the exception of the Afghan War, associated violence inside Pakistan, and the lingering Kashmir and Korean conflicts, the continent is largely at peace, a precondition for joint economic progress.

No single, overarching political body brought about the current Asian détente. What has happened can be seen as a test for integration theories, as presented in the present book's first chapter. The region had little economic, security, or social pluralism before the growth of regional cooperation. Economically, little intraregional trade existed in the early years; trade patterns were a carryover from colonial patterns. Efforts to develop security pluralism, such as through SEATO, were a complete failure. Geographic and language barriers reduced the likelihood of social interaction. U Nyun's effort to develop cultural pluralism, as especially practiced in ASEAN, was critical for the rise of Asian institutions.

There is little evidence for classical functionalism, as the creation of Asian organizations in one issue-area did not spill over to others; each was separately created. The most transformational event, the first and second ASEAN Summits in 1976 and 1977, changed the organization's focus from political to economic concerns, consistent with neofunctionalism's expectation. After those meetings of government heads, the organization acquired a Secretariat, expanded in scope, and became an arena for managing conflicts that has now expanded to the ambitious ARF. Staircase functionalism, in other words, has operated within Southeast Asia, bringing about ASEAN as a multifunctional body.

The pattern of organizational growth for Asia is not the same as for the Pacific region, however. The following chapter explains why.

4

Waves of Pacific Regional Cooperation

When regional organizations began to be formed in Asia, similar developments in the Pacific had already occurred. There were four South Pacific organizations before Asia's first regional body, the Colombo Plan, began in 1951.

Once again, the focus on waves is to determine what role, if any, pluralistic influences have had on regional cooperation among the Pacific Island nations. Social pluralism (social communication patterns) was nearly nonexistent when regional institutions were built in the region, since no landmass unites them. Security pluralism is inapplicable, as nations in the Pacific do not perceive military threats. Transactional linkages were imperial and lingered long after Asian countries achieved independence; increased prosperity through trade has been a goal. In other words, only cultural pluralism can explain why the climate existed for a profusion of almost 50 regional bodies in the Pacific.

If functionalism truly describes regional cooperation in the Pacific, the various regional organizations in specific issue-areas should exist side by side rather than being interconnected, with task expansion entirely sparked by the successes of experts. Neofunctionalists, however, would expect that organizational stability and growth is a result of decision by political leaders, not experts. Multifunctionalists expect that political leaders will expand the scope of a successful organization into many new issue-areas, not just more activity related to the original purpose. Institutional functionalism would link particular procedures to organizational growth. The present chapter provides a test of which theory best explains organizational developments in the Pacific.

The waves of leadership in the Pacific roughly resemble those operating in Asia. But Pacific Island leaders quickly established a forum for heads of government, something that has never occurred in Asia. They did so by first combining countries from Melanesia and Polynesia and later incorporated Micronesia.[1] More recently, countries of the Americas bordering on the Pacific have been embraced within some but not all organizations.

The lesser role of the UN is due in part to the fact that the Economic Commission for Asia and the Far East (ECAFE) initially had only two Pacific countries as members—Australia and New Zealand. Not until 1974 did ECAFE officially expand its geographic scope to Pacific Island countries, renaming itself the Economic and Social Commission for Asia and the Pacific (ESCAP).

Colonial Leadership

In the first wave of regional organizations, the period from the mid-1940s to the mid-1950s, Western powers created five regional institutions:

- **South Pacific Health Service** (1946)
- **South Pacific Air Transport Council** (1946)
- **Conference of Commissioners of Police of Australasia and the South West Pacific Region** (1947)
- **South Pacific Commission** (1948)
- **ANZUS Council** (1952).

The most prominent are the **South Pacific Commission** (SPC) in 1948 and the **ANZUS Council** of the Security Treaty Between Australia, New Zealand, and the United States in 1952. Less well known are two organizations formed in 1946—the **South Pacific Health Service** (SPHS) and the **South Pacific Air Transport Council** (SPATC), both of which later folded. The least prominent is the **Conference of Commissioners of Police of Australasia and the South West Pacific Region** (CCPASWPR), which was formed as a bilateral body comprising Australia and New Zealand in 1903, but became a trilateral body when Fiji joined in 1947.[2] CCPASWPR continues to the present and has many of the newly independent countries as members.

SPC, the most important early organization, began with all the region's colonial powers (Australia, Britain, France, the Netherlands, New Zealand, and United States) as members. The aim was to provide economic assistance for the peoples of the South Pacific. All six original countries met together in a body called the Session. The island peoples were only allowed to comment on their projects at a different body—the triennial South Pacific Conference. But as more Pacific Island states became independent, the two meetings were scheduled together for the first time in 1967, and the Session was abolished in 1973.

Meanwhile, countries in the North Pacific were still part of the American-administered UN strategic trusteeship. As they became independent and joined SPC, the organization was renamed the **Pacific Community** (PC) in 1997. The SPC acronym was retained as the administrative body for the Pacific Community—the Secretariat of the Pacific Community (SPC).

The **ANZUS Council** began with three members. But the United States booted New Zealand out of organizational aspects of ANZUS in 1984, when an American naval vessel was refused port entry in New Zealand because the newly elected prime minister required Washington to certify that the ship was not carrying nuclear weapons. Australia and the United States continue meetings known as the **Australia-United States Ministerial Consultation** (AUSMIN). Australia continued to cooperate bilaterally with New Zealand, but the Council itself ceased to meet. In 2010, however, there were vague signs that New Zealand might return to ANZUS (Callick 2010).

As in the case of Asia, most organizations formed by external powers fared poorly. Countries indigenous to the region were much more successful in responding to the needs of the countries.

Fiji-Sponsored Organizations

Regional cooperation promoted by external powers placed Pacific countries in roles of dependence. Regional powers wanted to construct their own edifice of cooperation, and the result was a wave of activity centered in Fiji, which became independent in 1970:

- **Pacific Islands Producers' Association** (1968)
- **South Pacific Chiefs of Police Conference** (1970)

- **University of the South Pacific** (1970)
- **South Pacific Forum** (1971)
- **Committee for Co-ordination of Joint Prospecting for Mineral Resources in South Pacific Offshore Areas** (1972)
- **South Pacific Board for Educational Assessment** (1981)
- **Tourism Council of the South Pacific** (1983).

Pacific Island countries harvest some cash crops for the world market, but have been hampered by commercial shipping companies that play one island country against another to keep purchase prices low. Even before independence, Ratu Mara, then Minister for Natural Resources of Fiji, went to neighboring island countries and persuaded them in 1968 to set up a secretariat to coordinate prices. The organization was called the **Pacific Islands Producers' Association** (PIPA). One of the crops was coconuts, so in 1971, Samoa joined the Asian Coconut Community (ACC) on behalf of PIPA countries, and ACC in 1975 became the Asian and Pacific Coconut Community in recognition of PIPA. But in 1974, PIPA was disbanded, largely because the Forum decided to absorb PIPA's functions.

Even though Fiji joined CCPASWPR before independence in 1947, the only other South Pacific member countries were the British Solomon Islands (which dropped out in 1959) and Papua New Guinea. In 1970, the Fiji police chief decided to form the **South Pacific Chiefs of Police Conference** (SPCPC), opening membership to already independent Nauru and Tonga as well as many other island states that were on the verge of independence. SPCPC started with seven members and grew quickly (cf. Boswell 2010). In 2000, the body was renamed the **Pacific Islands Chiefs of Police** (PICP).

A patchwork of institutions of higher learning existed during the colonial era in the South Pacific within Fiji, Papua New Guinea, and Samoa. The smaller states lacked facilities and finances to set up their own colleges. After the Commonwealth Secretariat commissioned a study on the problem, the decision was made to found the **University of the South Pacific** (USP) at Suva, Fiji, with sufficient resources to educate students from other Pacific Island countries. USP opened its doors in 1968, when 13 countries had signed the university's charter, pledging to provide appropriate share of funds on an annual basis. In 1970, the agreement was fully ratified. Subsequently, USP has established mini-campuses in nine countries outside of Fiji.

But who would attend USP? With government agencies so closely involved in USP finances, there was a temptation to send students who were politically connected but unqualified. After a study of the problem by the New Zealand Department of Education in 1975, a decision was made to set up the **South Pacific Board for Educational Assessment** (SPBEA), which began at Suva in 1981, when seven countries signed the organization's constitution. SPBEA is responsible for entrance exam screening of USP applicants.

Pacific Island countries are ideal locations for tourism, having pristine beaches and an ideal climate, yet they are remote from mainland America and Asia. Due to the obvious potential, the need to develop tourist markets prompted Malakai Gucake of the Fiji Visitor's Bureau to propose the **Tourism Council of the South Pacific** (TCSP), which was adopted at a conference in 1983. In 1998, the name was changed to **South Pacific Tourism Organisation** (SPTO), which is governed by representatives from member governments but also permits private tourism companies to join.

Asian and Pacific countries have vast offshore areas where oil and other minerals might be found, yet they lack adequate technology to engage in prospecting. Accordingly, ECAFE set up the Committee for Co-ordination of Joint Prospecting in Asian Offshore Areas (CCOP) in 1966. After oil was discovered in Tonga during 1968, Fiji asked ECAFE to allow a similar body for the South Pacific. The result in 1972 was the **Committee for Co-ordination of Joint Prospecting for Mineral Resources in South Pacific Offshore Areas** (CCOP/SOPAC) within ECAFE, though a Secretariat was established at Suva in 1974. In 1984, CCOP/SOPAC became an independent, intergovernmental body apart from the UN system, and in 1990 was renamed the **Pacific Islands Applied Geoscience Commission** (SOPAC). In 2010, SOPAC became a division within the Secretariat of the Pacific Community (SPC).

Leadership by the Forum

The most important regional organization in the Pacific emerged from efforts by Ratu Sir Kamisese Mara, Fiji's first prime minister. Known originally as the **South Pacific Forum** (SPF), he sought to bring heads of government of newly independent states into contact as an alternative to SPC.

Meanwhile, the United States administered the UN strategic trusteeship over Pacific islands north of the equator, which Washington called the Trust Territory of the Pacific Islands (TTPI). In 1986, that arrangement was abolished, and negotiations began for the countries to achieve independence. In 1990, the UN abolished TTPI. Washington then granted independence to most North Pacific countries, which in turn sought membership in the Forum. In 1999, the organization was renamed **Pacific Islands Forum** (PIF).

The Forum is in a strategic position to review problems of the region as a whole and then design organizational solutions. Several organs derived from Forum action are internal, while others are subsidiary bodies yet are semiautonomous because those involved hold high-ranking positions in Pacific Island governments. The South Pacific Bureau for Economic Co-operation (SPEC), formed in 1972, became the Forum's secretariat in 1975 and thereby the principal coordinating body that played a key role in spinning off new organizations, some of which later were renamed:

- **South Pacific Regional Meeting on Telecommunications** (1973)
- **South Pacific Regional Shipping Council** (1975)
- **South Pacific Regional Civil Aviation Council** (1976)
- **Pacific Forum Line** (1977)
- **Regional Committee on Trade** (1979)
- **South Pacific Trade Commission** (1979)
- **South Pacific Forum Fisheries Agency** (1979)
- **Melanesian Spearhead Group** (1986)
- **South Pacific Environmental Program** (1995)
- **Pacific Aviation Safety Office** (2002)
- **Smaller Island States Summit** (2002)
- **Pacific Directors of Civil Aviation Security Forum** (2012)
- **Polynesian Leaders Group** (2011).

The proliferation began in 1973, when SPEC convened communication ministers to form the **South Pacific Regional Meeting on Telecommunications** (SPECTEL). Although no ministerial-level conclave was held afterward, subministerial-rank officials met regularly up to 1988 to coordinate a regional plan to bring telephone service to the region, while a program coordinator within SPEC handled day-to-day operations. By 1999, the **Forum Communications Ministers Meeting**

(FCMM) superseded SPECTEL. In 1997, by which time new telecommunication firms provided services to the islands, the Pacific Islands Telecommunications Association (PITA), a nongovernmental body composed of the various regional telecommunication companies, was formed.

One problem identified by PIPA was irregularity of shipping. The region's transportation problems had been mostly irregular and uncoordinated. After discussion in SPF and ESCAP, the Forum charged SPEC with setting up a meeting of transportation ministers. The result was a meeting of the **South Pacific Regional Shipping Council** (SPRSC) in 1975 to determine priorities. In 1977, the body then agreed to establish the **Pacific Forum Line** (PFL), an autonomous corporation with eight countries as original shareholders in the corporation; later, four additional countries bought shares, though PFL links only eight countries today. In 1996, SPRSC was incorporated into the structure of the South Pacific Commission, and has been known from 2007 as the **Regional Transport Ministers Meeting**.

Similarly, the **South Pacific Regional Civil Aviation Council** (SPRCAC) emerged in 1976, when SPEC implemented a Forum resolution. Later, the body was renamed the **Pacific Islands Forum Aviation Ministers Meeting** (FAMM). Senior civil aviation officials formed a Standing Committee to undertake planning, leaving implementation to SPEC's Transport Division. In 2006, the functions of the Transport Division were transferred to SPC.

In 1998, meanwhile, FAMM agreed in principle to set up a **Pacific Aviation Safety Office** (PASO). In 2002, Vanuatu agreed to host PASO, and in 2004, a treaty on air safety was signed, formalizing PASO as an intergovernmental body. PASO's governing body is the Council of Directors, which appoints PASO's General Manager. PASO now undertakes safety audits in the region. In 2010, the **Pacific Directors of Civil Aviation Security Forum**, as successor to FAMM, was established by the Pacific Community to meet annually.

The economic viability of the island states of the South Pacific depends on income from trade. As SPEC was specifically set up to handle economic issues, trade concerns have been in the forefront. In 1944, Australia and New Zealand formed a bilateral trade agreement, and then strengthened the relationship into a free trade agreement in 1966. In 1975, when Australia granted independence to Papua New Guinea, the two countries also signed a free trade agreement.

The remaining South Pacific island states were eager to link with both Australia and New Zealand and saw the agreement with Papua New Guinea as a model.

In 1979, meanwhile, SPEC convened trade ministers to form the **Regional Committee on Trade** (RCT) to discuss trade issues at the highest policy level. In 1980, the Forum sponsored the **South Pacific Regional Trade and Economic Co-operation Agreement** (SPARTECA) as a framework, leaving details to be worked out within the Forum and RCT to identify products of Pacific Island governments that would be admitted to Australia and Zealand on favorable terms. The **Forum Trade Ministers Meeting** (FTMM) assumed that responsibility in 1999.

Australia decided to jump-start the process of trade promotion by volunteering to set up the **South Pacific Trade Commission** (SPTC) through an exchange of letters with SPEC in 1979. SPTC consists of an office in downtown Sydney with a Director who seeks to find markets for goods produced by Pacific Island countries. In 1988, the name changed to **Pacific Islands Trade and Investment Commission** (PITIC), with offices in China, Japan, and New Zealand as well as Australia.

SPEC planning also resulted in the **South Pacific Forum Fisheries Agency** (FFA) in 1979, an organization headquartered in Honiara, Solomon Islands, that enjoys complete autonomy. FFA licenses fishing vessels in the region and conducts research on fishing patterns and stocks and other matters. In 2004, the organization was renamed **Pacific Islands Forum Fisheries Agency** (PIFFA). In 1979, SPEC established the **South Pacific Regional Environmental Programme** (SPREP) in cooperation with the South Pacific Commission. SPREP later set up a head office in Apia. An agreement drawn up to make SPREP an independent IGO finally went into force in 1995. In 2004, the organization changed its name to **Pacific Regional Environmental Programme** (PREP). (The acronym remained SPREP by placing the letter "S" from the word "Secretariat" before the abbreviated new name of the organization.)

In 1986, heads of state of Papua New Guinea, Solomon Islands, and Vanuatu met together before a Forum summit. They were concerned that the main beneficiaries of the organization appeared to be Polynesian countries neighboring Fiji. Accordingly, from 1987 they declared their caucus to be the **Melanesian Spearhead Group** (MSG), at first only as a mini-summit. Later, MSG established an annual meeting of foreign ministers. A Secretariat in Vanuatu now parallels activities of the Forum in some respects. MSG remains an entirely independent intergovernmental organization.

In 1989, the Forum for the first time invited countries providing aid to the region to a **Post-Forum Dialogue** (PFD). The innovation was apparently based on the success of ASEAN's Post Ministerial Conference. In 1992, another innovation was the **Forum Regional Security Committee**, which meets before Forum summits to discuss international law enforcement and security matters.

For years, foreign policy and security considerations were the province of the annual Forum summit of heads of government. Then in 2000, a separate meeting of heads of foreign ministries began under the title **Forum Foreign Affairs Ministers Meeting** (FFAMM).

In 1994, meanwhile, MSG launched a limited free trade agreement among the member countries. Australia and Fiji signed a free trade agreement in 1999, when Fiji joined MSG, and the four countries agreed to increase the scope of the agreement to all products by 2005. Both actions goaded the rest of Forum member countries to negotiate the Pacific Island Countries Trade Agreement (PICTA). Adopted in 2001, PICTA is a free trade area among Pacific Island governments, governed by a trade ministers conference and implemented by the Forum's Secretariat.

Also in 2001, SPARTECA was supplemented by the Pacific Agreement on Closer Economic Relations (PACER), which provides a framework for future development of trade cooperation between Australia and New Zealand with the Pacific Island states. The structure developed for PACER was designed to manage PICTA. Accordingly, in 1998, the first **Forum Economic Ministers Meeting** (FEMM) was held.

In 2002, the Forum hosted a meeting of the smallest Pacific Island states. Known as the **Smaller Island States Summit** (SIS), the aim is to enable countries with very limited resources to consider their own needs apart from the larger states. SIS meetings have been held ever since, involving Cook Islands, Kiribati, Marshall Islands, Nauru, Palau, and Tuvalu.

MSG's formation puzzled some members of the Forum, who did not know how to react at first. In 2010, after a Forum meeting, some representatives from Polynesian countries met and decided to launch their own body. In 2011, the **Polynesian Leaders Group** (PLG) was formally launched in a meeting at Apia, Samoa, by three sovereign states (Samoa, Tonga, and Tuvalu) along with nonsovereign American Samoa, Cook Islands, French Polynesia, Niue, and Tokelau. Since Fiji is home to both Melanesians and Polynesians, the centrality of Suva may bring the two splinter groups together. But so far, the division complicates regional cooperation in the South Pacific.

In sum, the Forum has become a multifunctional organization. Its organizational chart reveals a large number of divisions that deal with technical matters. Having absorbed PIPA and SOPAC, the Forum has established a central place in the region. That centrality, in turn, resulted in the breakaway MSG, which also has aspirations to become multifunctional.

Hawai'i-Sponsored Organizations

The state of Hawai'i is one of the 50 states of the United States. Up to 1893, during the years of the Kingdom of Hawai'i, embassies were located in Honolulu, the capital. Today, however, diplomatic representation is by consulates. Except for New York and Washington, more international organizations are headquartered in Honolulu than in any other city of the United States. Most are nongovernmental bodies, but a few were set up to link governments:

- **Pacific-Asian Congress of Municipalities** (1971)
- **Pacific Islands Tourism Development Council** (1976)
- **Pacific Islands Conference** (1980)
- **Joint Commercial Commission** (1993).

Honolulu, with a population of nearly a million, has several "sister cities," as do most big cities throughout the world, but those intergovernmental relationship are bilateral. A truly "international" body must have at least three sovereign states as members. As Honolulu has more than two dozen sister cities, the need to coordinate that aspect of government in an efficient manner stimulated Mayor Frank Fasi to consider an umbrella organization for all cities in countries bordering on the Pacific. Accordingly, in 1971, he hosted the Founder's Session of the **Pacific-Asian Congress of Municipalities** (PACOM), with 81 cities representing 27 countries in attendance. (The Honolulu City

Council insisted on the term "Municipalities" so that city legislators as well as mayors would be welcome.) PACOM was a breakthrough in that for the first time countries in South America (Ecuador, Panamá, and Perú) attended an international organization that claimed to be centered in the Pacific. When Fasi was defeated for reelection in 1980, PACOM continued at a lower level of activity and nearly died out, but he won election in 1984 and revived the organization. In 1996, after he served his last term in office, the organization became moribund. In 2011, Honolulu hosted a Sister Cities Summit, inviting all sister cities to attend, but that was a one-time event.

Polynesian residents of Honolulu have long felt affinity for their kin in islands elsewhere in the Pacific. In 1972, Governor John Burns recruited Andrew Gerakas from a UN assignment in Apia, Samoa, to serve as executive director of a unit of Hawai'i state government to promote tourism development in the region. In 1976, after a series of conferences, the **Pacific Islands Tourism Development Council** (PITDC) was formed. But the body collapsed in 1979, when Pacific Island states realized that PITDC was too oriented to Hawai'i tourism. The body now known as SPTO, formed in 1983 as discussed above, excludes Hawai'i from membership.

In 1980, the Pacific Basin Development Council (PBDC) began where PITDC left off as an organization linking governors of American Samoa, Guam, Hawai'i, and the North Mariana Islands, all under American control. The organization, not a true international body of sovereign states, collapsed when the legislature of Hawai'i ceased financial support in 1986.

The fourth initiative from the Aloha State came from an entity located on the edge of the University of Hawai'i campus, colloquially known as the East-West Center (EWC). Founded in 1960 as the Center for Cultural Interchange Between East and West, President Barack Obama's mother received scholarship funding from the Center, and later was supported by its Technology and Development Institute. The same institute also provided research support for me while I began to prepare publications on Asian and Pacific regional cooperation (M.Haas 1974, 1979–1980, 1985, 1989a, 1989b).

Initially a unit of the University, EWC became an independent corporation in 1975 and changed its name by adding the words "and Technology" between "Cultural" and "Interchange." Fiji's Ratu Mara was a charter member of the new governing board. Everett Kleinjans, the president, then consulted with leaders in the region to determine how the EWC might best play a constructive role. As a result, EWC in 1980 sponsored the **Pacific Islands Conference** (PIC), where heads of governments and administrations of Pacific Island countries would, in Kleinjans's term, be "free to talk" in developing broad priorities for the region. PIC's secretariat remains at EWC. Observer status at PIC meetings has been extended to seven sister organizations—FFA, SOPAC, SPC, SPF, SPREP, SPTO, and USP. PIC now meets at three-year intervals.

PIC provided a forum in which a proposal emerged for a **Joint Commercial Commission** (JCC) to enhance trade between Pacific Island countries and the United States. After discussions at two PICs, the organization was launched in 1993.

Fish Stocks Organizations

Overfishing of tuna has been a concern for many years. The result has been the development of several organizations covering various parts of the world, including three relating to the Pacific:

- **Inter-American Tropical Tuna Commission** (1949)
- **Western and Central Pacific Fisheries Commission** (2004)
- **Commission for the Conservation and Management of Highly Migratory Fish Stocks in the Western and Central Pacific Ocean** (2004).

The first effort to provide a fish stock agreement was the **Inter-American Tropical Tuna Commission** (IATTC), which was created by a treaty of 1949 with a headquarters in San Diego, California. However, no island states in the Pacific were independent at the time, so the organization could not then be considered a regional organization alongside the others reviewed in the present chapter. In 2003, however, negotiations were undertaken to revise the original treaty and to include several South Pacific Island states. In 2010, the Convention for the Strengthening of the Inter-American Tropical Tuna Commission, known as the Antigua Convention, came into force. The headquarters is now in La Jolla, immediately adjacent to San Diego.

The Food and Agriculture Organization of the United Nations sponsored several conferences over the years, culminating in the

UN Fish Stocks Agreement of 1995. Five years later, the Western and Central Pacific Fisheries Convention was negotiated and opened for signature. A body known as the **Commission for the Conservation and Management of Highly Migratory Fish Stocks in the Western and Central Pacific Ocean** is responsible for implementation of the treaty. The short title is **Western and Central Pacific Fisheries Commission** (WCPFC), which was set up in 2004 with headquarters in Kolonia, Pohnpei, Federated States of Micronesia. IATTC is now understood to apply to the Eastern Pacific, whereas WCPFC covers the Central and Western Pacific.

Currently, the Commission for the Conservation of Antarctic Marine Living Resources (CCAMLR), the Commission for the Conservation of Southern Bluefish Tuna (CCSBT), and the Indian Ocean Tuna Commission (IOTC) also seek to preserve fishing stocks. They are not Pacific Island regional organizations in view of their geographic scope. The first two were discussed in the previous chapter.

Organizations Formed without Waves

Some organizations arose out of need rather than because of strong leadership. They arose individually rather than emerging in waves:

- **South Pacific Judicial Conference** (1972)
- **South Pacific Labour Ministers Conference** (1973)
- **Cook Islands/Niue/New Zealand Joint Shipping Service** (1975)
- **Pacific Island Law Officers' Meeting** (1981)
- **Association of Pacific Island Legislatures** (1981)
- **Customs Head of Administration Regional Meeting** (1986)
- **Pacific Islands Development Bank** (1989)
- **Pacific Island Tax Administrators Association** (2004).

Although the chief justices of American Samoa and Western Samoa originally proposed a bilateral conference, they took note of the formation of the South Pacific Forum and passed the idea along to other chief justices in the region. An initial conference, with attorneys general as well, was held in Apia, Samoa, in 1972. Afterward, meetings were held on a biennial basis under the label **South Pacific Judicial Conference**. The body was renamed **Pacific Judicial Conference** (PJC) in 2004.

Another meeting of government officials, the **South Pacific Labour Ministers Conference** (SPLMC), was convened by Australia's Prime Minister Gough Whitlam. Aware of the Conference of Labor Ministers (CALM), he thought that a Pacific counterpart was needed, as the International Labour Organisation (ILO) had no office in the South Pacific. Then in 1975, ILO set up an office in Suva, and in 1976, CALM was retitled the Conference of Asian and Pacific Labor Ministers (CAPLM), absorbing South Pacific Labour Ministers Conference (SPLMC) after 1983. Nevertheless, encouraged by ILO, the SPLMC meeting was revived in 2010, but retitled the **Pacific Islands Labour Ministers Conference** (PILMC) as the Marshall Islands from the North Pacific had joined ILO.

Exporters from Pacific Island states hope that ships will be available to pick up primary products. But for the diminutive Cook Islands and Niue, the irregular arrival of commercial vessels was so intolerable that New Zealand offered in 1975 to underwrite and supply the **Cook Islands/Niue/New Zealand Joint Shipping Service** (JSS). Both countries are self-governing but maintain an association with New Zealand, as those born in either territory qualify as citizens of New Zealand. Today, commercial vessels provide regular service, so JSS is no longer needed.

Although top police officials enjoyed two conferences, as noted above, the needs of police officials at mid-management levels remained. Accordingly, Vanuatu's attorney general organized the **Pacific Islands Law Officers Meeting** (PILOM) in 1981. The need to share information, as criminal gangs hop from island to island, has become increasingly important over the years. In 2007, the body was retitled the **Pacific Islands Law Officers' Network** (PILON).

In 1981, the Territory of Guam sponsored the **Association of Pacific Island Legislatures** (APIL), primarily as a body to bring together legislators from the newly independent states of the North Pacific that had once been governed by the United States within the UN Strategic Trusteeship. The organization continues that role and has also accepted members from Nauru, Kiribati, and the State of Hawai'i.

One proposal suggested at APIL was for a bank that would serve the region. In 1989, APIL members launched an undercapitalized **Pacific Islands Development Bank** (PIDB). Membership exclusively consists of APIL members.

One aspect of trade is the official processing of imports at ports of entry, known as customs. Delays occur when product classifications differ from country to country, especially if inspection for contraband is ongoing. In 1986, the **Customs Heads of Administration Regional Meeting** (CHARM) held an initial meeting to rationalize various aspects of customs procedures. In 1998, CHARM proved successful in drafting a comprehensive treaty regarding customs in the region. The treaty, in turn, established by the **Oceania Customs Organization** (OCO), which has superseded CHARM. OCO's Secretariat is in Brisbane.

The viability of Pacific Island governments depends upon their ability to have revenue to cover expenses, a problem dealt with in Asia by the Study Group on Tax Administration and Research (SGATAR). A counterpart in the Pacific is the **Pacific Island Tax Administrators Association** (PITAA), which has met since 2004. A frequent proposal at PITAA meetings is to fund a secretariat to implement priorities.

Coordination of Pacific Intergovernmental Organizations

The Economic and Social Commission for Asia and the Pacific provides some coordination of regional organizations within Asia but very little for Pacific Island bodies. For some years, rivalry existed between the South Pacific Commission and the South Pacific Forum despite conscientious efforts to avoid duplication of effort. In 1988, a decision was made to establish the **South Pacific Organisations Coordinating Committee** (SPOCC) to provide a formal basis for coordination. In 1999, the name was changed to the **Council of Regional Organisations in the Pacific** (CROP).

Currently, CROP has representation from several Pacific regional organizations. The largest are the Pacific Community (the renamed South Pacific Commission) and the Forum; the latter serves as CROP's secretariat. Six organizations, identified above, also have been members—the Forum Fisheries Agency, South Pacific Applied Geoscience Commission, South Pacific Bureau for Educational Assessment, South Pacific Regional Environment Programme, South Pacific Travel Organization, and the University of the South Pacific. In addition, CROP has representation from three nongovernmental international bodies—the Fiji School of Medicine, the East-West Center's Pacific Island Development Program, and the Pacific Power Association.

The existence of the Forum as a unifying political body has enabled careful planning, and CROP ensures that duplication and overlap are minimal. Expertise is shared within the various functional organizations. Pacific Island states seek a free trade area, though the resulting marginalization of inefficient producers could be unsettling. Thus, Pacific Island states seek some form of economic integration, but they are cautious in going on that route.

Testing Theories of Functionalism

Similar to the test of functionalist theories in the previous chapter, evidence in the present chapter can be used to determine whether technical organizations precede political-security IGOs (functionalism) or the opposite (neofunctionalism). Staircase functionalism predicts that technical bodies will both precede and follow political-security IGOS.

The evidence provides overwhelming support for staircase functionalism (see Table 4.1). The formation of ANZUS was the last gasp of colonial leadership. Fiji's efforts to launch the Forum came after three technical initiatives, as functionalists might expect, but the Forum has encouraged a multiplicity of new technical bodies.

Multifunctionalism, that is, the growth in new functions within a keystone organization, is also strongly supported. Strong political backing of the Forum as the central regional institution led to a proliferation of new functions inside the organization as well as to the formation of the CROP coordinating body.

Conclusion

Whereas Asian countries are often picky about aid projects, seeing them as possible neocolonial scams, independent Pacific Island countries consider foreign aid to be indispensible. Without attention to

Table 4.1 Evidence for theories of functionalism in the Pacific

Leadership	*Technical IGOs Formed Before Political IGOs*	*First Political IGO*	*Technical IGOs Formed After Political IGOs*
Colonial	4	ANZUS	0
Fijian/Forum	3	Forum	11+
Hawai'i	2	PIC	1

their economies, many countries would not have a chance to become viable states.

Testing pluralism theories presented in the first chapter, the Pacific region had little economic (transactional), security, or social pluralism before the growth of regional cooperation. Economically, intraregional trade among Pacific Island countries did not exist in the early years and still remains a goal. Trade patterns with former colonial powers were insufficient for prosperity, so an increase in Pacific Island country trade with Australia and New Zealand has long been an objective. Efforts to develop security pluralism, such as through ANZUS, had no impact upon regional cooperation because of a lack of a common threat, even during the Cold War. The region remains at peace externally, though internal conflicts have arisen and the Forum has been an important regional institution in dealing with security matters, as discussed in Chapter 6 below. Geographic barriers reduced the possibility for social interaction, whereas Ratu Mara's effort to develop cultural pluralism, as especially practiced in the Forum, was critical in launching so many Pacific institutions.

The South Pacific Commission grew in scope over the years largely because of generous funding from outside the region. But the most transformational event was the establishment of the Forum in 1971. Many organizations arose thereafter. During that first meeting, government heads agreed upon a Secretariat and prioritized economic issues.

Multifunctionalism receives strong support in part because the scope of the Forum expanded in later years, even absorbing SOPAC. The Forum served to promote much trust between political leaders and thereby had the capability to become an arena for managing conflicts when serious ethnic conflicts later broke out within some countries of the region. Nevertheless, the primary goal remains to seek prosperity.

Thus, both Asian regionalism and Pacific regionalism share cultural pluralism as primary preconditions and postconditions for organizational success. In addition, the evidence supports staircase functionalism in both regions. However, both ASEAN and the Forum have not only become central to their respective regions but also pivotal. The following chapter explains how they maneuvered themselves into indispensible organizations.

5

Pivotal Roles in Regional Cooperation

The history of regional cooperation in Asia and the Pacific has largely been one of growth in spurts during the last half of the twentieth century. Few new organizations have emerged during the twenty-first century. From the 1970s, three organizations have consciously tried to manage the proliferation of new institutions, playing pivotal roles—the UN Economic and Social Commission for Asia and the Pacific, the Association of South-East Asian Nations, and the Pacific Islands Forum. In the present chapter, turning points are identified in transforming Asia from a zone of conflict into an arena of peace and enabling the Pacific Island peoples to transcend a colonial past by enjoying peaceful and supportive relations with Australia and New Zealand.

Dead Ends

One way to understand the dynamics of regional cooperation in Asia and the Pacific is to examine the 19 organizations that folded:

- **Asian and Pacific Council** (ASPAC)
- **Asian and Pacific Maritime Cooperation Scheme** (APMCS)
- **Asian Judicial Conference** (AJC)
- **Asian Rice Trade Fund** (ARTF)
- **Economic Cooperation Center for the Asian and Pacific Region** (ECOSEN)
- **Indochinese Foreign Ministers Conference** (IFMC)

- **International Natural Rubber Organization** (INRO)
- **Ministerial Conference for the Economic Development of Southeast Asia** (SEAMCED)
- **Pacific-Asian Congress of Municipalities** (PACOM)
- **Pacific Islands Tourism Development Council** (PITDC)
- **Regional Cooperation for Development** (RCD)
- **Registry of Scientific and Technical Services for the Asian and Pacific Region**
- **South-East Asia Treaty Organization** (SEATO)
- **Southeast Asian Promotion Centre for Trade, Investment and Tourism** (SEAPCENTRE)
- **Southeast Asia Regional Organization for Inter-Governmental Cooperation and Coordination in Family and Population Planning in Southeast Asia** (IGCC)
- **Southeast Asian Tin Research and Development Centre** (SEATRADC)
- **South Pacific Health Service** (SPHS)
- **South Pacific Air Transport Council** (SPATC)
- **Taxation and Customs Cooperation Conference** (TCCC).

One obvious conclusion is that organizations sponsored by countries at the margin do less well than those at the heartland of both regions. Organizations formed for political reasons by Japan, South Korea, and the United States were terminated when political winds shifted and a more peaceful, less confrontational, approach was preferred. Some organizations ended because funds ran out. Iran's revolution of 1979 was the death knell for RCD. China's antipathy for an independent Taiwan killed TCCC. Vietnam ended IFMC to advance the Cambodian peace process. ESCAP's Asian Rice Trade Fund proved infeasible. Judges in the region lost interest in the value of AJC.

The Pivotal Role of the UN Office in Bangkok

The establishment of the UN's Economic Commission for Asia and the Far East (ECAFE) in 1947 was the first major step in bringing Asian countries together into what has been called the "economic parliament of Asia." ECAFE was formed in Shanghai but moved to Bangkok in 1949.

Each of ECAFE's administrative divisions organized multinational conferences, especially the Trade and Investment Division. In some cases, ECAFE projects resembled regional organizations because they were overseen by ministerial-level officials from Asian countries. The Asian Highway project, for example, set up a Coordinating Committee. The coining of the term "Asian Way" by U Nyun provided a cultural basis for giving preference to countries in the region to break free from external control.

A turning point was ECAFE's adoption of a commodity approach in 1966. Later, the UN Conference on Trade and Development helped ECAFE to advance more commodity organizations. The initial secretariat for all but two of the region's commodity organizations was at ECAFE/ESCAP headquarters in Bangkok until another country volunteered to provide funding.[1]

ECAFE's renaming as the Economic and Social Commission for Asia and the Pacific (ESCAP) in 1974 was another turning point. Previously, Australia and New Zealand had been the only Pacific countries included in ECAFE's scope. The Conference of Directors General for Civil Aviation had already existed from 1961. The Asian and Pacific Council had "Pacific" in the name but neither independent Nauru (1968) nor Fiji (1970) were invited to the functional organizations created by ASPAC. ESCAP did not want to be parochial, as the new states of the Pacific would otherwise be the only ones in the world to fall outside the UN's regional economic commissions, so five organizations in existence before 1974 were retitled to include the word "Pacific."[2] Organizations formed after 1974 have tended to include both subregions in their titles.

A third way ESCAP impacted the region was in establishing subsidiary bodies:

- **Asian Statistical Institute** (now the Statistical Institute for Asia and the Pacific)
- **Asian and Pacific Centre for Transfer of Technology**
- **Regional Co-ordination Centre for Research and Development of Coarse Grains, Pulses, Roots and Tuber Crops** (now the Centre for Alleviation of Poverty through Sustainable Agriculture)
- **Asian and Pacific Centre for Agricultural Engineering and Machinery**
- **Asian and Pacific Training Centre for Information and Communication Technology for Development.**

The Statistical Institute for Asia and the Pacific was made a subsidiary body of ESCAP 25 years after its founding. Others were originally created as subsidiary bodies. In all cases, the centers have governing bodies of their own, so they should be considered semiautonomous.

ESCAP leaders planned conferences to bring together technical experts throughout the region. In cases when independent organizations were launched, political leaders were brought into deliberations on the new bodies. ESCAP, in other words, followed the neofunctional path, offering proposals for technical organizations and then obtaining approval from member governments. Subsequently, various organizations failed to grow in functions, as expected by neofunctionalists, and have remained unifunctional rather than multifunctional. The increase in technical bodies is consistent with the "spillaround" expectations of functionalism, as after one ESCAP proposal was approved, others were based on the same model.

Whether staircase functionalism applies is doubtful, as ESCAP's launching of technical organizations did expand in members but seldom in new tasks. For example, ECAFE's crowning achievement, the Asian Development Bank, has developed many innovative ways to encourage regional economic growth, but never in direct response to an increase in members.

The Pivotal Role of ASEAN

While ESCAP was broadening its geographic region to include the independent island states of the Pacific, there was a subregional trend. Within Asia, the Association of South-East Asian Nations (ASEAN) became the linchpin for almost all Asian regional organizations. On the map, Southeast Asia occupies a middle position between East Asia and South Asia, but the manner in which ASEAN became so pivotal is more than a matter of location. ASEAN political leaders in fact created the climate for solid regional institutions, following the neofunctional path. Once formed, the region increasingly became "Aseanized."

The formation of ASEAN was primarily a result of Indonesia's desire to pry countries of the region from alliances with Western powers so that there would be an arena of peace in Southeast Asia. Nevertheless, Indonesia and the Philippines were both upset with the formation of Malaysia, in which Britain allowed Sabah and Sarawak to merge with the Federation of Malaya. Indonesia realized that a neutralized Southeast Asia required an end to bitter feelings over the formation of Malaysia, so Indonesian Foreign Minister Adam Malik approached Thai Foreign Minister Thanat Khoman, who agreed on the need for a new organization, and ASEAN was launched in 1967. The earlier Association of Southeast Asia was officially terminated soon afterward, having been superseded.

The five founding ASEAN countries (Indonesia, Malaysia, Philippines, Singapore, and Thailand) soon issued an invitation to Burma to join, but Rangoon refused, maintaining a policy of complete isolation. Indochinese countries were in turmoil, so the five members granted Observer status to the three noncommunist Indochinese regimes but not full membership. Then in 1975 the Indochinese countries ceased attending. Brunei joined in 1984, the year of its independence from Britain.

One of the unwritten rules of ASEAN, based on the Asian Way, is to seek unity by building consensus. The reason for seeking unity is so that ASEAN countries can vote as a bloc in UN organs, thereby assuring that they would never again be overlooked. The unity also cultivated a sense that organizations proposed among ASEAN countries would be successful, and about a dozen have indeed been launched exclusively with Southeast Asian countries, as noted in Chapter 3 above.[3] Meanwhile, East Asia and South Asia were divided, the former on Cold War lines, the latter because of continuing India-Pakistan tensions.

Four years after ASEAN began, Indonesia secured support for a resolution declaring that all foreign bases were temporary, known as the Zone of Peace, Freedom and Neutrality (ZOPFAN) Declaration of 1971. At that time, American bases in the Philippines and Thailand were being used to launch attacks in what Washington called the Vietnam War. So the implication of ZOPFAN was that support for the American effort was eroding in both Bangkok and Manila.

Thanks to the spirit of ASEAN, the **Association of Natural Rubber Producing Countries** (ANRPC) began at Kuala Lumpur in 1971, the first of several commodity-organizations. Other commodity-organizations were also formed at Kuala Lumpur but initially had some non-Southeast Asian members. Soon after the International Rubber Organization collapsed in 1999, Indonesia, Malaysia, and Thailand formed the International Natural Tripartite Rubber Organization.

ASEAN's only competitors in the political field were the Asian and Pacific Council, the Asian Parliamentarians' Union, and the South-East Asia Treaty Organization. One by one, they ceased to exist due to resignations from Southeast Asian countries. ASPAC folded in 1972. APU was reorganized as the Asian-Pacific Parliamentarians' Union (APPU) in 1980, reflecting growth to include South Pacific countries.

In 1973, when the United States made peace with Vietnam, SEATO continued at its Secretariat in Bangkok. The seeds for SEATO's abolition, sown by ZOPFAN, germinated in 1976, when American military aircraft flew from a base in Thailand to rescue an American commercial ship seized by the Khmer Rouge off the coast of Cambodia. Because the United States did not ask permission from the Thai government, the Thai public reaction was so negative that the government demanded an end to American bases and a shutdown of SEATO. Aseanization, the reshaping of Asian regional cooperation to fit ASEAN's perspectives, had prevailed.

Initially, ASEAN was a club of foreign ministers, a body now known as the ASEAN Ministerial Meeting (AMM). In 1976, the first ASEAN Summit of heads of government was held, and the 1977 summit resulted in formation of the ASEAN Economic Ministers meetings.

In the wake of the collapse of Japanese-sponsored organizations after 1975, the ASEAN Economic Ministers (AEM) met for the first time in 1977 and agreed to work together. AEM's aim was greater economic cooperation, and formation of a free trade area was an objective. Although there was a goal of catching up with economic integration efforts in Europe, an unlikely prospect, the immediate significance of AEM was that somewhere in Asia planning for an economic community was ongoing.

Donor countries had been attending foreign ministers meetings to talk bilaterally, so ASEAN multilateralized the event by forming a single Post Ministerial Conference (PMC) in 1979, thereby providing a new forum for discussions on conflicts in the region. Thus, ASEAN foreign ministers were hosting their opposite numbers from Australia, Canada, Japan, New Zealand, and the United States. In time, China, Papua New Guinea, Russia, and South Korea began to attend PMCs. Once again, Aseanization was occurring.

ASEAN also served as the catalyst for nongovernmental associated organizations, including industry clubs and business councils. The

ASEAN Chemical Industries Council and the US-ASEAN Business Council are examples of associated organizations. Two initially unaffiliated organizations borrowed the ASEAN name—the ASEAN Inter-Parliamentary Organization (AIPO) in 1975 and the Meeting of Chiefs of National Police of the ASEAN Countries (ASEANAPOL) in 1981. Subsequently, ASEAN designated ASEANAPOL as a "stakeholder organization." Other stakeholder organizations are the Federation of Institutes of Food Science and Technology in ASEAN, the Southeast Asian Fisheries Development Center, and the Working Group for an ASEAN Human Rights Mechanism. In 1983, ASEAN began to accredit civil society organizations, perhaps the best evidence of the pivotal role of the organization throughout the culture of the Southeast Asia.

In 1978, Vietnamese troops entered Cambodia to drive the genocidal Khmer Rouge from the country. ASEAN's response was to expel all three Indochinese countries from attending its meetings, and to pressure other regional organizations to do the same. A new form of Aseanization had arisen.

The new People's Republic of Kampuchea, set up by Cambodians in Phnom Penh after the Khmer Rouge was chased toward Thailand, was then denied a seat in the UN. Based on the ASEAN model, the Indochinese Foreign Ministers Conference was launched by Vietnam in 1980.

IFMC was not the only organization that copied the ASEAN model. A Bangladesh initiative resulted in the formation of the South Asian Association for Regional Cooperation in 1985, when heads of governments in the Indian subcontinent and adjacent island states had their first summit meeting. SAARC adopted the formal structure of technical committees and ministerial meetings based on the experience of ASEAN. SAARC, though administratively hydra-headed, similar to ESCAP and ASEAN, has lacked the dynamism of ASEAN because of the festering India-Pakistan conflict.

During the 1980s, ASEAN became so obsessed with the Cambodian conflict that the organization was constipated regarding the unfinished business of regional economic cooperation. The consensus was to establish a hard-line stance against Vietnam in order to support Thailand as a "front-line state" that feared invasion by Vietnamese troops. Indonesia, nevertheless, secured permission from the other foreign ministers to begin a dialog with Hanoi, and a peace process gradually emerged. In 1991, an agreement was signed to have the UN sponsor elections in Cambodia. The UN-supervised election of 1993 then legitimized a Phnom Penh government (M.Haas 1991, 2011b), and the last vestige of the Cold War in Southeast Asia thus ended. Soon, Indochinese countries applied for membership in ASEAN.

In 1992, an ASEAN Free Trade Area (AFTA) agreement was signed, but was not self-executing. Accordingly, the Common Effective Preferential Tariff (CEPT) arrangement was adopted as part of AFTA to enable tariffs on specific products to be lowered one by one as they were agreed upon. By 2011, more than 99 percent of the items in the CEPT inclusion list had been accepted by the first six ASEAN countries (Brunei, Indonesia, Malaysia, Philippines, Singapore, and Thailand) at the 0–5 percent tariff range. The later-joining Indochinese countries and Myanmar have lowered 80 percent of the products to the 0–5 percent level. AFTA, thus, now exists, shattering the expectations of those who were skeptical when planning began in 1977.

ASEAN heads of state, meeting in 1992, agreed upon the need for a security dialog. The remaining threat in the region was the rising strength of China, which threatened to annex islands in the South China Sea claimed by Brunei, Malaysia, the Philippines, Taiwan, and Vietnam. After diplomatic efforts, the ASEAN Regional Forum was launched during the annual Foreign Ministers Meeting in 1994. ASEAN foreign and defense ministers then began to host opposite numbers from its "Dialog Partners" (Australia, Canada, the European Union, Japan, South Korea, New Zealand, United States), two "Consultative Partners" (China, Russia), two observer countries (Laos, Vietnam), and one special observer (Papua New Guinea), who agreed to attend ARF on an annual basis. In due course, Bangladesh, Cambodia, India, North Korea, Pakistan, and Timor-Leste joined ARF.

In 1995, ARF countries identified the parameters for discussion to include the Korean conflict, the South China Sea friction, China's nuclear weapons testing, and France's nuclear tests in the South Pacific. Many countries in the region wanted China's military capabilities to become more transparent and less belligerent, as Beijing had threatened military action in the Spratly Islands and against Taiwan (Garver 1992; Lam 2003). Later, Middle East conflicts, terrorism, and transnational crime were added to the issues for discussion at ARF. ASEAN, thus, has given birth to the largest regional security dialog in the world.

With the dissolution of the Soviet Union, the Central Asian "stans" were desperate to establish what they had before—a common market and assured security. Accordingly, they drew upon the ASEAN model, notably through the Shanghai Cooperation Organization in 2001 and the Organization of Central Asian Cooperation in 2002.

ASEAN was silent when Indonesia tried to annex East Timor in 1975. The territory had been a colony of Portugal, which departed without providing security for its former colony. For the next two decades, Jakarta's forcible occupation was not on ASEAN's agenda. But after a new government came to power in Jakarta, Indonesian forces withdrew to allow East Timor (Timor-Leste) to enjoy independence, which arrived in 2002 after a UN transitional arrangement. Due to its economic situation, Timor-Leste lacks the resources to provide contributions on a par with other countries, so ASEAN countries have been reluctant to admit Timor-Leste as its newest member. Accordingly, Australia and Indonesia agreed to form a Southwest Political Dialogue (SwPD) in 2002 in which Timor-Leste has found community with adjacent countries, including Papua New Guinea and the Philippines.

Over the years, heads of various ministries in Southeast Asian countries have met together under the ASEAN framework. At the Bali summit in 2003 ASEAN agreed in principle to organize several related ministerial bodies under the labels ASEAN Political-Security Community and ASEAN Economic Community. The Philippines insisted on inclusion of the ASEAN Sociocultural Community as a third component of the multifunctional body. The reorganization was completed by 2007 (see Table 5.1).

East Asia, despite great wealth, has never been able to develop subregional institutions. From the mid-1970s ASEAN countries met after the annual foreign ministers meetings with China, Japan, and South Korea bilaterally as Dialogue Partners, which was renamed the Post Ministerial Conference in 1979. In 1997, ASEAN invited China, Japan, and South Korea to join a ministerial forum known as the East Asian Economic Caucus to discuss economic issues. Now East Asia was being Aseanized. In 2005, heads of state agreed to upgrade the meeting to an annual East Asia Summit.

In 2009, the ASEAN Intergovernmental Commission on Human Rights was launched, with membership from all ten ASEAN countries. In so doing, ASEAN eclipsed yet another IGO, the Asia Pacific

Table 5.1 Ministerial meetings of ASEAN

Years Active	*Communities and Ministerial Meetings*	*Acronym*
	Political-Security Community	APSC
1967–	ASEAN Ministerial Meeting	AMM
1986–	ASEAN Law Ministers Meeting	ALAWMM
1994–	ASEAN Regional Forum	ARF
1997–	ASEAN Ministerial Meeting on Transnational Crime	AMMTC
2006–	ASEAN Defense Ministers Meeting	ADMM
	Economic Community	AEC
1977–	ASEAN Economic Ministers	AEM
1979–	ASEAN Ministerial Meeting on Agriculture and Forestry	AMAF
1980–	ASEAN Ministers on Energy Meeting	AMEM
1991–	ASEAN Free Trade Area Council	AFTA
1996–	ASEAN Transport Ministers Meeting	ATM
1996–	Ministerial Meeting on ASEAN Mekong Basin Development Cooperation	AMBDC
1997–	ASEAN Finance Ministers Meeting	AFMM
1998–	ASEAN Tourism Ministers Meeting	M-ATM
2001–	ASEAN Telecommunications and IT Ministers Meeting	TELMIN
2005–	ASEAN Ministerial Meeting on Minerals	AMMin
	Sociocultural Community	ASC
1976–	ASEAN Committee on Women[a]	ACW
1977–	ASEAN Education Ministers Meeting	AEMM
1979–	ASEAN Labor Ministers Meeting	ALMM
1980–	ASEAN Health Ministers Meeting	AHMM
1980–	ASEAN Ministers Meeting on Science and Technology	AMMST
1981–	ASEAN Ministerial Meeting on Environment	AMME
1989–	ASEAN Ministers Responsible for Information	AMRI
1993–	ASEAN Ministerial Meeting on Youth	AMMY
1998–	ASEAN Ministers Meeting on Rural Development and Poverty Elimination	AMRDPE
2003–	ASEAN Ministerial Meeting on Disaster Management	AMMDM
2003–	ASEAN Ministers Responsible for Culture and Arts	AMCA
2003–	Conference of the Parties to the ASEAN Agreement on Transboundary Haze Pollution	COP to AATHP
2006–	ASEAN Ministerial Meeting for Social Welfare and Development	AMMSWD

[a] Originally the Sub-Committee on Women; retitled in 2002.

Forum of National Human Rights Institutions (APF), which had been formed in 1996.

Although Malaysia and the Philippines engaged in joint military maneuvers within the first decade of ASEAN (van den Kroef

1978a:144), they were not officially sanctioned by ASEAN. Informally, ASEAN countries had been helpful in conflict resolution, as when Indonesian diplomacy ignited the Cambodian peace process. Then in 2011, the ASEAN Summit committed the organization to interstate conflict resolution as well as toward combating transnational crime and working toward nuclear disarmament, consistent with the Treaty on the Southeast Asian Nuclear Weapon-Free Zone.

ASEAN, in sum, became a multifunctional organization when government heads decided that more was needed than the original club of foreign ministers. Although staircase functionalism applies to ASEAN's growth, multifunctionalism accounts for the organization's peacemaking capabilities. Yet Aseanization has advanced beyond Asia itself, as discussed next.

Aseanization of APEC

In 1980, a meeting among academics, businesses, and government officials from 11 countries was held to explore ways to promote trade across the Pacific. The initiative came from Japanese Prime Minister Masayoshi Ohira and Australian Prime Minister Malcolm Fraser. One result was the formation of the Pacific Economic Cooperation Council (PECC), which in turn convened annual meetings and called for the establishment of a trade organization (Kim and Young 2005). Instead of member governments, PECC had member committees.

Bob Hawke, elected Australia's prime minister in 1983, sought to orient the foreign policy of his country more toward Asia and continued to explore options relating to international trade in the region. Although leaders in Japan and the United States had considered the advantages of Asian-Pacific economic cooperation for decades, such innovations had always been opposed by ASEAN leaders, who were understandably annoyed that more aid was not being channeled to Southeast Asia (Rostow 1986:106). But their main fear was that the economic superpowers would dominate the region again through PECC (Gordon 1981; Khoman 1983; Soesastro 1983:46–50; Sopiee 1983).

During the 1990s, dramatic international events took center stage—the end of the Cold War, the Cambodian peace agreement, the Uruguay Round of the General Agreement on Tariffs and Trade (GATT), preparations for the European Union (EU), and negotiations for the

Canadian-American bilateral North American Free Trade Agreement (NAFTA), which by 1992 included México. ASEAN welcomed China, Indochina, and Russia to partnership in the Asia-Pacific region, but negotiations for EU and NAFTA appeared to be dividing the world into trade blocs that would establish barriers to trade from Asia.

In January 1989, Hawke asked ASEAN to indicate an acceptable framework for an economic organization that would include East Asia, Southeast Asia, and North America. When ASEAN countries realized that they could have their cake and eat it too by strengthening ASEAN while agreeing to a wider economic forum, they responded, and the inaugural **Asia-Pacific Economic Cooperation** (APEC) conference was held at Canberra in November 1989. All ASEAN countries attended, along with all PMC countries (which by then included South Korea) but not the European Community. Inviting the Soviet Union seemed unrealistic without China, and Beijing hinted that separate representation for Hong Kong and the Republic of China was out of the question. Nevertheless, APEC was publicized as an example of "open regionalism" in contrast to the closed membership of the EU and NAFTA, which were deemed stumbling blocs for a world free trade area (Bergsten 1997).

When the first session of APEC convened, economic and foreign ministers attended. Although US Undersecretary of State for Economic Affairs Joan Spero later claimed that the meeting "frankly, had no goal" (Awanohara and Chanda 1993:16), three objectives were identified—(1) enhance prospects for the Uruguay Round, (2) assess prospects and obstacles for trade and investment in the region, and (3) identify common economic interests. To define objectives more clearly, the meeting focused on the structure and potential projects of APEC. Whereas the industrialized countries wanted a highly structured organization similar to the Organization for Economic Cooperation and Development (OECD), ASEAN insisted on a looser structure (Higgot, Cooper, and Bonner 1994:11,23). ASEAN prevailed, so no permanent committees were set up. Instead, APEC decided that future meetings would discuss reports of working groups, which in turn would draw upon PECC task force experience.

At the second session, held at Singapore in July 1990, APEC foreign ministers identified ten working groups in areas for possible technical cooperation. Specific projects and study groups in such fields as conservation of marine resources, energy technology cooperation, and trade were formed as well. In September 1990, a meeting of APEC trade ministers at Vancouver discussed developments in the Uruguay Round.

Dissatisfied with progress in the Uruguay Round and reports of the tone of the Vancouver conference, which appeared to portend a future marginalization of ASEAN by APEC, Malaysia's Prime Minister Mahathir startled the region by proposing an East Asia Economic Group (EAEG) in December 1990. His proposed grouping, aimed initially at providing more clout for less developed Asian countries in the Uruguay Round (Economist 1991), was to include ASEAN, Burma (Myanmar), Indochina, China (including Hong Kong and Macau), Japan, and South Korea. Although Mahathir hinted that Australia and New Zealand might ultimately be admitted to EAEG, he definitely wanted to exclude NAFTA countries, and he was firmly opposed to APEC as a future trade bloc. His view was openly shared by the Philippines and Thailand (FEER 1991).

Expecting more increased trade with Asia than with Europe in the 1990s, Washington was strongly opposed to Mahathir's proposal, and American pressure persuaded Japan and South Korea to demur, though Tokyo suggested that the grouping might serve a useful purpose as a caucus within APEC. Indonesia, miffed that Mahathir's idea was not cleared within ASEAN first, quickly convened a meeting of APEC officials in early March and a meeting of senior officials from ASEAN countries later in March to discuss the idea. Responding to objections to his proposal, Mahathir (1992:16) modified the EAEG concept, instead urging formation of a "noninstitutional" **East Asian Economic Caucus** (EAEC) within APEC that was "not intended to be a trade bloc." EAEC, which would meet just before or after APEC sessions, was then endorsed in principle at both the ASEAN Economic Ministers meeting in October 1991 and at the ASEAN Summit in Singapore during January 1992. The possibility of a much lamer EAEC proved initially acceptable to US Trade Representative Carla Hills (Vatikiotis 1991:65). But one month later, Secretary of State James Baker rejected EAEC as having a negative effect on APEC.

APEC membership expanded at its Seoul meeting, held in October 1991, which the foreign ministers of China and South Korea attended for the first time. Beijing understood that representation was of economies, not governments, so Taiwan was able to join as "Chinese Taipei," and Hong Kong was admitted as well (Awanohara and Chanda

1993:17). In addition, applications were received from Argentina, Chile, Ecuador, India, México, and Perú.

During the APEC meeting at Bangkok in 1992, the ministers agreed to establish a Secretariat with a modest staff, mostly seconded from government ministries. Singapore agreed to donate accommodations and about a dozen local staff to accommodate the organization's Secretariat for the first three years with a $2 million budget to spend.

In 1993, APEC appointed an Eminent Persons Group (EPG) of 12 business executives, former politicians, and scholars (increased in 1994 so that all member countries would have one representative) for a two-year term to prepare a brief study on the future of the organization. The report, released later that year with the title *A Vision for APEC Towards an Asia-Pacific Economic Community*, urged APEC "to pursue an active program of regional trade liberalization... to help create an Asia Pacific Economic Community" (1993:26–27). The EPG proposal was endorsed by Australian Prime Minister Paul Keating, who called for a summit conference of APEC heads of government, an EU-style integrated market for Asia, and a change of the "C" in APEC from "Cooperation" to "Community" (Rees 1993). In part as a form of pressure on stalled Uruguay Round talks and as an opportunity to score a foreign policy triumph, President Bill Clinton supported Keating's ideas for changing the name and holding a summit. In July, Clinton issued invitations for a summit to be held immediately after the APEC ministerial meeting in November at Seattle. Fred Bergsten, who represented the American Chamber of Commerce, continued to push for trade liberalization, abrasively in the opinion of some (Ravenhill 2001:131).

Mahathir at this point felt that his worst fears about APEC had been confirmed. If APEC showed more concern for the prerogatives of hegemonic leadership and formal institutional structures than for the real needs of poorer Asian countries, he intended to boycott the 1993 meeting. He urged other Asian countries to follow suit and to develop the EAEC concept instead. ASEAN's Secretariat was then busy at work designing how the EAEC would operate, and the idea was discussed during a meeting of the ASEAN-US Dialogue. Washington seemingly warmed up to the idea. Later in 1993, the judgment changed, and American officials denounced the idea, fearing that EAEC would evolve into an exclusive trade bloc.

An American proposal for a Trade and Investment Framework Agreement (TIFA) emerged at an APEC subministerial meeting at Williamsburg, Virginia, during March 1993. TIFA contained a provision for a permanent APEC Committee to further trade and investment liberalization, but the text of the proposed agreement used the words "integrated market." Due to ASEAN and Japanese opposition, the text was watered down into a "vision statement" during an APEC subministerial meeting at Honolulu in September 1993. All hints about the formation of a trade bloc were dropped, and the economic ministers agreed to continue reducing barriers to trade and investment. Southeast Asian countries were reassured when the summit meeting was declared to be "informal," that is, without a fixed agenda in accordance with Asian Way principles.

At the fifth APEC session in Seattle during November 1993, Malaysia was represented at the ministerial level. With the addition of México and Papua New Guinea, APEC membership rose to 17. To increase the number of developing member countries, Indonesia and Malaysia backed Chile for membership (Awanohara 1994:13). Santiago was then assured of membership by November 1994 and allowed to participate during the year in working group meetings. With active membership applications pending from Colombia, Ecuador, and Russia, and Observer status applications from Argentina and Perú (Hoon 1991), a three-year moratorium on new members was imposed until 1997, leaving some 15 countries and organizations knocking on the door, seeking to be represented at APEC meetings.

Malaysia was the only country that refused to attend the "informal summit" on Blake Island in the Puget Sound after the Seattle meeting of APEC. Hong Kong and Taiwan were represented by senior economic officials. At American insistence, a Vision Statement was issued from the summit, lauding the "deepening in our spirit of community" and calling for a meeting of finance ministers, the formation of a Pacific Business Forum as a temporary working group, the establishment of an APEC Business Volunteer Program, and the development of an APEC Educational Program. But the effort to transform APEC into an economic policy-setting body was nixed by ASEAN, so APEC remained a forum for consultation and discussion operating by consensus. EAEC was kept alive, especially with the quiet but cautious endorsement by China and Japan (FEER 1994; Tasker 1994).

Perhaps the most important APEC meeting was held in 1994 at Bogor (when Chile was accepted as a member). APEC agreed to work toward three goals—(1) trade and investment liberalization, (2) business facilitation, and (3) economic and technical cooperation. The major aim was for free and open trade and investment in the Asia-Pacific by 2010 for industrialized economies and by 2020 for developing economies. A Free Trade Area of the Asia-Pacific was also proposed.

Then in 1995, APEC agreed to establish a business advisory body, named the APEC Business Advisory Council, to be composed of three business executives from each member economy. Visa-free business travel among APEC countries was endorsed. For economic and technical cooperation, the organization then authorized APEC Study Centers. One hundred such centers soon operated in twenty member countries within a consortium framework.

APEC is credited with serving as a forum that broke the deadlock in negotiations on agricultural products between EU and NAFTA, thereby assuring the success of Uruguay Round negotiations (Yue and Pangetsu 2006). The World Trade Organization (WTO) was then formed in 1995. Because WTO's establishment heralded a worldwide free trade regime that fulfilled APEC's original quest, the organization has tried ever since to refocus on a wide variety of issues.

APEC, however, utterly failed to deal with the 1997/1998 economic crisis. The most prosperous APEC members did little to respond to liquidity problems in Indonesia, Malaysia, South Korea, and Thailand.

Accordingly, ASEAN went ahead to form an EAEC in 1997, established summits with each country separately in 1998, and upgraded EAEC to the **East Asia Summit** (EAS) in 2005. The latter initially included China, Japan, and South Korea (the ASEAN+3 countries) along with Australia, India, and New Zealand. In 2010, Russia and the United States were invited as full members of EAS.

In 1998, Perú, Russia, and Vietnam joined APEC, but new memberships were again put on hold. New Delhi was the most insistent among more than a dozen applications, so APEC allowed the country Observer status, though India does not have a Pacific Ocean border.

APEC meetings from 1999 have been largely technical. The terrorism threat from 2001 and worldwide economic slowdown in 2008 focused the attention of members on domestic matters. Nevertheless, in 2007, ASEAN government heads agreed to a blueprint for a common market, to be called the ASEAN Economic Community, by 2015.

An Asian monetary fund had been proposed by Japan in 1997 in the midst of the financial crisis of Korea and several Southeast Asian countries. But in 2009, the idea was Aseanized. In 2010, the **Asian Monetary Fund** (AMF), with a Secretariat in Singapore, was unveiled as an alternative to the International Monetary Fund. AMF, however, is only capitalized at $120 billion.

ASEAN, thus, has consistently taken decisive action on problems within Asia, whereas APEC was designed for profit making by countries outside Southeast Asia. In short, APEC was Aseanized.

The Pivotal Role of the Forum

Whereas ASEAN played hardball to establish its primacy in Asia, maneuvering by the Pacific Islands Forum has been a softball effort to achieve the central role in the region encompassing Pacific Island states.

Fiji's Ratu Mara set the tone in 1968 by establishing the Pacific Islands Producers Association two years before Fiji's independence. He then organized the South Pacific Forum as a body exclusively for independent South Pacific states, subliminally encouraging the colonial powers to release their control over the region. Attending the first Forum in 1971 were Australia, Cook Islands, Fiji, Nauru, New Zealand, Tonga, and Samoa. As the remaining South Pacific countries (Kiribati, Niue, Papua New Guinea, Solomon Islands, Tuvalu, and Vanuatu) achieved independence, they became full members of the Forum. In addition, when the United States granted independence to Micronesian countries (Federated States of Micronesia, Marshall Islands, Palau) in the North Pacific, they were admitted as well, occasioning the name change from South Pacific Forum to Pacific Islands Forum.[4] Pointedly excluded from the Forum were France's colonies (New Caledonia, Tahiti).

The South Pacific Commission (SPC), founded in 1948, is headquartered in Nouméa, New Caledonia. Mara had been displeased that external countries met together in the annual SPC Session to decide SPC aid priorities for the region and then invited representatives from

Pacific Island countries to react in a separate body, the triennial South Pacific Conference. Mara felt that the island peoples should come first in any such discussion, and due to his leadership the South Pacific Conference became the plenary body in 1973.

Later, as noted in the previous chapter, 18 organizations were sponsored by the Forum.[5] Ratu Mara's approval also enabled the East-West Center to sponsor meetings of the Pacific Islands Conference (PIC). However, after the Honolulu-based Pacific Islands Tourism Development Council (PITDC) started in 1976, the feeling in Suva was that the initiative was more about Hawai'i tourism and less about Pacific island tourism, so PITDC collapsed in 1979 and was replaced in 1983 by the Tourism Council of the South Pacific, which was renamed the South Pacific Tourism Organisation in 1988.

Most South Pacific organizations have been unifunctional, so the rise of bodies on aviation, shipping, and telecommunications could be understood as functionalist "spillaround" encouraged by Fiji. However, the various coups in Fiji (1987, 2000, and 2006) meant that the island state disappointed democracies elsewhere in the region.

What happened next are two extraordinary developments. In 2000, the Forum adopted the Biketawa Declaration, which developed a framework for regional conflict resolution. The impetus was the emergence of coups in Fiji as well as civil strife in Papua New Guinea and the Solomon Islands.

Then in 2005, the Forum adopted the Pacific Plan for Strengthening Regional Cooperation and Integration. Although the document includes the objective "recognize and protect cultural values" (Huffer 2011), the Plan is based on four pillars—economic growth, sustainable development, good governance, and security.[6]

The Forum thus became the most pivotal factor in the Pacific, even taking the extraordinary step of expelling Fiji in 2009. The Forum began modestly but in time acquired more scope, even absorbing SOPAC. The Forum, in other words, can best be appreciated as a multifunctional organization.

Conclusion

Since formation of the Association of South-East Asian Nations, regional cooperation has blossomed in Asia, though ESCAP undeniably primed the pump until Asia was Aseanized. Ratu Mara's influence in regional cooperation in the Pacific was also profound, having established the organization now known as the Pacific Islands Forum. Although his influence faded as Fiji coups arose, the Forum remained pivotal.

The present chapter has provided more evidence for the thesis that cultural pluralism is at the foundation of regional cooperation in Asia and the Pacific. The critical role of decisions by lower-level government leaders supports ESCAP's functionalist approach, but higher-level government heads in ASEAN and at the Forum have bypassed neofunctionalism and staircase functionalism for multifunctionalism. The two regions did so in response to differing situations. ASEAN was primarily formed to handle foreign policy questions associated with the civil war in Vietnam; when that war ended, government heads decided to branch out by bringing forward the prior economic agenda of the Association of Southeast Asia that had been frustrated during that war. The Forum, meanwhile, had an economic focus in the beginning, as the Pacific was at peace, but leaders added security issues when civil strife in some of the member countries could not be ignored. Thanks to pioneering efforts of ECAFE, both ASEAN and the Forum remain central and pivotal to regional cooperation in Asia and the Pacific, respectively.

Part III

Effectiveness

Three organizations in the Asian and Pacific region have been pivotal—ESCAP, ASEAN, and the Forum. The next question is whether any political-military regional organizations have served in positive conflict resolution roles.

Chapter 6 identifies conflicts within each subregion and then assesses how well intergovernmental organizations have used their diplomatic, economic, political, and even military tools of statecraft in conflict resolution. "Political-military" organizations are those that discuss issues relating to conflicts between countries in the region as opposed to functional (nonpolitical) IGOs that exclusively deal with such issues as banking, economic development, education, fertilizer development, judiciary concerns, maritime issues, police, and science cooperation.

Comparative empirical research has rarely been attempted in studying regional organizations, but tests of hypotheses requires rigor. Chapter 7 presents results of a systematic quantitative analysis designed to shed light on factors that account for successful organizations as security communities, using indicators for concepts proposed by scholars who have advanced significant theories. Statistical tests will enhance theory building with important policy implications.

6

Creating Arenas of Peace

From Zones of Conflict to Arenas of Peace

Many zones of conflict have become arenas of peace in Asia. No region-wide organization arose in Asia, in part because the Cold War initially divided the vast region. From the 1970s, the Forum served the South Pacific region as a whole, since the Cold War did not intrude, undoubtedly because the United States maintained a dominant presence (cf. Crone 1993; Duffield 2001).

Subsequently, regional cooperation has been crucial in the transformation of some though not all conflicts. Some have been resolved, but others are frozen, simmering, or ongoing. The multifunctional organizations—ASEAN and the Forum—have played major roles.

In the discussion below, the "intervener" role is assigned to the country or organization that has helped to promote peace. The analysis proceeds by subregion, primarily identifying interstate conflicts but also including conflicts inside countries that have an impact either on a second country or on the subregion. What the narrative below allows is a test of the hypothesis that countries belonging to intergovernmental organizations are less likely to engage in militarized disputes with each other (Russett, Oneal, and Davis 1998). Of course, countries engaged in such conflicts are unlikely to form IGOs, so a serious test is whether pre-IGO conflicts are reduced after countries join IGOs.

Conflicts in East Asia

China has been involved in most disputes within East Asia. The civil war ended in 1949 with a victory for the People's Republic of China, whereupon leaders of the defeated Republic of China left to govern Taiwan. Ever since, China has insisted on recovering territories lost during the time when the country was weak and signed "unequal treaties." As a result, China undertook major military action in previously independent Tibet, on the Russian border, and over the islands of Quemoy and Matsu held by the Republic of China while insisting that Taiwan revert to control from Beijing (cf. Heo and Horowitz 2003:Ch2–4). Due to American naval vessel action and Russian diplomacy, Beijing stopped shelling Quemoy and Matsu in 1958. China also claims all islands in the South China Sea, but that is of concern primarily in Southeast Asia rather than East Asia.

In March 1969, Chinese troops ambushed Russian border guards at Zhenbao Island at a section of the contested border along Xinjiang Province. (The dispute evidently prompted President Richard Nixon to plan his famous trip to Beijing). Clashes continued for five months; then bilateral negotiations began. In 1991, Russia agreed that the island belonged to China (Weitz 2008). Other border disputes with Russia were resolved by 2008.

The World War II settlement deprived Japan of three Kuril islands north of Hokkaido that are now held by Russia, which has proposed compromise settlements at various times. In 2006, when a Japanese fishing boat was fired upon for intruding in Russian waters, one person died (BBC 2006a).

China and Taiwan also lay claim to the Pinnacle Islands, otherwise known as the Senkaku or Diaoyutai Islands, which had been owned by private Japanese citizens but were leased to the Tokyo government until 2012, when Japan bought them back (Pan 2009; Reuters 2012). Japan claims that the islands were unclaimed when they were taken over as the spoils of victory in the Sino-Japanese War in 1895, when China signed the Treaty of Shimonoseki. Tokyo believes that Beijing only became interested in the islands after prospecting for natural gas and oil began. Although Japan, as a condition of its surrender, accepted the Potsdam Declaration of 1945, which called upon Tokyo to return all territories historically taken from China, the United States governed them during the postwar occupation of Japan, and they are included in the scope of the bilateral US-Japan security treaty of 1960 (Kyodo 2012b). Claiming that the islands were discovered, named, and occupied in the fourteenth century and that Japan agreed to relinquish them in the China-Japan Joint Statement of 1972

(China Daily 2012), Beijing prefers low-level economic sanctions to goad Tokyo into relinquishing them. Neither country favors submitting the case to the International Court of Justice (Asahi Shimbun 2012). The islands are close to Ishigaki Island, which China recognizes as part of Japan. But the islands are also near Taiwan, which disputes Tokyo's claim. After histrionics on all sides, with landings in various years (Bradsher and Jacobs 2012) and a water cannon skirmish in 2012, the two countries held talks, and the acrimony has died down (Fackler 2012).

The Liancourt Rocks are held militarily by South Korea. Tokyo intermittently asks for their return (Stephan 1974). Known as Dokdo in Korea and Takeshima in Japan, they were seized by newly independent South Korea during the post–World War II Japanese occupation (Choe 2012). Seoul argues that Japan grabbed the islands from Korea in 1905 soon after winning the Russo-Japanese War of 1904–1905 (Harlan 2012). Nevertheless, both countries are allies of the United States, and Tokyo has proposed settling the dispute at the International Court of Justice (Kyodo 2012a).

The most dangerous East Asian conflict is between North and South Korea. As the Soviet Union was absent at a meeting of the UN Security Council in 1950, a UN force was authorized to defend South Korea. China and the Soviet Union provided military support for North Korea, and the United States commanded the multinational UN operation on behalf of South Korea. Although there was an armistice in 1953, the North has since undertaken several aggressive moves. One was the killing of 17 South Koreans accompanying President Chun Doo-Hwan in 1983 due to a bomb planted by North Korean government agents at a monument in Rangoon, Burma. More recently, warlike incidents have occurred along the contested maritime boundary with the South involving naval battles, the torpedoing of the South Korean ship *Cheonon*, and the exchange of gunfire over Yeonpyeong Island (Chang 2010; Haas 2012). In effect, the civil war continues.

In 1979, Vietnamese troops entered Cambodia to expel the Khmer Rouge. When they stayed, China decided to deliver a "lesson" in the form of a border attack later in 1979 and a few times thereafter. During the Cambodian peace process, largely due to ASEAN diplomacy, China agreed to make peace with Vietnam.

A naval incident occurred in 2007. Russian observers presumed that two Japanese fishing vessels, the *Hoshinmaru* and the

Tomimaru, were in their territorial waters. The boats were seized, and the crew and catch were held. Rather than responding militarily, Tokyo decided to submit the dispute to the International Tribunal for the Law of the Sea (ITLOS), which in 2007 ruled that Russia should return the *Hoshinmaru* ship and crew to Japan along with a cash settlement. Japan, having already referred the *Tomimaru* case to a Russian court, however, was asked by ITLOS to abide by the determination of that court. The cases appear to establish an important global precedent.

In sum, East Asian regional organizations have been ineffective (see Table 6.1). Fourteen countries in the ASEAN Regional Forum outside East Asia (ASEAN countries, Australia, India, New Zealand, and the United States) have the potential to mediate, but militarized disputes continue nonetheless. The East Asia Summit, set up without North Korea or Taiwan, has not dealt with any of the disputes, spending time on economic issues instead. What has kept the peace, in the absence of a strong subregional forum, has been the deterrent effect of military power in East Asia, not memberships in IGOs.

Table 6.1 Disposition of conflicts in East Asia

Conflict	*Years*	*Intervener*	*Outcome*
China-Taiwan	1949–	USA	simmering
Korean Civil War	1950–1953	UN, USA	armistice
China-Tibet	1951	none	victory
Kuril Islands	1951–	none	frozen
Quemoy/Matsu	1954, 1958	Russia, USA	frozen
Sino-Russian border	1969–2008	none	resolved
Pinnacle Islands	1971–	bilateral talks	intermittent
Liancourt Rocks	1972–	none	intermittent
China-Vietnam	1979–1991	ASEAN	reconciliation
Rangoon bombing	1983	none	frozen
ASEAN Regional Forum began in 1994			
Korean naval battles	1998	none	frozen
Korean naval battle	1999	none	frozen
Korean naval battle	2002	none	frozen
East Asia Summit began in 2005			
Hoshinmaru and *Tomimaru* seizures	2007	ITLOS	judgment
Korean naval battle	2009	none	frozen
Cheonon torpedoed	2010	none	frozen
Yeonpyeong Island, Korea	2010	none	simmering

Conflicts in South Asia

South Asia has been dominated by four wars between India and Pakistan, including the Bangladesh War of 1971 (Dixit 2002). Pakistan-based terrorists have committed violent acts in India from time to time, most recently in Mumbai during 2010, but India has not counterattacked. The ASEAN Regional Forum has recently tried to mediate.

The Sino-Indian border war of 1962, in which China seized disputed territory at high altitudes during the Cuban Missiles Crisis, ended when Beijing declared a ceasefire and agreed to withdraw some but not all forces. Six countries at the first meeting of nonaligned nations at Bandung later in 1962 called for China to disengage (cf. Rediff 2002). In 1993 and 1996, the two sides inked the Sino-Indian Bilateral Peace and Tranquility Accords, though the border still remains largely undefined.

In 1953, Britain and the United States provided the wherewithal for a coup that ended democratic rule in Iran. Today, Washington contemplates military action on Iran that might be launched by Israel.

There have been two major civil wars in the region. The Sri Lankan civil war almost became a proxy war between India and Pakistan (Deegalle 2006); although the UN sought to mediate (Mackey 2012), Norway was more successful. The royalist government of Nepal had to deal with a Maoist insurgency (Hutt 2004), but UN intervention stabilized the situation; the government agreed to let Maoists take part in government, and the insurgents placed their weapons under UN monitoring (BBC 2006b).

India has dealt with insurgencies, too, but they have not impacted a third country or attracted much outside concern. Peoples in India's Northeast region, feeling neglected by the Indian government, have demanded autonomy from the mid-1960s. The largest group, the Naxalites, began to build support for Maoist ideology in West Bengal during 1967 and in time spread throughout many provinces along the Bay of Bengal (Duyker 1987). Their most violent terrorist attack occurred in 2010 (Al Jazeera 2010).

In recent years, Bangladesh has had conflicts with left-wing extremists but also with militant Islamic groups. After many years of conflict, the Bangladesh government finally signed a peace agreement in 1997 with representatives of the indigenous insurgents operating in the Chittagong Hill Tracts. Nevertheless, government forces still instigate violence on behalf of Bengali settlers (Acharya 2009a).

The Indian Border Security Forces have killed and injured hundreds of civilians along the border with Bangladesh in recent years. In 2009, Bangladesh and India set up a Joint Task Force to deal with militants inside Bangladesh (Acharya 2009a).

Bangladesh has also sustained attacks from Myanmar, provoked by attacks by Burmese exiles. In 2008, Myanmar deployed more than five thousand troops in an area along the border that Dhaka considers its own. That same year, Bangladeshi war vessels deterred an attack by Myanmar's navy on an island in the Bay of Bengal held by Bangladesh. In 2009, Myanmar's security forces fired on a Bangladeshi fishing boat and Bangladeshi troops clashed with Myanmar-based insurgents.

Until 2007, landlocked Bhutan largely allowed India to handle its foreign relations. Possibly in response to China's incursion in 2005 into disputed territory along the undemarcated border to build roads and bridges, a treaty that year permitted Bhutan to handle its own foreign policy. Bhutan, which then had no formal relations with China, approached Beijing on the matter, and India interceded. China then promised to work out the issue peacefully (News China 2005).

From 2004, American unmanned aerial (drone) attacks within Pakistan should have occurred. Although the airplanes initially took off from bases in Pakistan, the Islamabad government has regularly objected to the injuring or killing of civilians. In 2011, Pakistan revoked permission to launch attacks from bases on its soil. Drone attacks on Pakistan territory, which Islamabad still criticizes, nevertheless continue from bases in Afghanistan today.

One other country should be mentioned—Sikkim. In 1947, the landlocked territory voted to opt out of the newly formed India. But in 1973, Sikkim asked for India's protection when riots broke out in front of the royal palace. Although some commentators have objected to India's use of military force in the country as an excuse for annexation (Datta-Ray 1984), Sikkim voted to join India in 1975.

The South Asian Association for Regional Cooperation, however, has played no visible role in conflicts that have arisen after

Table 6.2 Disposition of conflicts in South Asia

Conflict	*Years*	*Intervener*	*Outcome*
Kashmir War	1947–	UN	simmering
Iran coup	1953	UK, USA	ruler deposed
Sino-Indian War	1962	none	frozen
Indo-Pakistan War	1965	none	simmering
Indian insurgencies	1966–	none	simmering
Bangladesh War	1971	none	victory
Sikkim riots	1973	India	annexation
Sri Lanka Civil War	1983–2009	Norway, UN	victory
SAARC began in 1985			
ASEAN Regional Forum began in 1994			
Nepal Civil War	1996–2006	UN	reconciliation
Indo-Pakistan War	1999	ARF, EU	frozen
India-Bangladesh War	2001–	bilateral task force	simmering
India-Myanmar	2001–	none	continuing
United States-Pakistan	2004–	none	continuing
Bhutan-China	2005	India	frozen

its formation (see Table 6.2). SAARC's primary interest is in economic issues, but has achieved little progress. Nevertheless, the European Union, the UN, and Norway have been willing to mediate in South Asia. In addition, ARF's recent involvement in efforts to defuse Pakistan's incursion into the part of Kashmir controlled by India may bode well for the future. But again the data contradict the hypothesis that IGO membership makes militarized conflicts less likely. The same conflicts have existed before and after SAARC was formed.

Conflicts in Central Asia

Most countries in the "stans" of Central Asia have enjoyed peace before and after new IGOs have arisen in the region. The major exception, Afghanistan, has not benefited from any of the Asian regional organizations that might have played a role on its behalf (see Table 6.3). The current aim of the North Atlantic Treaty Organization is to carry out UN Security Council resolutions to provide stability for the country, and non-NATO countries, such as Thailand, have provided civilian

Table 6.3 Disposition of conflicts in Central Asia

Conflict	*Years*	*Intervener*	*Outcome*
Afghan-USSR	1979–1989	none	victory
Afghan Civil War	1989–2001	none	victory
Tajikistan Civil War	1992–1997	Russia, UN, USA	armistice
Uighur insurgency	1997–	none	simmering
Afghan Civil War	2001–	NATO, UN	ongoing
Shanghai Cooperation Organization began in 1995[a]			
Collective Security Treaty Organization began in 2002			
Kyrgyzstan riots	2010	SCO, UN	repression

[a] Originally, the Shanghai Five.

assistance. Many observers question whether outside intervention has had a positive result, and the role of Pakistan has been ambiguous at best (West 2011).

Although China brought what is now called Xinjiang Province under control in 1755, the population is mainly Uighur, a Turkic Muslim people. During China's civil war, a Republic of East Turkestan was established in the province, but China reestablished control after the People's Republic of China defeated the Nationalist Chinese and began to encourage Han Chinese to resettle in the province. Protests in the 1990s morphed into clashes in 1997, and unrest has continued, with some refugees pouring into neighboring countries. Turkey has made critical comments of the treatment of Uighurs but has not taken any concrete action (Kaltman 2007).

Although the Shanghai Cooperation Organization and the UN calmed the situation in Kyrgyzstan (Weir 2010), the coexistence of both China's SCO and the Russian-sponsored Collective Security Treaty Organization promises to assure Central Asian peace prospects. Russia's linchpin in the region is its base in Tajikistan. From 1993, diplomatic efforts involving both Russia and the United States hastened the UN-brokered agreement for Tajikistan (Slim and Hodizoda 2002), which lost nearly one hundred thousand lives in its civil war. In 2012, more internal unrest emerged but was quickly suppressed. Afghanistan, meanwhile, belongs to neither CSTO nor SCO, and Central Asian regional organizations have not played a role in mitigating its civil war.

Conflicts in Southeast Asia

Southeast Asia has had to cope with more conflicts over the years than all other subregions combined (see Table 6.4). But peace has prevailed as the scope of the conflicts has declined from bloody wars to occasional incidents.

After World War II came wars of independence. Those in Indonesia (Taylor 1960) and Vietnam (Addington 2000; Fall 1963) ended, the latter despite intervention from outside the region.

Several conflicts have involved insurgencies, which sometimes have involved other countries. For Indonesia, two problems (1965 coup; Aceh uprisings from 1976 to 2004) were dealt with internally (Hughes 2002; Siddharth 2005). Conflict with pirates (nonstate actors) prompted formation of the Tripartite Council in 1971 to better coordinate measures to stop the disruption of the Straits of Malacca.

Hanoi's efforts to unify the country were blocked by Washington from the Geneva Accords partition in 1954 until the American military withdrawal in 1973. Contrary to the view that civil wars inhibit IGO formation (Haftel 2012:Ch5n111), the South-East Asia Treaty Organization was formed because of the Vietnamese civil war. Joining the United States on the Vietnamese battlefield were SEATO allies Australia, New Zealand, the Philippines, and South Korea. A member of SEATO, Britain, stayed out; its public was opposed. Charles de Gaulle disparaged the SEATO alliance. Karachi, upset because SEATO failed to support its role in the Bangladesh War of 1971, had already withdrawn from SEATO and sent no troops to Vietnam. In 1975, Hanoi achieved victory over the South and effected unification of the country in 1976.

From 1967, Mao-styled Communists in Cambodia, known as the Khmer Rouge, began to build an insurgent army, which with some Chinese assistance became strong enough to seize power by 1975. The United States, which backed Lon Nol's coup of Prince Sihanouk in 1970, did not come to the aid of Lon Nol's government when the Khmer Rouge triumphed. Some claim that American efforts in Cambodia to install Lon Nol fueled support for the Khmer Rouge (cf. Sihanouk 1980:35).

A civil war in Laos, which began in 1954, provoked American intervention but ended with a Communist victory in 1975 (Conboy

Table 6.4 Disposition of conflicts in Southeast Asia

Conflict	*Years*	*Intervener*	*Outcome*
Malacca Strait piracy	historic	TC	reduction
Indonesia-Netherlands	1945–1949	UN	victory
Vietnam-France	1946–1954	Geneva Conference	partition
Burmese civil wars	1948–	ASEAN	partial ceasefire
Malayan insurgency	1948–1960	UK	victory
South-East Asian Treaty Organization active in 1954–1977			
Vietnamese Civil War	1954–1975	Australia, New Zealand, Philippines, South Korea, USA	victory
Laotian Civil War	1954–1975	USA	victory
Preah Vihear	1962	ICJ	judgment
Indonesia-Malaya	1963–1965	Thailand	reconciliation
Anglo-Malayan/Malaysian Defence Agreement active in 1957–1971			
Sabah dispute	1963–	Thailand	simmering
Indonesian coup	1965	none	repression
Thai Communist insurgency	1965–80	China	withered
Association of South-East Asian Nations began in 1967			
Khmer Rouge insurgency	1967–1975	none	victory
Corregidor incident	1968	none	closed
Philippine Communist insurgency	1968–	Norway	simmering
Cambodian coup	1970	USA	victory
Five Power Defence Arrangements began in 1971 Tripartite Council began in 1971			
Mindanao insurgency	1972–	Malaysia	partial resolution
Battle of the Paracel Islands	1974	none	victory
SEAFDEC vessel seizure by Burma	1975	none	reflagged ship
Cambodia-Vietnam	1975–1978	none	victory
Cambodian autocide	1975–1979	Vietnam	regime change
East Timor seizure	1975–2002	UN	reconciliation
Reed Bank	1976–	none	simmering
Cambodian Civil War	1979–1991	ASEAN, Australia, Indonesia, UN, Paris Conferences	reconciliation
Sabah fishing boat	1980	none	closed

Table 6.4 Continued

Conflict	*Years*	*Intervener*	*Outcome*
	Indochinese Foreign Ministers Conference active 1980–1989		
Thailand-Vietnam	1984	none	withdrawal
Maddanas Island	1985	none	closed
Laos-Thailand	1987–1988	Vietnam	resolved
Malaysia-Philippines	1988	none	closed
Pedra Branca	1992	ICJ	judgment
	ASEAN Regional Forum began in 1994		
Mischief Reef	1994, 1999	none	simmering
Philippines-Vietnam	1995, 1996	none	closed
Johnson South Reef Skirmish	1998	none	victory
Ligitan and Sipadan	1998–2002	ICJ	judgment
Philippines-Vietnam	1998–1999	none	closed
Myanmar-Thailand	1998–1999, 2001, 2002	none	closed
Pattani insurgency	2001–	Malaysia	ongoing
	Southwest Pacific Dialog began in 2002		
Malaysia-Singapore	2003	ITLOS	judgment
Indonesia-Malaysia	2005–	ICJ, ASEAN	ongoing
crackdown on Burma protest	2007	Singapore	stopped
Cambodia-Thailand	2008–	ASEAN	ongoing
East London Reef	2011	none	simmering
Scarborough Shoal	2012	none	capitulation

1994). In late 1987, Thai troops moved into territory claimed by Laos, which responded militarily; after the Vietnamese army came to the aid of Vientiane, Bangkok backed down in a few months and agreed to a ceasefire. In 1996, as Laos was negotiating entry into ASEAN, the Thai-Lao Joint Boundary Commission was established to demarcate the exact border between the two countries.

Regarding the Communist insurgency in Thailand, civilian aid by SEATO up to 1977 was aimed at winning villages over to the Thai government (M.Haas 1989a:37). The insurgency ended in 1980, when China offered to stop aid to the insurgents in exchange for having Thailand allow Chinese arms to reach the Khmer Rouge so that Vietnam would not control the entire territory of Cambodia. As a result, the Vietnamese fended off attacks from the Cambodian resistance in a civil war that occasionally appeared to spill over into Thailand (M.Haas 2011b:110).

The Philippines has had to cope with Communist insurgents in Luzon as well as the Mindanao insurgency by Muslims (Fernandez 2011). In 2011, after several mediation attempts over the years, Norway offered to engage the Communist movement and the Manila government (International Crisis Group 2011). From Philippine independence in 1948, Muslims on Mindanao and in the Sulu Archipelago have claimed that they were never part of the Spanish Philippines and thus did not revert to American control after the Spanish-American War of 1898. The dispute turned violent in 1972 and remained unresolved until 2012, when Malaysian Prime Minister Najib Razak brokered a framework accord between the Manila government and the Moro Islamic Liberation Front to create an autonomous region, Bangsamoro, for Muslim majority areas (BBC 2012b; Fitch 2012). But one of the rebel Muslim groups has not signed on.

In southernmost Thailand, seeds for an insurgency were sown in 1905, when the Thai military annexed territory that was formerly the Pattani kingdom. In recent years, Malay Muslims have felt ignored by Bangkok, and the result has been a campaign for better treatment that escalated into an insurgency by 2004. A Thai army crackdown in 2006 only increased the discontent. Incidents continue to occur to the present, sometimes involving bombs and shootings (McCargo 2008).

The Communist insurgency in Malaya began in 1948 as the insurgents redirected their violence against Imperial Japan in World War II to the return of Britain to maintain its Malaya colony. Britain fought the insurgents in an operation known as the Emergency until 1960. As the insurgency waned, Britain formed the Anglo-Malayan Defence Agreement in 1957, the year when the Federation of Malaya was granted independence. In 1973, the Federation of Malaysia was formed with the addition of Sabah, Sarawak, and Singapore, but Kuala Lumpur expelled Singapore in 1975. Singaporean police dealt with its own Communist dissidents after independence but later exaggerated their strength to justify extreme repression of legitimate political opposition (M.Haas 1999).

Beyond internal conflicts, Southeast Asia has also been plagued by border conflicts, which have rarely escalated beyond individual incidents. There have been three bloody exceptions. One was the confrontation over the inclusion of Sarawak into the Federation of

Malaysia. As a result, Indonesia mobilized its army against Malaysia, and several hundred soldiers died during the *confrontasi* of 1963–1965 (Gordon 1966; Jones, Bremer, Singer 1996; Lyon 1969). Manila was also unhappy that Sabah was included as a new state in Malaysia and temporarily withdrew its ambassador from Kuala Lumpur until ASEAN was formed.

Adam Malik, appointed Indonesia's foreign minister in 1966, sought to end the tension with Malaysia and the Philippines with a much larger vision for the region, consistent with Jakarta's long-standing policy of nonalignment. After consultation with his opposite number in Thailand, Thanat Khoman, the result was formation of the Association of South-East Asian Nations in 1967, including acceptance of Sabah and Sarawak within Malaysia (Jeshuran 2007; Samad and Bakar 1992). Kuala Lumpur later returned the compliment by assisting Manila in dealing with the Mindanao insurgency (Fernandez 2011).

In 1968, nevertheless, Malaysia sent an aircraft and two gunboats into Philippine waters on learning that an insurgent force in Corregidor was preparing to invade Sabah (Brown 1994: 102; Caballero-Anthony 1998: 54; Jones, Bremer, and Singer 1996). Other Malaysian-Philippine incidents have emerged from time to time (Indorf 1984:18; Jones, Bremer, and Singer 1996; Mak 2009; Simon 1990:128). In 1980, for example, a Philippine naval boat shot at a fishing boat homeported in Sabah. In 1985, Malaysian gunboats and helicopters raided Maddanas Island, claimed by the Philippines. In addition, in 1988 Malaysian forces seized a Filipino fishing boat in the South China Sea.

A more serious conflict came in 1975, as Portugal withdrew from its colony in East Timor. Rather than welcoming the territory as a newly independent state, Jakarta forcibly tried to annex East Timor without the approval of the people. ASEAN was silent, accepting the explanation that the former colony might become a communist hotbed—a sort of Southeast Asian Cuba. The Indonesian army massacred some sixty thousand in the initial attack, and the bodycount ultimately rose beyond 100,000–150,000 (Kiernan 2003). Ultimately, the UN intervened, set up a transitional administration, and facilitated the country's independence in 2002 (Robinson 2010). The new country, Timor-Leste, may never forget that ASEAN did nothing to stop Jakarta, but Indonesia made some amends by agreeing to include the new country within the formation of the Southwest Political Dialogue in 2002.

Another major border war came in 1978. ASEAN was insensitive to Khmer Rouge attacks on Vietnam, which pleaded in vain for international intervention as residents along the border were massacred. Phnom Penh even declared an irredentist intention of annexing Khmer Krom, that is, South Vietnam, and in 1978 the Khmer Rouge army began marching toward Saigon (M.Haas 2011b:132). In response, Vietnamese troops entered Cambodia at the end of 1978, and the Khmer Rouge was swept from power by the end of 1979.

With refugees pouring from Cambodia into Thailand, Bangkok asked for support to handle both the refugee population and the danger of having the Vietnamese army close to its border. Beijing then withdrew support for the Communist insurrection in Thailand in exchange for Bangkok's willingness to allow arms to flow to the Khmer Rouge, thereby preventing Vietnam from enjoying total victory in Cambodia (M.Haas 2011b:110).

During the 1980s, ASEAN unanimously insisted that the new government in Cambodia, which began operation to replace the Khmer Rouge in Phnom Penh, was unworthy of UN membership. ASEAN persuaded the UN to allow the defeated Khmer Rouge to occupy the Cambodian seat in the UN while military forces supplied by arms from China and the United States kept the Vietnamese army at bay during the 1980s. Nevertheless, in 1984 Hanoi's army got close enough to the Thai border for Bangkok to mobilize troops.

But soon a remarkable transformation occurred. Indonesia, still mired in East Timor, got ASEAN approval in 1980 to begin separate negotiations with Hanoi, which all along wanted an international force to maintain peace in the country so that Vietnamese troops could depart. A peace process developed that ultimately found Australia stitching together pieces of an agreement for a conference at Paris during 1991. China and the United States then accepted having the UN set up a framework for a ceasefire, and free elections were held in 1993 (M.Haas 2011b).

ASEAN's two-track diplomacy toward the Cambodian civil war was significant because for the first time the Asian Way trumped the ASEAN Way. According to the latter, ASEAN countries had pledged never to meddle in the internal affairs of its fellow member countries. But the Pan-Asian spirit of the Asian Way saw things differently: Consensus slowly developed from initial disagreements within ASEAN on how to bring peace to Southeast Asia to a peace process and finally to a peace agreement. Whereas ASEAN ignored the East Timor problem, the Cambodian conflict offered a choice between absolute support for Thailand as a vulnerable frontline state and a broader view of how to bring the long-held ASEAN goal of building a Zone of Peace, Freedom, and Neutrality (ZOPFAN) within Southeast Asia.

Initially, ASEAN was regarded cynically as a dictator's club. Coups arose in many countries, notably Thailand, so the "ASEAN Way" originally involved noninterference in the internal affairs of member countries. Nevertheless, people power demonstrations in Thailand (1976), the Philippines (1986), and Indonesia (1998) brought new leaders to the fore who championed democracy and human rights. ASEAN then woke up to play a central role in providing mediation.

Even though ASEAN followed a policy of "constructive engagement" with Burma, some ASEAN leaders were unhappy with Rangoon's human rights record. Border clashes with Thailand were also an irritant. An odd incident occurred in 1975, when a research vessel of Singapore's office of the Southeast Asian Fisheries Development Center was seized for straying into Burmese waters and incorporated into the Burmese fleet (M.Haas 1989a:99). In December 1998, a Burmese naval ship attacked a Thai naval vessel, killing two Thais. The following month, Thai patrol boats killed three Burmese aboard frigates in an exchange of fire (Collins 2003:104–105; Palmer and Bremer 2004). Several Burmese have also died in clashes along the Thai border from time to time (Collins 2003:100; Ghosn, Palmer, and Bremer 2004; Haacke 2003:210–211).

Nevertheless, after being invited as a guest at the ASEAN foreign ministers meeting in 1994, Burma (renamed Myanmar in 1989) applied for ASEAN membership in 1995. Burma's admission to ASEAN in 1997 was designed to pressure Rangoon from within ASEAN meetings rather than continuing the failed Western policy of maintaining isolation and sanctions.

In 1998, ASEAN foreign ministers dropped the noninterference principle, namely, that internal conflicts of ASEAN countries should never be discussed. Instead, they substituted the principle that "enhanced interaction" or "flexible engagement" would be used (Emmerson 2008:75). Accordingly, Aung San Suu Kyi wrote to ASEAN in 1999, urging further diplomatic action (Zaw 2008). ASEAN then began to pressure Burma to adopt democratic reforms. One instance came in

2006, when ASEAN might have allowed Burma to chair the annual meeting of foreign ministers, as traditionally that honor is determined by alphabetical order. However, for Burma to do so might serve as a blight on ASEAN, so Myanmar was skipped, and the honor rotated to the next country in line. In 2008, another form of pressure came from Singapore's Foreign Minister George Yeo, who denounced Burma's crackdown on peaceful demonstrations (the "Saffron Revolution"), though he spoke outside an ASEAN meeting.

When Burma gained independence in 1948, many ethnic groups in the provinces had resisted rule from Rangoon (now Yangon), so the army's assignment had long been to unify the country by triumphing in various civil wars within the provinces. But as the army got stronger, they decided to dominate civilian institutions, adding another layer of civil discontent in the capital, which in turn led to military crackdowns. In 2012, ASEAN's pressure succeeded with the release of political prisoners, a ceasefire with most of the dissident rural ethnic groups, and a free election that allowed an opposition to contest and win a few seats in parliament (Wade 2009; McElroy 2012).

With the most land borders in the region, Thailand has encountered problems with other neighboring states. In 2005, for example, Kuala Lumpur reacted to the arrival of Muslim refugees in Malaysia who were fleeing in order to escape repression by the Thai army in the south of Thailand. Former Prime Minister Tun Dr. Mahathir bin Mohamad then conducted negotiations with Thai Prime Minister Taksin Sinawatra to come up with a modus vivendi (AsiaViews 2010), but he did not succeed.

Yet another border conflict is about Cambodia's access to an historical monument. After the International Court of Justice ruled in 1962 that Cambodia had sovereignty over the eleventh century Hindu temple Preah Vihear, the issue seemed settled. But access to the temple was blocked by members of the Thai military in 2008, and some battle deaths ensued until 2011, when Cambodia took the conflict back to the ICJ. The court then ruled that both sides should remove their troops and establish a demilitarized zone (LaRocco 2011). After an informal ASEAN discussion, Indonesia agreed to send observers so that nothing untoward would happen until the matter could be resolved bilaterally (Padden 2011). In other words, Phnom Penh allowed ASEAN and ICJ to intercede, and Jakarta responded in a manner that Bangkok would accept.

Even the border between Malaysia and Singapore has been in dispute. When Singapore planned to add a landfill that might intrude into Malaysian waters, the parties in 2003 agreed to submit the case to the International Tribunal for the Law of the Sea (ITLOS), which ruled that Singapore should abandon its plan because of potential damage to the marine environment.

Perhaps the most intractable conflicts in Southeast Asia involve sea boundaries.[1] China's efforts to show muscle on behalf of a claim of sovereignty in the South China sea, with ships deployed to more than one hundred reef-associated islands in the Paracel and Spratly islands, have angered Brunei, Indonesia, Malaysia, the Philippines, Taiwan, and Vietnam despite a vague Chinese-ASEAN "code of conduct" declaration of 2002 (Thayer 2007:27). The problem arises because China lays claim to all the islands (Paracels, Spratlys, and Scarborough Shoal). Although a portion of the Paracel Islands lies within China's 200-mile exclusive economic zone, China's larger claim is based on a fifteenth century visit by a Chinese military force.

In the first incident, the Battle of the Paracel Islands, Chinese warships defeated a South Vietnamese naval contingent in 1974 (Cutler 2009). China has remained under control of the Paracels ever since. In June 2012, Beijing declared that Sansha City on Woody Island in the Paracels is the capital of its possessions in the South China Sea, and in July a military garrison was homeported in the town.

In the Spratlys, the situation is more complicated. The Philippines occupies 7 islands and 3 reefs; Vietnam has 6 islands, 17 reefs and 3 banks; Taiwan is in charge of 1 island and 1 reef; the Malaysian flag is on 1 artificial island and 5 reefs; and the People's Republic of China governs 8 reefs. Brunei, also a claimant, does not have a foothold anywhere.

In 1970, the Philippines began exploring for oil in the area and in 1976 discovered gas in Reed Bank, the largest seamount in the Spratlys. Although Reed Bank is only 85 miles from the Philippine island of Palawan and 600 miles from the China coast, Beijing objected, and drilling stopped after Chinese vessels fired warning shots; they continue to intrude at Reed Bank.

Another notorious example of unilateral territorial acquisition involves Mischief Reef, only 130 miles from Palawan Island, where China built some dwellings on stilts in 1994 and again in 1999. Manila decided not to counter the move, fearing that war might result (Bordadora and Burgonio 2008).

China's intention to use force became clear in the Johnson South Reef Skirmish of 1998, when a Vietnamese ship arrived at the reef only to discover a Chinese troop encampment, whereupon both sides called for reinforcements. A firefight ensued, China sunk one of Vietnam's vessels, and China then took over seven more reefs in the area (cf. Cheng and Tien 2000). In 2011, Chinese naval vessels fired on Vietnamese fishing boats off East London Reef (BBC 2011), and they cut exploration cables of a Vietnamese exploration ship.

After harassing a Philippine exploration ship, China warned Southeast Asian countries not to engage in oil exploration in the region (Richburg, Wan, and Branigin 2011). A Philippine coast guard ship was forced to retreat from Scarborough Shoal by two Chinese maritime surveillance ships in 2012 (Perlez 2012). An arms race appears inevitable in the region.

Several incidents in the Spratlys over the years have also brought Southeast Asian countries into conflict with each other. In 1979, a Malaysian task force occupied a Spratly reef coveted by the Philippines (Jones, Bremer, and Singer 1996; Mak 2009). Singaporean and Malaysian patrol boats clashed in 1992 near the disputed island of Pedra Branca (Jones, Bremer, and Singer 1996; Tan 2000: 22–23), but in 2007, ICJ awarded the island to Singapore.

Philippine and Vietnamese naval vessels exchanged fire in the Gulf of Thailand during 1995 (Collins 2003:105; Ghosn, Palmer, and Bremer 2004). The Philippines increased patrolling near the Spratlys to the chagrin of Vietnam in 1998 (Ghosn, Palmer, and Bremer 2004), and the following year, Vietnamese troops shot at a Philippine air force plane in the Spratlys (Collins 2003:197; Ghosn, Palmer, and Bremer 2004; Mak 2009).

Indonesian and Malaysian naval ships clashed near the disputed sea block of Ambalat in 2005 and 2009 (Mak 2009). Due to the moderating influence of membership in ASEAN (Emmerson 2005:175), Indonesia and Malaysia agreed to submit their disputed claims, never contested by force, over the Ligitan and Sipadan islands to ICJ, and Malaysia was granted sovereignty by the court.

On the pretext of assuring the security of shipping routes in the South China Sea, the United States decided in 2012 to dispatch Marines to Darwin, Australia, not far from the area of conflict (McDonell and Brown 2012). Whether Washington's decision was a response to ASEAN is unknown, but American and Philippine marines conducted war games in the Spratlys during 2011 to show support for Manila's proposal to turn the region into a Joint Marine Peace Park (Pazzibugan and Esplanada 2011).

Reviewing conflicts in Southeast Asia (see Table 6.4 above), SEATO played no role in preventing or lessening militarized conflict. ARF has been useful outside Southeast Asia. Members of the Five Power Defence Arrangements and the Tripartite Council have focused on conflicts outside the membership. The Southwest Political Dialogue was set up to smooth relations between former enemies, Indonesia and Timor-Leste.

Originally, under the ASEAN Way, countries agreed never to get involved in internal or bilateral disputes among the members. More recently, ASEAN has become involved in disputes that might earlier have been left alone. Since ASEAN leaders know one another so well on a personal basis, they can work toward solutions informally whereas a more formal institutional framework might bring out contentiousness over details. There lies a major reason for identifying ASEAN as having established an arena of peace. Given ASEAN Regional Forum's intervention in the latest India-Pakistan conflict, bringing about an arena of peace in the rest of Asia may now be within ASEAN's destiny.

Conflicts in the Pacific Islands

In contrast with Asia, the Pacific islands have long been an arena of peace. The main international conflict has been over the western part of New Guinea, an island second only to Greenland in size.

In 1961, Indonesia fought the Netherlands, an initial member of the South Pacific Commission, to gain control of Irian Jaya, the Dutch province west of Papua New Guinea now known as West Papua (van der Kroef 1978b). In 1969, the UN organized a vote of leaders to accept Indonesian sovereignty, but resistance by the Free Papua Movement has continued ever since, and the Jakarta government reportedly has become increasingly repressive in Papua (Harvey 2009). The Forum has ignored the issue despite protests on behalf of West Papua outside a recent Forum meeting. In 2011, UN Secretary-General Ban Ki-Moon suggested that the matter should be taken up by the UN General Assembly Committee on Decolonization (Yamo 2011), but the conflict continues. The eastern half of the island, now known as Papua New Guinea, was granted independence by Australia in 1975.

France is reluctant to grant independence to colonies in New Caledonia and French Polynesia (Tahiti).[2] Unlike Tahiti, New Caledonia has a history of opposition to colonial rule. When the French brought outsiders to mine nickel deposits, the indigenous Kanaks were herded into reservations. In 1878, High Chief Atal united many of the central tribes and launched a guerrilla war, resulting in the death of two hundred Frenchmen and one thousand Kanaks. France continued to rule until World War II, when the island was a staging area for battles against Japan. In 1953, all residents of New Caledonia were granted French citizenship. Due to the nickel boom of 1969–1972, more workers were imported, and Kanaks became a minority in their own country. From 1976, France adopted the first of several governing statutes for New Caledonia, but the Kanaks objected, even organizing a violent protest in 1985, when I first visited. In 1987, a referendum on independence was rejected by a large majority. But in 1988, the minority protest took the form of hostage taking. Then, in 1988, the dissidents signed the ten-year Matignon Agreements, agreeing not to agitate for independence in return for economic assistance, the establishment of local government units for the Kanak population, amnesty for those involved in the hostage incident, and a decision to allow a vote on self-determination as early as 2014. As Matignon was about to expire, the Nouméa Agreement was signed, providing for a 20-year transition in which more authority would be transferred to local governments, including those with Kanak majorities, followed by the granting of self-governance in 2018. However, the future arrangement is for a French protectorate, as Paris will retain control of the courts, defense, finances, and security after 2018. Both the Matignon and Nouméa accords were negotiated with the intervention of Paris and accepted by the voters (cf. Chappelle 2005).

Although the region was at relative peace when the Forum was established in 1971, internal conflicts among members subsequently arose within Fiji, Papua New Guinea (Bougainville), and the Solomon Islands. They have provided important challenges for the Forum.

The imprint of Ratu Mara, elected Fiji's prime minister in 1970, on South Pacific regional organizations continued until the election of 1987, when his party lost reelection. Many indigenous Fijians were dissatisfied over the political strength of the Indian population in that election, and two military coups occurred that year. The indigenous Fijians feared that they might lose control of the country.

In 1987, the interim government asked Ratu Mara to continue as prime minister, which he did until 1992. He then resigned, ran for vice president, and became president when the president became incapacitated. But in 2000, Fiji had another coup, and he was forced to resign. Four years later, he died. In 2006, yet another coup occurred, and Fiji has been under military rule ever since (Firth, Fraenkel, and Lal 2009). Although internal coups, they have presented a challenge to the Forum because its Secretariat is in Suva, the Fiji capital.

South Pacific countries interpreted the Ratu Mara saga of 1987 as Fiji's abandonment of democracy. Having adopted a republican form of government, Fiji parted ways with the Commonwealth in 1987, giving the country further diplomatic isolation. Although the Forum ignored the Fiji coup of 1987, after the coup in 2000 Forum leaders met to review options. The result was adoption of the Biketawa Resolution, which established a framework for conflict resolution and implied that democratic rule would become a precondition to membership in the Forum. But, of course, the action was consistent with the its longstanding objection to colonial rule: New Caledonia and Tahiti remain ineligible to join the Forum.

When civil conflict emerged in the Solomon Islands during 1999, the Forum did not act, but the violence continued. In 2003, in accordance with Biketawa principles, a Forum peacekeeping force, the Regional Assistance Mission to Solomon Islands, was organized by Australia, New Zealand, Fiji, and Papua New Guinea (Kabutaulaka 2005). The situation then calmed down.

Insolvent Nauru was the second beneficiary of the Biketawa Resolution, but for economic reasons. From 2004 to 2009, the Forum established the Pacific Regional Assistance to Nauru to recapitalize the bankrupt country.

In 2005, the Forum adopted the Pacific Plan for Regional Integration and Cooperation. One of the four pillars is to provide regional security.

Then, after the Fiji coup of 2006, the Forum tried to intervene so that democratic elections could be held, but the Fiji government was defiant. Fiji then joined the Melanesian Spearhead Group in 2007, in part to avoid regional isolation, and MSG did not intervene.

In 2009, the Forum took the extraordinary step of suspending Fiji from membership. Thus, the Forum had not only taken over diplomatic leadership in the region but was attempting to hold a government to a democratic standard.

Similar to ASEAN's blindness over the conflict in East Timor, the Forum ignored the Bougainville secessionist movement in Papua New Guinea for many years. In 1975, the province had issued an independence declaration two weeks before Australia granted independence to Papua New Guinea. But Canberra paid no attention to the declaration, and the newly elected Port Moresby government did not even designate Bougainville as a distinct province. Increasingly, residents objected to environmental damage caused by copper, gold, and silver mining companies, and a second grievance was a demand for increased royalties from the mining profits.

However, Papua New Guinea did pay attention to renewed independence demands when the Bougainville Revolutionary Army became more violent in 1985. Then a civil war erupted in 1989, claiming at least fifteen thousand lives. In 1990, Papua New Guinea security services placed an embargo on the Bougainville island province, whereupon Bougainville issued a second independence declaration and began to set up a formal government. In response, Port Moresby asked the Forum and the UN to send a peacekeeping mission. Yet the UN Security Council did not rate the conflict as important. In 1994, a regional peacekeeping force was instead set up instead under Tongan leadership, supported by Australia, Fiji, New Zealand, Solomon Islands, and Vanuatu (Leadbeater 2011), and a peace process developed. In 1997, a peace agreement was brokered by New Zealand on behalf of the Forum in which monitoring of the ceasefire was assigned to the UN from 1998 to 2005. Currently, Bougainville is an autonomous province of Papua New Guinea, sometimes referred to as the North Solomons, pending a plebiscite vote on independence. The Forum sent election observers to the territory in 2005 and 2010.

No militarized interstate conflicts preceded the formation of Pacific regional organizations, and none have followed. Although not originally set up to handle conflict resolution, the Forum has nevertheless seized the opportunity in recent years (see Table 6.5). There is a fear that the apparent split between Melanesians and Polynesians will disrupt the unity that has enabled the Forum to be the pivotal organization in the Pacific. Meanwhile, ANZUS remains irrelevant to the Pacific Islands region.

As a postscript, in 1999 Australia and New Zealand filed ITLOS cases against Japan for overfishing. After ruling that Tokyo must pay litigation expenses of Canberra and Wellington, and abide by

Table 6.5 Disposition of conflicts in the Pacific

Conflict	*Years*	*Intervener*	*Outcome*
	South Pacific Commission began 1948[a] **ANZUS Council active 1952–1985**		
West Papua	1961–	UN	ongoing
	South Pacific Forum began in 1971[b]		
New Caledonia uprising	1985–1988	France	peace
	Melanesian Spearhead Group began in 1986		
Fiji coups	1987	none	frozen
Bougainville	1989–2007	Forum	reconciliation
Japanese overfishing	1999	ITLOS	judgment
Solomon Islands	1999–2003	Forum	frozen
Fiji coup	2000	none	frozen
Fiji coup	2006	Forum	ongoing

[a] Later retitled Pacific Community.
[b] Originally, the South Pacific Forum.

maximum catch requirements, but an arbitration panel reversed the ITLOS decision.

Conclusion

Conflicts in Asia and the Pacific do exist, but most have been frozen or resolved rather than left to fester. Examining regional organizations over time, mere co-memberships have not served to reduce the likelihood of militarized disputes, contrary to a frequently cited cross-sectional statistical study (Russett, Oneal, and Davis 1998), as active intervention is required. Although military-security organizations forming a security community have played a significant role in conflict resolution, the cooperative spirit promoted by technical organizations should not be overlooked. Indeed, I was once told in 1978 that ministerial-level delegates of two Southeast countries resolved their differences on the sidelines during a meeting of the Southeast Asian Ministers of Education Organization.

Clearly, in recent years, an arena of peace has increasingly been forged in Asia and the Pacific through IGO-sponsored diplomacy, especially in Southeast Asia and the Pacific Islands (see Table 6.6). Prospects for peacemaking in Central Asia, East Asia, and South Asia

Table 6.6 Conflict resolution in Asia and the Pacific

Subregion	*Conflicts*	*Resolution Efforts*[a]	*Third-Party Interveners*
Central Asia	6	5	NATO, Russia, SCO, UN, USA
East Asia	17	4	ASEAN, bilateral talks, ITLOS, Russia, UN, USA
South Asia	14	8	ARF, EU, India, Norway, UK, UN, USA
Southeast Asia	43	25	ASEAN, Australia, China, France, Geneva Conference, ICJ, IFMC, Indonesia, ITLOS, Malaysia, New Zealand, Norway, Paris Conferences, Philippines, Singapore, South Korea, TC, Thailand, UN, UK, USA, Vietnam
Pacific Islands	8	5	Forum, France, ITLOS, UN

[a]Numbers in this column refer to cases where intervention was involved; some had several interveners.

are more promising today than before, as ASEAN has begun to look outward at the rest of the region.

The advance toward democracy in Asia has been slow, and there has been some retrogression in the Pacific. In an unprecedented move, the Forum decided to suspend Fiji in 2009 because the Suva government refused to restore democracy. In 2012, meanwhile, despite Myanmar's longstanding internal and external conflicts, the country appeared to be moving toward greater democracy by holding a free and fair election. ASEAN's policy of engagement with Myanmar has worked, whereas the policy of isolation by Western powers has not. Multifunctional regional organizations (ASEAN and the Forum) are doing their part to turn countries as well as regions in conflict into arenas of peace (see Table 6.7).

Both ASEAN and the Forum have rethought their basic principles, adopting tacitly a vision that peace in Asia and the Pacific can best be accomplished when all countries become democracies. Such an idea has had a long lineage, as Immanuel Kant (1795) had first proposed a league of republics (countries without despotic monarchs and hereditary aristocracies), and President Woodrow Wilson saw a post–World War I settlement as a pathway for making the world "safe for democracy," thereby promoting world peace.

The idea of a separate IGO of democracies was reborn after the collapse of the Cold War and the so-called "end of history" (Fukuyama

Table 6.7 Conflict resolution modes in Asia and the Pacific

Conflict Resolution Actors	*Cases*
bilateral negotiations	5
international conferences	2
international tribunals	7
mediation: American/European actors	3
mediation: Asian-Pacific actors	8
mediation: UN	10
military forces	10
regional organizations	12
conflicts with no resolution actor	39

1992) as an alternative to the concept of a perpetual "clash of civilizations" (Huntington 1993). In the year 2000, President Bill Clinton and Secretary of State Madeleine Albright even championed a caucus of democracies within the UN. The idea was viewed as a way to get around the UN veto in the Security Council by authoritarian China and Russia, which opposed the American-led Kosovo War of 1999 that sought to prevent further ethnic cleansing by Serbia. Instead, a Community of Democracies might authorize military action to stop serious human rights violations around the world, an idea that has gained support from some human rights scholars (Ikenberry and Slaughter 2008).[3] Alternatively, as one scholar has argued, the UN Charter could be interpreted as allowing regional organizations to resolve breaches of the peace when the UN Security Council fails to do so (Slaughter 2012).

Such ideas have excited some Western thinkers, but leaders within Asia and the Pacific have gone beyond mere ideas, albeit cautiously. Meddling in ASEAN member country internal conflicts, once vetoed by the ASEAN Way, is being transcended. The Forum has long demanded an end to colonial rule in the region, so the expulsion of Fiji is similar to the long-time refusal of membership to French-controlled New Caledonia and Tahiti. Democratic Asian and Pacific leaders are now changing the region from a zone of conflict into an arena of peace.

7

Successful Security Communities

The thesis of the present volume is that Asian and Pacific regional organizations have turned zones of conflict into arenas of peace. What has been presented thus far has proved that thesis: The Association of South-East Asian Nations and the Pacific Islands Forum have played pivotal and crucial roles in mitigating conflicts and now are embarked on formal conflict resolution.

Why have ASEAN and the Forum succeeded so well and other organizations in the Asian and Pacific have continued without fanfare, failed, or languished? Information presented in the volume above provides a quantitative database for answering that question, so the present chapter undertakes a statistical approach to provide additional insight.

Hitherto most studies on regional cooperation have tended to describe individual organizations or sets of organizations in a particular region of the world without developing a theory of success or failure—or testing a theory comparatively. However, an early attempt to perform such a test was a study by Karl Deutsch and associates, *Political Community and the North Atlantic Area* (1957), which compared 12 attempts at political unification, 7 unified states that broke apart, and 14 cases of pluralistic security communities (groups of countries for whom war was unthinkable) within Europe and the North Atlantic.

There have been some dissents from the Deutschian framework. Stanley Hoffmann (1965) argued that the entire idea of preconditions missed the point—that governments in the last analysis agree to form, expand, contract, and abolish IGOs on the basis of national interest. His theory, now characterized as **intergovernmentalism**, has been echoed more recently (Moravscik 1991; Garrett and Tsebelis 1996; Tsebelis and Garrett 2001).

In an implied critique, political scientists Ernst Haas and Philippe Schmitter (1964) compared ten economic IGOs in Africa, Europe, and Latin America, advancing the theory of **neofunctionalism**. Sociologist Amitai Etzioni (1965), explicitly critiquing Deutsch, used organization theory concepts to contrast two cases of successful unification with two unsuccessful attempts. Later, Haas (1975) used a sample of 30 IGOs. Their studies were primarily within Europe.

A decade later, I attempted a comparison between five existing organizations and two defunct cases in Asia and the Pacific to test the theoretical approaches of Deutsch, Etzioni, and Haas with statistical methods (M.Haas 1986). I first made judgments based on my extensive knowledge of the organizations. I then correlated each judgment with a dichotomous measure based on whether the IGO was defunct or still existed, using two versions of Kendall's tau as the appropriate way to calculate correlations involving dichotomous variables. I then computed measures of statistical significance to contrast stronger from weaker correlations.

Intergovernmentalists might have predicted that I would find either no correlations or spurious correlations, but that was not the case. What I found is that organizations that fail or become defunct have the following major characteristics: (1) lack of mutual compatibility of main values, (2) a quest for only goal harmonization rather than integration, (3) low popularity in the public, (4) loss of members, (5) decreased cooperativeness, (6) decision making not centralized, and (7) failure to enhance prosperity. Organizations that survive have the opposite characteristics.

More recent efforts have attempted to find the keys to the success of regional organizations. One scholar used public opinion data to compare ASEAN, the European Union, and Mercosur but did not find any consistent predictors for organizational success (Tusicisny 2007). As noted in Chapter 1 above, data assembled by three Korean economists identified cultural factors as preconditions to success in political-security matters within six regions (Kim, Kim, and Park 2011). A third empirical study, involving 25 economically oriented

IGOs in various regions, found that intraregional conflict resolution by economically oriented IGOs in several regions is positively related to whether they have regular meetings of high-level officials (Haftel 2007, 2012). The latter study also reported a strong relationship between a wider scope of joint economic activity within IGOs and efforts at intraregional conflict resolution. Trade patterns, however, were unrelated.

Accordingly, I have decided to retest my earlier study herein with a sample of 22 Asian and Pacific security-oriented organizations.[1] The following organizations, listed in chronological order, have discussed strategic (military-security) issues and in some cases have actually deployed military force:

- **Council of the Security Treaty Between Australia, New Zealand and the United States** (ANZUS Council)
- **South-East Asia Treaty Organization** (SEATO)
- **Five-Power Defence Arrangements** (FPDA)
- **Asian-Pacific Parliamentarians' Union** (APPU)
- **Asian and Pacific Council** (ASPAC)
- **Association of South-East Asian Nations** (ASEAN)
- **Tripartite Council** (TC)
- **Pacific Islands Forum** (PIF)
- **ASEAN Inter-Parliamentary Assembly** (AIPA)
- **Pacific Islands Conference** (PIC)
- **Indochinese Foreign Ministers Conference** (IFMC)
- **Association of Pacific Island Legislatures** (APIL)
- **South Asian Association for Regional Cooperation** (SAARC)
- **Melanesian Spearhead Group** (MSG)
- **Asia Pacific Parliamentary Forum** (APPF)
- **ASEAN Regional Forum** (ARF)
- **Indian Ocean Rim Association for Regional Cooperation** (IOR-ARC)
- **Shanghai Cooperation Organization** (SCO)
- **Asia Pacific Forum of National Human Rights Organizations** (APF)
- **Forum for East Asia-Latin America Cooperation** (FEALAC)
- **Southwest Political Dialogue** (SwPD)
- **Collective Security Organization** (CSTO).

Table 7.1 Success and failure of Asian and Pacific regional organizations

Types of IGOs	*Asian IGOs*	*Pacific IGOs*
Technical		
total IGOs formed	56	32
total IGOs defunct	15	6
defunct/formed	.27	.19
Political-Security		
total IGOs formed	17	6
total IGOs defunct	4	1
defunct/formed	.24	.17

Security Community Theory

Before embarking on a fresh empirical analysis, some general comments on Asian and Pacific regional cooperation are in order. Contrasting IGOs with political aims and those with technical purposes, the rate of success and failure is roughly equal (see Table 7.1). Technical organizations in Asia and the Pacific have collapsed mostly due to lack of funding, whereas policy divergences account for the failure of such political-security IGOs as ANZUS, ASPAC, and SEATO.

To probe more deeply, I invoke the security community theory of Karl Deutsch. According to Deutsch (1953), the unification of Germany and Italy from an assortment of smaller states occurred in the nineteenth century because the peoples spoke the same languages and communicated across borders. In a later publication, Deutsch and his associates (1957) referred to German and Italian unification as the achievement of **amalgamated security communities**. They hypothesized that countries in the North Atlantic, particularly those forming what became the European Union, were achieving security communities without amalgamation because crucial factors were present. But not all scholars agreed (cf. Fisher 1969).

By **pluralistic security community**, Deutsch referred to organizations formed by independent states that sought to avoid war and engaged in peaceful change—that is, took cooperative measures together without seeking confederation, federation, or political unification. A later distinction was that **comprehensive security communities** avoided not only war but also civil war, whereas **interstate security communities** avoided war but might have civil wars (Väyrynen 2000). In both cases, Deutsch and associates believed that the route to peace was the establishment of an increasing number of subregional security communities, not the perilous Cold War containment preference to form alliances opposing other alliances.

One scholar later identified the concept of **security regime**, where countries agree to avoid war but might remain political rivals (Jervis 1982). In practice, the key difference between security communities and security regimes is that the former consist of organizations within a larger context of several potentially complementary or overlapping organizations. Environmental regimes, for example, might consist of all the treaties that impose certain requirements on signatories (e.g., Breitmeir, Underdal, and Young 2011), but a security regime is a much looser concept that might operate without treaty obligations.

Studies of security communities have mushroomed in recent years, though mostly descriptively rather than as a way to test theory.[2] Those advocating constructivist interpretations of world politics have embraced the concept of security community (Adler and Barnett 1998; Bearce and Bondanella 2007).

The ASEAN Summit in 2004 explicitly agreed to develop the components of a "security community" by 2020, and the Biketawa Declaration of 2000, as augmented in 2005, similarly transformed the Forum into a security community. I also consider the other 20 organizations listed above as de facto security communities, since they discuss strategic issues regarding war and peace. Accordingly, a study of the factors crucial for the success of security communities is very timely.

Dependent Variables

To determine the success of international organizations seeking to serve as security communities, several conceptual variables can be measured, using scale assignments (see Table 7.2). Without an empirical analysis based on operationalizations of relevant conceptual variables, there is no way to determine which factors are crucial in successful security communities.

But "success" can be measured in many ways. Amitai Etzioni (1965) should be given credit for developing a very useful set of dependent variables to measure "success":

Survival. Etzioni characterizes the most important dependent variable as the "stability" of an organization. IGOs that have been

Table 7.2 Indicators of successful political-security IGOs

Indicator	*Scores*
survival	years of operation (0 = defunct)
decisiveness	0 = talkathons
	1 = concrete actions to defuse conflict
budgets	0 = no financial commitments
	1 = financial commitments beyond secretariat offices
members	number of initial members
	newer members/maximum members
	members pulling out/max members
strength	0 = conflicts within
	1 = nascent
	2 = ascendant
	3 = mature: loosely coupled
	4 = very mature: tightly coupled
scope	1 = political issues alone
	2 = political and security issues
scope	2 = spillover to economic issues
	1 = economic issues in original mandate
	0 = no economic issues

abandoned score the lowest, whereas those that still exist are judged the most stable. I prefer to use the term "survival" and assign a zero for the demise of ANZUS, ASPAC, IFMC, and SEATO on that variable. The other organizations are scored by the years that they have existed since formation.

Decisiveness. A most important measure of success in determining why zones of conflict have become arenas of peace in Asia and the Pacific is "decisiveness." Etzioni suggests that the more the organization conciliates conflicts, as described in Chapter 6 above, the more decisive an IGO. Military exercises and planning for military contingencies can also show decisiveness in regard to security issues. Ernst Haas (1975) refers to "binding decisions," "implementation of decisions," and "increasingly cooperative decisions" along the same lines. However, no IGO in Asia and the Pacific has made a binding decision, which would occur in a supranational organization. Some organizations are only talkathons, just passing unimplemented resolutions, but successful IGOs implement resolutions in one form or another. The most glaring example of an organization still operating that has been blocked from action is the ASEAN Regional Forum, which has unsuccessfully prodded China to be more cooperative about military matters. Accordingly, the 22 IGOs considered herein are classified either as talkathons or as organizations that have taken concrete actions to resolve conflicts.

A second measure of decisiveness is the agreement by IGO member countries to pay for the cost of subsidiary bodies beyond a secretariat after an organization is formed. In 2009, for example, the East Asia Summit agreed to establish the Economic Research Institute for ASEAN and East Asia beyond relying on ASEAN for its secretariat. Ernst Haas identifies "centralized decision making" as an important element of an effective organization and seeks to determine whether budgets remain flat or increase over time. Some countries may be generous in paying the cost, but most IGOs beg for money, particularly in Asia and the Pacific. Conferocracies, international organizations consisting of regular conferences with no permanent bodies, are inherently indecisive. IGOs with formal Secretariats plus other structures are judged decisive. To avoid autocorrelation with a variable measuring the existence of formal Secretariats (see below) "decisiveness" is measured as a substantial budgetary commitment.

Membership. Some organizations start with a large number of members. Others do so well that they attract new members. A negative measure would be the number of countries that leave an IGO as a percentage of the largest total membership ever attained by that organization, even before dissolution. For example, ASEAN started with a modest five countries but in time doubled in membership, whereas half the members deserted ASPAC before South Korea stopped sponsorship. Although Ernst Haas (1975) identifies increased membership as a positive sign, in several studies IGOs with large membership had more internal conflict (Acharya and Johnson 2007; Langhammer and Hiemenz 1990:69; Mansfield and Milner 1999:615–616). But that may be the point of having large organizations—to have a forum for discussion and potential mediation among rival governments.

Strength. The power of security communities can also be scaled across a continuum. Etzioni proposed "level of integration" as one way to distinguish efforts at mere goal harmonization from serious attempts to achieve political integration. Ernst Haas and Philippe Schmitter (1964) identify a similar variable—organizational power. Emanuel Adler and Michael Barnett (1998) identify the most successful security communities as "tightly coupled" if they have supranational elements in which countries cede some sovereignty to the intergovernmental body. In a "loosely coupled" organization, countries are committed to come to one another's assistance and actually do so. At the other end of the scale are organizations that have pairs of members in conflict with each other. ARF, for example, is attended by both North and South Korea. Adler and Barnett characterize a "nascent" organization as one in which members that have recently pledged to avoid war with one another, whereas an "ascendant" organization is one that has avoided war for perhaps a decade or more.

Scope. Another indicator of success is the number of issue-areas that an IGO is established to handle. Some IGOs focus entirely on political issues, such as the Asian-Pacific Parliamentarians' Union. Others just focus on security matters, such as the Tripartite Council, which is concerned with piracy in the Straits of Malacca and Singapore. Increased scope—"broadening," which Haas calls "spillover"—is another measure of organizational success. Broadening of political-security organizations had a statistically significant correlation with organizational survival in my previous study (Haas 1986). Haftel (2012) argues the familiar hypothesis that organizations with a strong economic focus are likely to develop such elaborate benefits that military conflict among its members would disrupt the economic payoff. SEATO tried to prolong its existence by providing some economic aid and technical assistance, yet such generosity was overshadowed by its Cold War posture. I therefore positively code the 22 political-security IGOs on the variable "scope" if they also handle economic questions.

Other measures of organizational success could be used, and Deutsch does not use conflict resolution.[3] The present study prefers parsimony.

Independent Variables

Many possible predictors of organizational success have been articulated over the years. The force of a particular leader, whether U Nyun, Adam Malik, or Ratu Mara, cannot be denied, but alas there is no objective way to measure charisma.

Several scholars (esp. Ravenhill 2002:169) have classified motives for forming regional political-security organizations as follows. (1) Some are started by dominant (hegemonic) states (cf. Hurrell 1995), such as the formation of SEATO under the nuclear umbrella of the United States, because of common threats. (2) Smaller states may form an organization to contain the hegemons, notably the South Asian Association for Regional Cooperation, which countries around India initiated to gain collective clout. (3) Smaller states may want to counterbalance hegemons, which will not be invited to join, as was the case with ASEAN. (4) States may form an organization while a hegemon appears in decline (Crone 1993), as when ASEAN forged ARF to protect the status quo of an existing region in order to forestall a loss of interest by the United States amid the rising regional power of China. But the classification is not mutually exclusive, does not explain the formation of seven organizations (APF, APIL, ASEM, FEALAC, PIC, SwPD, and TC), and offers too little statistical variability for quantitative analysis.

A fifth motivation is pursuit of tangible economic benefits (Deutsch et al. 1957; Etzioni 1965; Keohane 1982; Kindleberger 1981). Organizations formed primarily for economic reasons are not among the 22 under examination in the present chapter, though economic benefits may have been a secondary motivation. ASEAN had political goals in mind when formed in 1967, did not seriously seek economic goals until the 1977 summit, and only recently has focused on conflict resolution. The earliest Forum priority was to end colonialism in the region, though economic considerations were also obvious; security interests came later.

To determine the ingredients of successful security communities, I primarily test conceptual variables from *Political Community and the North Atlantic Area*, though many overlap with variables proposed by Ernst Haas and his associates (Barrera and Haas 1969; Schmitter 1969a,1989b; Barrera 1969). Deutsch and his associates refer to 12 conditions that may account for successes (Deutsch et al. 1957:46–60) and related factors that cause breakups (ibid., 60–64). Their contribution appears to have emerged from diverse perspectives of the eight scholars involved, as if by committee. What they appear to say is that some conditions are necessary to start a security community, but that security communities thrive only when tangible benefits are derived from joining (see Figure 7.1). I have thus reformulated that framework somewhat by defining "success" by the dependent variables identified above, and all the proposed necessary and helpful conditions are hypothesized as preconditions (independent variables).

preconditions → formation of communities → benefits → successful communities

Figure 7.1 Deutsch's conditions for security communities.

Accordingly, my operationalization proceeds cautiously, as some Deutschian conceptual variables could serve both as independent and as dependent variables. Preconditions (independent variables), as derived from his taxonomy, are explained below (see Table 7.3) and then quantified along with the dependent variables (see Table 7.4):

Compatibility of main values. Countries join security communities because they have common goals but may resign when policies change. Ideally, member elites of an IGO trust one another and share a distinctive way of life—a "we" feeling—that has developed from common past experiences. Deutsch's first principle, in other words, recognized shared cultural values as predictive of IGO formation: Compatible political and social values lead to joint decisions between countries when elites depoliticize their differences. Arguably, organizations formed entirely within a subregion are somewhat more likely to have members with compatible values than those with biregional or multiregional memberships. An intermediate coding is for organizations combining two subregions, such as the Southwest Political Dialogue, which combines three Pacific Island states with three Southeast Asian countries. In my earlier study, mutual compatibility of main values had a statistically significant correlation with organizational survival (Haas 1986). Value compatibility can increase after an IGO has formed and has acted decisively, as evidenced by glowing accounts about the ASEAN Way.

Mutual responsiveness. Security communities are strong when IGO member countries have a habit of quickly and adequately assisting

Table 7.3 Classifying concepts by theory

Concept	*Theory*
mutual compatibility	cultural regionalization
responsiveness	security regionalization
predictability	neofunctionalism
expectations	multifunctionalism
organizational strength	institutional functionalism
economic growth	transactional regionalization
communication links	social regionalization
democratization	sociopolitical regionalization
mobility	social regionalization
transaction range	functionalism
elite units	intergovernmentalism

Table 7.4 Predictors of successful political-security IGOs

Indicator	*Scores*
value compatibility	2 = membership inside a subregion 1 = membership entirely in a region 0 = membership outside a region
mutual responsiveness	1 = no prior rivals in new IGO 0 = prior rivals in new IGO
mutual predictability	1 = formed at higher levels 0 = formed at lower levels
economic expectations	1 = economic gain anticipated 0 = no economic gain anticipated
institutionalization	1 = IGO begins with Secretariat 0 = no Secretariat in the beginning
economic growth	1 = main states grow before IGO 0 = mixed economic performance –1 = main states decline before IGO
communication links	1 = linguistic familiarity 0 = need for translators at meetings
political incorporation	democratic members/initial members
mobile population	common land borders/members
transaction range	prior regional IGO memberships/initial members
role interchange (number of elite units)	0 = equalitarian membership 1 = one dominant country 2 = two or more elite units

other countries, such as passing resolutions that show sensitivity to the needs of one or more specific countries. Successful security communities have an institutional framework for mutual consultation prior to taking action to promote security. Insofar as Deutsch believed that mutual responsiveness could operate as an independent variable, he ascertained if there was a history of countries working together as allies prior to joining IGOs, similar to the concept of security pluralism identified in the first chapter herein. In contrast, Japan's early initiative in forming the Ministerial Conference for the Economic Development of Southeast Asia failed because most countries remembered what the Japanese military did during World War II. Organizations to which rival states belong are unlikely to be mutually responsive unless the organization plays a conciliatory role to defuse the rivalry after the IGO is formed. For example, China and Russia achieved a détente when the latter joined the Shanghai Cooperation Organization, though Russia has blocked Chinese aspirations to expand SCO to economic matters.

Accordingly, the independent variable "mutual responsiveness" will be scored low when such rivalries have been present during the decade before an organization is launched.

Mutual predictability of behavior. Every member country in a successful security community should be able to anticipate that other states will follow through when joint decisions are made. In other words, previous elite interaction can serve to develop a sense of trust that other countries will be aboveboard and never renege on prior agreements. Organizations formed at summit conferences or at key ministerial levels, thus, should be more productive than those formed at lower levels because decisions at the subministerial level could be disavowed by leaders of their respective countries. IGOs of legislators, thus, are scored lower than those formed by foreign ministers. Exponents of intergovernmentalism and institutional functionalism expect organizations created at higher levels to be more successful than those formed at lower levels (Haftel 2012).

* * *

All security communities, according to Deutsch and associates (1957:66–67), must have the three characteristics identified above. The same analysis found that the next conditions, though essential for the continuation of amalgamated security communities, can also be helpful in ensuring the success of pluralistic security communities:

Expected economic ties or gains. Countries may join a political-security organization if they anticipate that one benefit might be increased prosperity due to expansion in trade because lowered trade barriers within the community offers an increased economy of scale. In other words, members of political-security IGOS may have their sights on establishing a multifunctional IGO. For evidence to rate organizations on this conceptual variable, I examined the founding documents of the 22 IGOs to ascertain whether economic goals are stated. The founding ASEAN Declaration, for example, focuses on political and security goals, and the organization did not focus seriously on economic goals until a decade later. SAARC, however, was viewed in economic terms from the start and only ventured into security issues after its formation. Deutsch and associates insisted that successful security communities must not delay providing members a "down payment" to ensure loyalty (1957:49). The prospect of immediate military burdens, he says, can doom a security community (p. 60). Functionalists expect that world peace will emerge when countries perceive their self-interest in economic terms before turning to overtly political concerns. Neofunctionalists hold the opposite view. Multifunctionalists argue that successful IGOs operating in many issue-areas, including conflict resolution, offer something positive for all member countries, thus lessening the probability of war among members (cf. Bearce 2003; Copeland 1996; Mansfield 2003). The opposite view is that some countries will inevitably derive much less economic benefit than others, so they will withdraw from an organization that plays favorites (Mytelka 1973:240; Nye 1971:78; Foroutan 1998:156–160).

Marked increase in political and administrative power. Institutionalization attracts members to join IGOs in order to enjoy a collective clout that was not present separately. The existence of a central Secretariat along with the formation of additional organizational structures, such as study centers, is one indicator of how much institutional power is initially bestowed upon an IGO. A permanent structure gives members the structural capacity to act together as a bloc, a concept stressed by neofunctionalists and institutional functionalists. However, Haftel (2012) warns that a Secretariat that acts too independently could produce conflict within the IGO. Thus, ASEAN would be scored low on organizational power in 1967, when the organization was a conferocracy, consisting only of rotating ministerial conferences.

Superior economic growth. Transactional pluralists predict that successful organizations are formed among members experiencing economic progress. IGOs formed in bad economic times would have a negative value on the economic growth variable. Deutsch and associates apply that standard to the "core" units of the security community (1957:51), so they are interested in economic growth of the dominant members of an IGO as a positive sign in building a security community. Indeed, Tokyo forged a half dozen organizations while the Japanese economy boomed in the 1970s but only two (the Asia Pacific Parliamentary Forum and the Forum for East Asia-Latin America Cooperation) during the doldrums of the 1990s. The ambiguity of Deutsch's formulation is that he intended to make economic growth a condition for maintaining successful political unification, thus as both an independent and a dependent variable. As an independent variable, I rate economic growth of the most important country at the time when a political-security IGO was formed.

Unbroken links of social communication. Consistent with Deutsch's long-time interest in social pluralism, he reported that effective organizations capitalized on preexisting informal ties of dense communications—contact between strata within member countries as well as with other countries. But during the Cold War, as IGOs blossomed in Asia and the Pacific, there was a lack of prior regional sociocultural ties, in part because travel to other countries is largely by air or sea rather than land. Ordinary citizens in both regions were unlikely to have ties with geographically distant neighbors. Accordingly, I propose linguistic familiarity as an operationalization of unbroken social communication linkages. The linguistic legacy of colonial rule has produced many bilingual English speakers within Asia and the Pacific. Accordingly, I have calculated the percentage of the number of countries with an English-speaking background out of the total number of initial countries joining the organization. Exceptions are the Collective Security Treaty Organization and the Shanghai Cooperation Organization, as most members were republics in the Soviet Union not long ago, and Russian is their second language, and the Indochinese Foreign Ministers Conference, formed of former French colonies. Deutsch, of course, expected dense social communication to cement political unions. His favorite measure was intraregional postal traffic, which of course presupposed linguistic familiarity.

Broadening of economic, political, or social elites. Deutsch and associates hypothesized that IGOs can achieve an increasingly solid footing as member countries democratize. They identify successful security communities as those with member countries that broaden leadership positions to more strata in the population. However, they caution that too much democratization may bring to the fore ethnic groups opposed to a political union with other countries. Consistent with Deutsch's insight, transitional democracies have been empirically demonstrated to be more conflict-prone than either autocracies or full-fledged democracies (Mansfield and Snyder 1995; 2002). Although some researchers report that democracies are more likely to form and join IGOs (Kahler 2000; Mansfield, Milner, and Rosendorff 2002; Mansfield and Pevehouse 2000), ASEAN was widely disparaged as a "dictator's club" in its early years. To measure this concept, I calculate the number of multiparty democracies among members at the time when each IGO was formed as a percentage of total members.

Mobility of populations. Organizations are more successful if member countries open their doors to citizens from countries that have joined a security community, allowing them to resettle or work on a temporary basis, thereby creating conditions for social pluralism. Stiff visa requirements discourage travel to other members of an organization. But so do vast distances between members. For mobile populations to be an independent variable, an appropriate measure in Asia and the Pacific is the number of land borders between initial members of an IGO. Some borders are easier to cross than others, though capitals and major cities are usually at some distance from the land borders. If borders are easy to cross, the resulting economic activity can bolster transactional pluralism. Trade can trump politics when serious planning has occurred for growth areas throughout Asia, such as Sijori, the economic zone between parts of Indonesia, Malaysia, and Singapore (cf. Tiglao 1994). However, the previous chapter provides detailed evidence of the fact that borders are often disputed and the source of conflicts that could challenge an IGO's effectiveness in conflict resolution. For many years, the ASEAN Way involved a pledge not to discuss border conflicts, but in recent years ASEAN has reconsidered that maxim. In addition to land borders, I count as common borders the two causeways in the region—connecting India with Sri Lanka and Malaysia with Singapore.

Multiple range of communications and transactions. To ensure organizational solidarity, according to Deutsch and associates, there should be increased functionalist cooperation between member countries in such matters as postal traffic, immigration customs procedures, commercial laws, and sharing of cultural, educational, and literary experiences. Functionalists understand the "multiple range" concept as a prediction that successful intergovernmental cooperation in "low politics" will eventually encourage organizations in "high politics." Haftel (2012), however, finds that the more similar countries' diplomatic portfolios, the greater their conflict, whereas countries with similar alliances and UN voting patterns form more IGOs together. In a recent study, common membership in IGOs is found to be a factor in shortening interstate conflicts (Shannon, Morey, and Boehmke 2011). Although Deutsch measures the range of communication and transactions with statistics on postal traffic and trade (1957:205–207), I average prior membership in regional nonpolitical IGOs for each of the 22 organizations studied in the present chapter, thereby testing the spillaround hypothesis—that cooperation in technical IGOs builds trust for the forming of political-security IGOs

(SEATO's score, for example, would equal the number of SEATO countries that also belonged to the first technical Asian organization, the Colombo Plan).

Interchange of group roles. The top roles of a security community, according to Deutsch and associates, should rotate. All member countries should have a hand in guiding an organization so that no country is left out or is treated as a minority. Haftel (2012) finds that dominant countries may keep the peace but may not be enthusiastic about organizations formed for that purpose. If a formerly dominant country cannot get accustomed to playing a more collegial role, the community will be in jeopardy. Similarly, some scholars hypothesize that successful security communities should have "balanced multipolarity," that is, an absence of dominant units (Ikenberry 2001; Smith 2000; Wæver 2011), similar to ASEAN. But other researchers expect that IGOs dominated by one country will be more peaceful (Buzan and Wæver 2003; Lemke 2002; Mansfield and Pevehouse 2000). In conferocracies, the venue and temporary secretariat for annual meetings rotates sequentially within members. Etzioni proposes the number of elite units as an important independent variable, roughly similar to Deutsch's "role interchange" concept. IGOs with just one dominant country, such as Japan, are hypothesized to differ from those with two or even three, notably ARF. The distinction between equalitarian and nonequalitarian IGOs is important to intergovernmentalists, who expect that successful security communities will reflect power realities.

Other variables. Benefits from a successful organization should presumably be equitably shared by member countries; no country should receive considerably more rewards than any other, and no country should be unduly burdened. For Deutsch and associates, "balance of rewards," a twelfth independent variable, is a later development in the variable "expected economic gains" and therefore is not used in the present analysis. Amitai Etzioni's *Political Unification* (1965) formulates clear independent variables, some of which have been used above.[4] Similarly, Ernst Haas and Philippe Schmitter (1964) proposed conceptual variables that have some similarities and differences from Deutsch. I have repackaged many of their proposed conceptual variables herein.[5,6]

Operationalizing the diversity of approaches of Karl Deutsch and Ernst Haas has an important advantage. Rather than testing just one theory, they can be combined into a single study to offer a critical test of competing theories and subtheories—whether intergovernmentalism, four types of pluralism (regionalizations), or four types of functionalism best account for organizational success. Ideally, more variables would be used to operationalize the various concepts, but at least those chosen herein have conceptual validity.

Empirical Analysis

To quantify the conceptual variables, I make informed judgments and computations for all 22 political-security organizations in Asia and the Pacific, excluding the ASEAN European Meeting and the Forum for East Asia-Latin America Cooperation, which focus on international rather than regional issues. I then compute correlations and factor analyze the correlation matrix (see Table 7.5). Using a vari max rotation, I stop at the eighth factors, by which all variables have high loadings (factor correlations) on at least one factor.[7] Factor analysis identifies correlation pairs or clusters that remain highly related when all other variables are held constant. The statistical test is quite rigorous but requires careful interpretation.

Theorists of security communities have long assumed that indicators of organizational success would go hand in hand. Deutsch and associates expected all 12 explanatory factors to be helpful in ensuring the success of a security community, though three (compatibility, responsiveness, and predictability) were the most essential. Statistically, therefore, we would expect the variables created above to consist of a single cluster of measures of IGO success and one or two sets of clusters of preconditions to success that would be intimately related to the success cluster. But that is not what the data demonstrate. Although each variable has a high value on at least one factor, the correlational picture is more complex than theorists may have expected, yet seems endemic in the potpourri of concepts that were incorporated into the Deutschian framework.

A correlational interpretation of the results would focus on which preconditions are associated with each dependent variable. In bivariate terms, the factor analysis results are as follows: (1) Organizations best **survive** when there are few elite members even though members experience little initial economic growth. (2) IGOs that **lose members** have only one major power, which experiences economic growth before joining. (3) IGOs with **many initial members** do not include rival countries. (4) To attract **new members**, an IGO should have a permanent

Table 7.5 Factor analysis of variables representing Asia-Pacific organizations (loadings over ±.4 emphasized)

	Empirical Perspectives	*Variables*	*1*	*2*	*3*	*4*	*5*	*6*	*7*	*8*
	Organizational Success	**Dependent Variables**								
1		survival	**–.70**	.16	–.15	.31	.29	.26	–.01	–.19
2		initial members	.10	.38	–.12	.07	**–.70**	.12	**.42**	–.23
3		new members	.11	.19	**.80**	.03	.18	–.12	.03	.17
4		members departed	**.86**	.01	.00	.12	.12	–.21	.04	–.06
5		strength	**.62**	–.39	.02	–.07	.18	–.17	.24	–.32
6		scope: military	–.00	–.18	.05	–.07	.21	–.24	.18	**.78**
7		scope: economic	**.89**	–.25	–.01	.07	.16	.16	.05	–.03
8		decisiveness	.10	–.12	.11	–.12	–.03	.03	**.90**	.21
9		budgets	.25	.01	**–.74**	.10	.28	**–.47**	.00	.09
	Theoretical Perspectives	**Independent Variables**								
10	cultural pluralism	compatibility	.21	**.54**	.36	.33	–.23	**–.47**	.12	–.14
11	security pluralism	responsiveness	.24	–.06	.04	.01	**.87**	.07	.10	–.01
12	neofunctionalism	predictability	–.23	.27	–.06	**.45**	-.25	.21	.08	**.62**
13	multifunctionalism	expectations	.01	–.10	.04	**.96**	-.05	.03	–.07	.07
14	institutional functionalism	organs	.03	.10	**.66**	.25	.13	.30	**.43**	–.16
15	transactional pluralism	economic growth	**.60**	.20	–.22	**.40**	.13	.16	**–.46**	–.08
16	social pluralism	communications	–.14	**.93**	.10	–.02	.00	–.07	–.03	.05
17	sociopolitical pluralism	democratization	.22	**–.92**	–.07	.08	.18	–.02	.12	.10
18	social pluralism	mobility	**–.43**	.01	**–.40**	**–.58**	–.28	.25	.25	.14
19	functionalism	transaction range	–.09	–.06	.15	.05	.01	**.91**	.05	–.10
20	intergovernmentalism	elite units	**–.70**	.16	.15	.31	.29	.26	–.01	–.19

Secretariat. (5) **Strong organizations** have two or more major powers that have achieved solid economic growth. (6) Political-security organizations that contemplate or use **military** means in conflict resolution have regular summit conferences. (7) If the most prominent members are doing well economically, a political-security IGO will expand to **economic** issues. (8) **Decisive** IGOs have permanent Secretariats even though the largest members are not economic powerhouses. (9) IGOs with the greatest **financial commitments** are the most effective in political-security matters.

But the above findings are bivariate. The advantage of factor analysis is a multivariate picture in which clusters of variables end up on single factors.

The most important source of statistical variation in the factor analysis is **organizational survival** (Factor 1). Organizations that become defunct are led by a prosperous major power, consider economic issues, and yet lose many countries even before their demise. Surviving organizations, in contrast, retain their initial membership, avoid economic issues, have countries with many common borders, focus politically, and lack major powers as members. What explains the division between defunct and thriving organizations is quite subtle: In defunct IGOs, lead countries are prosperous yet from outside the core region, whereas IGOs that survive are closer together, are not doing well economically, and have few conflicts between members. SEATO's problem, in short, was that an outside country was coercing subregional countries on matters of policy, and they ultimately differed. ASPAC floundered by trying to appeal to the disparate interests within East Asia, Southeast Asia, and the two large ANZUS Pacific powers. ASEAN's formation doomed ASPAC. On a theoretical level, transactional regionalization (increasing prosperity of lead countries) does not guarantee organizational survival but social regionalization (common borders) does. The high politics road of intergovernmentalism can become be a dead-end street if one or more superpowers dominate an organization.

Three predictor variables have high loadings on Factor 2, which primarily differentiates **sociocultural** (linguistic familiarity within a subregion) little **sociopolitical** regionalization (democratization). Organizations with many democracies tend to be transregional and need translators at meetings. IGOs composed of authoritarian regimes within subregions, such as IFMC and CSTO, tend to have common linguistic traditions. Yet organizational success is only weakly related to whether membership consists of either subregional nondemocracies or transregional democracies, mostly because democracies from outside the region initiated the earliest IGOs, and their pretensions to leadership were rebuffed. Nevertheless, IGOs with many democracies tend to advance internal organizational growth more than those composed of nondemocracies. Cultural regionalization appears to predict more initial members in an IGO, but the association is weak. The theoretical implication is that sociocultural regionalization encourages countries in subregions to form IGOs despite lack of democratization. IGOs with many democracies have slightly more institutional strength.

Factor 3 (**popularity**) identifies organizations that attract new members after their formation, most of which are nonadjacent to existing members. IGO popularity appears based on the absence of economic burdens on members beyond setting up a formal Secretariat. When countries believe that an organization has potential for collective action, they join. The factor appears to vindicate the institutional functionalist argument that IGOs thrive when they begin with sufficient political commitment to finance a Secretariat but then do not ask members to finance costly new structures.

Factor 4 identifies great **economic expectations** of transregional IGOs led by economically prosperous members that hold summit meetings. Such expectations are related to organizational survival: IGOs that break up are composed of subregional members in the economic doldrums who cannot afford to pay their dues. For example, ASEAN and the Forum offered the prospect of more prosperity but not IFMC. Multifunctional IGOs, thus, are more likely to flourish if they promise economic rewards even if they lack social regionalization (measured herein as the presence of common borders).

Factor 5 (**security regionalization**) contrasts IGOs that begin with a few friendly countries. TC works collaboratively on behalf of shared objectives, but ARF is still struggling to play a constructive role.

Factor 6 (**joiners**) identifies IGOs composed of members that previously belonged to many prior regional organizations. Such organizations have low budgets and little cultural regionalization. In other words, their membership is too diverse to be successful in any respect.

Decisiveness, which is the most important variable with regard to conflict resolution, defines Factor 7. Yet no clear pluralistic or functionalist precondition for decisiveness is evident. Two variables have moderate loadings on the factor: One shows that IGOs involved in concrete actions tend to have Secretariats. The other indicates that members of decisive IGOs are not economic powerhouses. ASEAN was merely a club of foreign ministers until a decision one decade later to form a Secretariat, and ASEAN became involved in formal conflict resolution much later. Indecisive IGOs are talkathons that have prosperous members but lack a permanent Secretariat. Transactional regionalization, in other words, does not explain IGO interest in conflict resolution, but institutional functionalism does.

Military-focused organizations (Factor 8) can be easily predicted: Preexisting allies formalize IGO relations at summit conferences. For neofunctionalists and institutional functionalists, the factor reveals what to them is a self-evident, if trivial, proposition.

Discussion

Security communities, that is, groupings of states that have pledged mutual nonaggression, are needed for world stability. They can start at subregional levels and build toward regional and transregional security communities. Theorists who have tried to suggest ways to bring about security communities have hitherto assumed that the most important factors were identified in 1957 by Karl Deutsch and associates, who assumed that 12 important factors were embedded within an undislodgeable conceptual ball of wax.

The present study has found otherwise. Different approaches lead to different results. Intergovernmentalism, pluralism (regionalization), and various forms of functionalism have long competed as practical pathways to security communities, but without an empirical test. The quantitative analysis herein finds that each approach contributes something, yet not the full story.

Intergovernmentalism expects that security organizations will be created by existing allies, who will attract other countries motivated by power realities. Some theorists believed that such a prescription was appropriate during the height of the Cold War. But today the situation is quite different, with ethnic unrest and terrorism more common than the threat of war. Summit conferences can bring leaders together on behalf of a common military cause, but countries are likely to split up when the adversary changes its spots. The data show that political-security IGOs formed by several likeminded major powers are more likely to persist than those with only one major power, provided that they are not distracted by economic development issues.

World pluralism expects that various forms of regionalization are preconditions for successful security communities. Yet differing types of regionalization have unique consequences.

Deutsch stressed **social regionalization** as the best explanation for the unifications of German- and Italian-speaking states into single states during the nineteenth century. But social regionalization, measured herein by countries that share common borders or have linguistic familiarity, fails to predict robust organizational success on any of the dependent variables. However, social pluralism has a slight association with enduring if weak organizations that barely grow in membership.

Data on **sociocultural regionalization**, which is more likely in IGOs whose members are drawn from subregions, parallel the findings of social regionalization. **Sociopolitical regionalization**, however, differs substantially from both social and sociocultural regionalization. Members of IGOs composed of democracies tend to speak different languages, few initial members, and—as commonly observed[8]—build strong organizations.

Transactional regionalization, which economists stress is the basis for such economic arrangements as common markets, can predict strong IGOs but that they often lose members. Pushed by particular economic superpowers, there is only a 50–50 chance that politically oriented IGOs which seriously embark on economic goals will also consider military matters, and are more likely to be talkathons.

Security regionalization exists when IGOs among friendly countries are mutually responsive. But such organizations have few initial members. The checkered history of ANZUS and SEATO bears out the empirical results that security-oriented regional IGOs do not last, thus predicting that CSTO's days are numbered.

Functionalist theories have also been tested herein. Some scholars believe that the key to world peace is how organizations are run institutionally rather than those constructed due to cultural, economic, political, or social regionalization.

Classical functionalism assumes that peace will result from the formation of many technical organizations in a variety of issue-areas, and that each IGO will inevitably suggest the need for another in a continuing process. Technical organizations, however, tend to have small budgets and many members from beyond subregions. An array of technical bodies does not build momentum for political action to deal with militarized disputes.

The **neofunctional** view is that organizations formed for economic reasons can only become stronger when political leaders support an increase in their scope of concerns. The data herein indicate that security communities dealing with military solutions must be formed and sustained by summit conferences, a finding entirely consistent with research by Yoran Haftel (2012).

Multifunctionalism is the view that IGOs focused on a wide range of international problems are more likely to consist of solid security communities, offering something for all member countries. The data show that organizations that promise future economic benefits tend to last somewhat longer than other types of IGOs, have members from more than one subregion, and can indeed play constructive roles because they are sustained by summit conferences.

Institutional functionalism, as measured by IGOs that have formal Secretariats, identifies organizations that attract new members but tend to have limited budgets. Such IGOs collapse if they fail to develop common norms, contrary to expectations of some theorists (Adler and Barnett 1998:50–51). Similarly, Haftel's study of multifunctional organizations (focused both on economic and security concerns) identified institutional elements, especially Secretariats and summits, as crucial in accounting for success in conflict resolution.

Staircase functionalism, a variant of institutional functionalism, requires time-series data for empirical testing. The process described in Chapter 5 above, through which ASEAN and the Forum have evolved, is entirely consistent with staircase functionalism. Over time, they deepened their scope after top-level officials met on a regular basis. They are now committed to resolve even internal conflicts, but their growth in members is unrelated to their progress toward multifunctionalism.

Implications

The main question of the present volume is how and why zones of conflict have become arenas of peace in Asia and the Pacific over the past six decades. As the present study focuses on case studies as well as quantitative analyses of dozens of IGOs, findings herein challenge previous studies on regional organizations.

Karl Deutsch and associates felt that a dozen key variables jointly ensured the success of security communities. Considering the 22 IGOs studied herein as a collective "security regime," the analysis has yielded a more complete picture of why the Asian zone of intense conflict became an arena of relative peace and how the Pacific has maintained a peaceful state of affairs while insisting on respect for human rights.

First of all, ASEAN and the Forum play crucial roles today for two reasons. They are founded on sociocultural regionalization, that is, the development of common norms presented in Chapter 2 above. In addition, they have maneuvered themselves diplomatically so that they play crucial roles in their respective regions (Chapters 3–6 above). When ASEAN and the Forum are studied along with other political-security organizations, theories of intergovernmentalism, world pluralism, and functionalism are exposed as simplistic.

The view that leaders of major powers alone can guarantee the success of security communities (**intergovernmentalism**) is naïve; The days of peace through big-power hegemony are long past. Nevertheless, regular summit conferences, important for institutional functionalists, ensure that strategic matters will be given serious attention. ASEAN and the Forum, which have no dominant major powers, could not have expanded to deal with military security issues without summit conferences.

Theorists of **world pluralism** believe that successful security communities can be developed only after various types of regionalization. But sociocultural regionalization is only linked to IGOs with many initial members. Sociopolitical regionalization, notably acceptance of democratic norms, results in IGOs with few initial members but does not preclude later organizational growth. Transactional regionalizationists, who sing the praises of IGOs that seek economic progress through increased trade, do not provide a direct pathway to conflict resolution capabilities. Security regionalization (IGOs without rival members) also does not assure organizational success.

ASEAN and the Forum had sociocultural affinity and started with few members. The Forum consisted of democracies, while ASEAN's governments were initially authoritarian but have increasingly democratized. Both sought economic benefits, but later for ASEAN and immediately for the Forum. ASEAN began with rivalries, especially the Philippine claim to Malaysia's state of Sabah, but Manila buried that issue for the sake of the organization. The Forum incorporated no rival countries. Thus, theories of sociocultural pluralism explain why ASEAN and the Forum became successful.

Functionalist theories, similarly, provide some insight into successful security communities, but they provide only pieces of a puzzle. Classical functionalists hope that a peaceful world will emerge as technical IGOs multiply over time, involving more countries in a tangled web of depoliticized cooperation. But the quantitative data only suggest that a proliferation of increased IGO memberships results in conferocracies with low budgets. Neofunctionalists expect that technical organizations can only become stronger after they get high-level political backing, and the data show that IGOs supported by summit meetings develop beyond mere political-security discussion to focus on how to employ military means in conflict resolution; in other words, IGOs based on summit conferences do not need to grow from technical bodies. For institutional functionalists, Secretariats and summit conferences are vital if IGOs are to engage in serious conflict resolution, and the data show that they are correct, as high-level meetings are necessary conditions. Nevertheless, formal Secretariats are not sufficient conditions.[9] Multifunctionalists insist that the most successful IGOs offer many kinds of benefits, technical and nontechnical.

Conclusion

The history of intergovernmental organizations in Asia and the Pacific indicates that peace emerged as countries increasingly began to talk within diplomatic and technical bodies. But both regions have gone beyond mere détentes into active conflict resolution modes, particularly ASEAN and the Forum. Why?

ASEAN and the Forum were formed after only three technical bodies were founded within their respective regions, hardly a ringing endorsement of functionalism. What brought them together was a common culture, which in turn encouraged them to expand their cooperation. Consistent with neofunctionalism, ASEAN languished until the first summit conference nearly ten years after its formation and then grew dramatically, while the Forum began as a top-level body and quickly spun off many new IGOs. ASEAN and the Forum delved into conflict resolution several decades after they established formal Secretariats and held summit conferences, so institutional functionalism is an incomplete explanation for their development into security communities. What is most important is that they became multifunctional IGOs. ASEAN and the Forum followed a staircase functionalist scenario.

The evidence indicates that a common ingredient in organizational success is institutional functionalism. After several decades, ASEAN became attentive in time to human rights issues; the original five countries have applied that perspective while screening undemocratic Brunei, Myanmar, and the three Indochinese countries for membership in the organization. Indeed, the ASEAN Charter of 2007 now commits the organization to adhere to the "principles of democracy, the rule of law, and good governance." Meanwhile, the Forum's commitment to democratic rule in the region, formalized by the Biketawa Declaration, has established the framework for dealing with undemocratic developments. Although it may be an exaggeration to refer today to the original five ASEAN countries as mature democracies today, over time they have been democratizing.[10] In a nutshell, ASEAN and the Forum have followed a staircase functionalist path (see Figure 7.2).

Thus, a shared culture appears essential, especially when viewed as integral to the Asian Way or the Pacific Way. Moreover, the interpersonal consensus building process in the Asian Way and the Pacific Way brought the two organizations to the point when they began to champion democracy.

Ideally, an IGO will be based on a likemindedness that transcends regional differences and a genuine desire to turn zones of conflict into arenas of peace. The Forum, initially composed of democracies, developed organizational strength quite early due to a common cultural understanding, the Pacific Way. ASEAN's initial bond was cultural,

security concerns → ASEAN formed 1967 → summit 1976 → economic goals + summits + gradual democratization → regional conflicts → conflict resolution efforts

economic concerns → summit 1971 → democracies form Forum → secretariat + summits → regional conflicts → conflict resolution efforts

Figure 7.2 Growth of ASEAN and the Forum.

the Asian Way, but the organization grew stronger as the initial members democratized (cf. Kahler 2000; Pevehouse and Russett 2006).

Today, ASEAN is consciously trying to develop a strong security community. The Forum has moved beyond ASEAN to take bold action in that regard. What we have learned is that common cultures assure that organizations can build mutual trust. ASEAN and the Forum also developed technical subsidiary bodies to satisfy needs of their member countries and thereby assured member loyalty. But institutional growth was cautious before conflict resolution was on the agenda. Twenty political-security organizations in Asia and the Pacific operating on more simplistic models of how to be effective, thus have been eclipsed by ASEAN and the Forum. Other regions around the world should take note.

Notes

1 International and Regional Cooperation

1. The official spelling of ASEAN, according to the founding Bangkok Declaration of 1967, is "Association of South-East Asian Nations."
2. For a time in the late 1960s, these scholars began to propose operationalizations of neofunctionalist concepts but never followed through to put their proposals into practice (Barrera and E.Haas 1969; Barrera 1969; Schmitter 1969a,1969b). There were several reasons: None showed quantitative sophistication, as they sought single measures as composites of many variables rather than screening the latter with factor analysis to determine whether they were unidimensional or multidimensional. In addition, they differed among themselves.
3. What they call financial integration (equivalent to what I call transactional pluralism) is measured by intraregional trade and intraregional investment, direct and portfolio. Institutional integration (social pluralism) is indexed by financial and monetary cooperation, regional IGOs, treaties, and sectoral cooperation. Political-security integration (security pluralism) indicators are security, absence of military threats, free markets, and political leaders favoring regional IGOs. They equivalence sociocultural integration (cultural pluralism) with cultural homogeneity (linguistic, racial, religious homogeneity), telephones per capita, and the maturity of civil society (Kim, Kim, Park 2011:46–47).
4. Countries lumped together are as follows: ASEAN (Brunei, Burma, Cambodia, Indonesia, Laos, Malaysia, Philippines, Singapore, Thailand, Vietnam), East Asia (ASEAN countries, China, Japan, South Korea), European Union (Austria, Belgium, Bulgaria, Cyprus, Czech Republic, Denmark, Estonia, Finland, France, Germany, Greece, Hungary, Ireland, Italy, Latvia, Lithuania, Luxembourg, Malta, Netherlands, Poland, Portugal, Romania, Slovakia, Slovenia, Spain, Sweden, United Kingdom), Mercosur (Argentina, Brazil, Paraguay, Uruguay), North America (Canada, México, United States), and Northeast Asia (China, Japan, both Koreas, Mongolia, Far East Russia).

2 The Asian Way and the Pacific Way

1. Another source of confusion is the Singaporean concept of "Asian Values," the view that Asian countries prioritize economic and social rights over civil

and political rights (cf. Zakaria 1994), thus arguing that Westerners have a biased view of human rights. Nevertheless, the interlude of the Asian Values, an ideological façade hiding authoritarian predilections, appears to have ended as democracy has spread in the region (Caryl 2012).

3 Waves of Asian Regional Cooperation

1. Traditionally, Europeans considered Asia to begin on the eastern side of the Bosporus, which separates the modern city of Istanbul. That would make the Middle East a region called "Western Asia." The UN regional offices in Bangkok did not originally include Western Asia in their scope. I follow that convention herein, though three countries in the Caucasus (Armenia, Azerbaijan, and Georgia) have recently been allowed membership in ESCAP.
2. The subregions of Asia are as follows: **Central Asia**: Afghanistan, Kazakhstan, Kyrgyzstan, Tajikistan, Turkmenistan, Uzbekistan; **East Asia**: China, Korea (North, South), Japan, Mongolia, Taiwan; **South Asia**: Bangladesh, Bhutan, India, Iran, Maldives, Nepal, Pakistan, Sri Lanka; **Southeast Asia**: Brunei, Burma (Myanmar), Cambodia, Indonesia, Laos, Malaysia, Philippines, Singapore, Thailand, Timor-Leste, Vietnam (North, South).
3. ESCAP has established several divisions with semiautonomous structures—the Asian Center for Development Administration, Asian Highway Coordinating Committee, Asian Institute for Economic Development and Planning, Asian Statistical Institute, Committee for Coordination of Joint Prospecting for Mineral Resources in the Asian Offshore Areas (CCOP), and a similar body for the Pacific (CCOP/SOPAC), and the Typhoon Committee.
4. SEAMEO's regional centers are the following, with dates of formation parenthesized: Regional Centre for Tropical Biology (1968), Regional Centre for History and Tradition (2000), Regional Centre for Educational Innovation and Technology (1970), Regional Centre for Quality Improvement of Teachers and Educational Personnel in Language (2009), Regional Centre for Quality Improvement of Teachers and Educational Personnel in Mathematics (2009), Regional Centre for Quality Improvement of Teachers and Educational Personnel in Science (2009), Regional Centre for Food and Nutrition (2010), Regional Centre for Education in Science and Mathematics (1967), Regional Language Centre (1968), Regional Training Centre (1996), Regional Center for Higher Education and Development (1993), Regional Open Learning Centre (1997), Regional Centre for Graduate Study and Research in Agriculture (1996), Regional Centre for Special Education (2009), Regional Centre for Archaeology and Fine Arts (1978), Tropical Medicine and Public Health Network (1966), and Regional Centre for Vocational Education and Training (1990). The tropical medicine network, in turn, consists of three specialized research centers.

5. I have left out the institutions associated with economic "growth areas" that have formed across borders, such as Sijori (between Indonesia, Malaysia, and Singapore), since few have gone beyond the planning stage (cf. Thant, Tang, and Kakazu 1998).

4 Waves of Pacific Regional Cooperation

1. **Melanesia** consists of *Bougainville*, Fiji, *New Caledonia*, Papua New Guinea, Solomon Islands, Vanuatu, and *West Papua* (Irian Jaya). The countries of **Micronesia** are *Guam*, Kiribati, Marshall Islands, Nauru, Northern Marianas, and Palau. **Polynesia** consists of *American Samoa*, Cook Islands, Fiji, *Hawai'i*, Niue, *Pitcairn*, *Rapa Nui* (Easter Island), *French Polynesia* (Tahiti), *Tokelau*, Tonga, Western Samoa, Tuvalu, and *Wallis and Futuna*. (Italics identify nonsovereign entities that are part of other states.)
2. When CCPASWPR began in 1903, only Australia and New Zealand were involved, so the body was bilateral, not international. With Fiji's membership in 1947, the organization became a truly regional body but was not an international grouping until Fiji's independence in 1970.

5 Pivotal Roles in Regional Cooperation

1. Malaysia sponsored the natural rubber and tin organizations. The rest (coconut, jute, pepper, silk, and timber) were headquartered at ECAFE/ESCAP from inception.
2. The Asian **and Pacific** Coconut Community, Conference of Asian **and Pacific** Labor Ministers, Statistical Institute for Asia **and the Pacific**, Asian-**Pacific** Parliamentarians' Union, and the Asian-**Pacific** Postal Union.
3. They are as follows: ASA, SEAMEO, ASEAN, COORDCOM, SEATAC, ACC, RIHED, TC, ANRPC, PC, AIPO, AIPA, SEATRADC, ASEANAPOL, and ITRO.
4. In addition to the name change of the Forum itself, several other bodies changed their names at various times: from South Pacific Commission to Pacific Community, from South Pacific Trade Commission to Pacific Islands Trade and Investment Commission, from South Pacific Forum Fisheries Agency to Pacific Islands Forum Fisheries Agency, from South Pacific Environmental Program to Pacific Regional Environmental Program.
5. The Forum launched the following: South Pacific Regional Meeting on Telecommunications, South Pacific Regional Shipping Council, South Pacific Regional Civil Aviation Council, Pacific Forum Line, Regional Committee on Trade, South Pacific Trade Commission (as later renamed Pacific Islands Trade and Investment Commission), South Pacific Forum Fisheries Agency (as later renamed Pacific Islands Forum Fisheries Agency),

Forum Energy Ministers Meeting, Foreign Finance Ministers Meeting, South Pacific Regional Environmental Program (as later renamed Pacific Regional Environmental Program), Forum Economic Ministers Meeting, Forum Aviation Ministers Meeting, Forum Communication Ministers Meeting, Forum Trade Ministers Meeting, Forum Foreign Affairs Ministers Meeting, Forum Education Ministers Meeting, Pacific Islands Energy Policy, and the Pacific Island Energy Policy and Pacific Energy Ministers Meeting.

6. Examples of ongoing initiatives are as follows: economic growth (educational requirements survey), sustainable development (climate change maintenance), good governance (financial audits), and security (maritime surveillance). See Solomon Times (2012).

6 Creating Arenas of Peace

1. For a useful map, see BBC (2012a).
2. In 1977, French Polynesia (Tahiti) was granted partial internal autonomy; in 1984, the autonomy was extended. French Polynesia became an "overseas collectivity" of France in 2004, a classification that also applies in the South Pacific to the small French colony of Wallis and Futuna.
3. The idea came to fruition in 2000, when the Community of Democracies was founded by 25 countries with a headquarters in Warsaw.

7 Successful Security Communities

1. I exclude CENTO from the sample because Turkey, a non-Asian country, supplied the headquarters.
2. The following have been studied as security communities, though descriptively rather than with rigorous empirical testing as performed herein: Canada-United States, Gulf Cooperation Council, Organization for Security Cooperation in Europe, México-United States, South Asia, Southeast Asia (Adler and Barnett 1998); ASEAN, EU/OSCE/NATO, Gulf Cooperation Council (Bellamy 2004); ASEAN, EU, Mercosur (Tusicisny 2007); and the Black Sea (Wæver 2011). Although one statistical study reports no correlation between IGOs and peaceful outcomes (Goldsmith 2007), the study has unfortunate design flaws that will be obvious to any reader of the present volume.
3. For Haas and Schmitter (1964), the best predictor of a dynamic organization, which increases activities within a particular sector, is whether the countries were committed to deepen activities from the start. As most IGOs start optimistically, their concept has little variability and thus is not used as a variable herein. Ernst Haas (1975) also notes that successful organizations will have an impact on national government bureaucracies, businesses, or nongovernmental organizations. But of course the opposite can be true: Bureaucrats and business executives can pressure IGOs. An analysis of technical organizations studied in the present volume would be needed to measure the impact of organizations on governments and nongovernmental entities.

4. I have used some of Etzioni's ten proposed variables but not all. My reasoning is as follows. (a) **Level of integration**: Etzioni identified policy harmonization as one part of a continuum. Some Asian-Pacific IGOs have gone beyond political discussions to deal with military-security matters, so I code one aspect of the independent variable "scope" to give points to organizations that deal with both issues. (b) **Scope of integration**: For Etzioni, the more issue-areas pursued, the more scope, and I have adopted two variables beyond politically oriented IGOs based on his concepts: one point for military-security matters and the other for economic issues. (c) **Decisiveness**: My distinction between talkathons and active IGOs comes from Etzioni. (d) **Stability**: What Etzioni called "stability" is what I use as organizational survival. (e) **Identive power**: Etzioni defined "identive power" as the popularity of the organization within the general public. That is what Andrej Tusicisny (2007) measured in his study of ASEAN, the EU, and Mercosur, albeit without conclusive results. Alas, public opinion is not available for all IGOs studied in the present chapter, but there was a statistically significant relationship with the survival of five out of seven organizations in my previous study (M.Haas 1986:Table 4). (f) **Utilitarian power**: An important element is whether an international organization has the economic resources to impose effective sanctions. Alas no IGO in Asia and the Pacific has ever had that power; effective economic sanctions require a global commitment. (g) **Coercive power**: Etzioni referred to the ability of an organization to achieve goals by using military or police power. Several IGOs have been set up to promise military defense, as coded in the "scope" variable, though only Australia has sent troops in accord with a decision by a regional IGO, the Forum. (h) **Number of elite units**: Deutsch's dependent variable concept of role interchange is equivalent. (i) **Economic impetus**: None of the Asian-Pacific political-security IGOs analyzed herein were formed for exclusively economic reasons, but my Deutschian variable "economic expectations" is equivalent. (j) **Rewards before burdens**: What Deutsch called a "down payment" is what Etzioni referred to as "rewards before burdens." In most organizations, assessments to pay for the cost of a Secretariat are based on a sliding scale, taking into account the size of each country's gross domestic product (M.Haas 1989a,1989b). Accordingly, burden sharing is only disproportionate in organizations that lack Secretariats, as measured by the "budgets" variable.
5. Ernst Haas and Philippe Schmitter originally proposed eight conceptual variables, some of which are similar to those of Deutsch. The first four were called "background conditions"—in other words, independent variables: (a) **Functional similarity in size of units**: When member countries have an equal distribution of resources, they predicted success. The variable applies more to ASEAN than to the other organizations and is similar to the Deutsch's "role interchange" and Etzioni's "number of elite units." (b) **Rate of transactions**: Deutsch's "range of transactions" and "population mobility" are two variables subsumed by "rate of transactions." The present study, thus, ascertains whether the two operationalizations of transactions differ. (c) **Balance of pluralism**: When Haas and Schmitter wrote, some countries

were engaging in import substitution and thus imposed tariffs on outside goods. In the era of the World Trade Organization, that variable is obsolete and would bias statistical results to favor more recent IGOs. (d) **Elite complementarity**: The Deutschian "value compatibility" is what Haas and Schmitter applied to elites.

Haas and Schmitter also felt that two conditions at the time of the formation of an IGO were useful in predicting organizational success: (e) **Commitment to higher levels of cooperation**: My variable "scope" is equivalent. (f) **Organizational power**: My "budget" variable is one way of measuring what they had in mind.

Finally, Haas and Schmitter contrasted three process conditions after an IGO is formed: (1) **Expert decision making**: Haas and Schmitter fervently expected more progress when decisions are assigned to experts rather than to contentious political leaders. The use of experts is more extensive in economic matters rather than within political-security organizations, which could but rarely relies on military experts; but security communities might be more successful if their activities spilled over to economic matters. Accordingly, reliance on expert decisions has already been measured as one aspect of the dependent variable "scope." (2) **Transaction growth**: Haas and Schmitter distinguished between "rate of transactions," as previously discussed, and "transaction growth." "Rate" refers to absolute levels, "growth" to changes over time. I equate the latter term with my operationalization of Deutsch's "transaction range." (3) **Adaptibility**: Some organizations respond to new realities. ASPAC was formed to block China's admission to the UN, but in 1971 the Taiwanese government was unseated. ASPAC did not adapt and failed. Accordingly, my variable "survival" is an excellent rendering of adaptability.

But, having traced the Haas-Schmitter formulation, Mario Barrera and Philippe Schmitter later tried a more comprehensive set of operationalizations. See my comment on their efforts in note 2 of Chapter 1 above.

6. Ernst Haas (1975) undertook a later study to assess factors producing changes in 30 organizations. Five concepts defined changes in scope: (a) **Increased issue-areas**: My two "scope" variables capture broadening, which is what he had in mind. (b) **Increased intensity**: Some organizations deepen their focus, finding new ways to carry out activities in the same issue-areas, such as by adopting new interpretations of the mandate in the form of declarations and memoranda. Some Asian-Pacific IGOs have done so, but not enough to produce variability in a statistical coding. (c) **Increased budget or personnel**: It is a pity that data are not readily available for all Asia-Pacific organizations to measure such an excellent variable. (d) **Increased IGO-government consultation**: Haas was trying to determine whether organizations operate in a vacuum or interact with government officials. Organizations without formal Secretariats are much less likely to have an impact on governments, so my "budgets" variable would be one type of operationalization. (e) **Increased IGO-NGO consultation**: Many NGOs use ASEAN in their title, ASEAN

Bankers Association for example, so ASEAN would score high on his fifth concept. However, few Asian-Pacific IGOs rise to that level of visibility.

Ernst Haas's last five factors focused on increases in levels of activity: (f) **Increased membership**: I have adopted this concept as a dependent variable. In my earlier study, increased membership was significantly correlated with organizational survival (M.Haas 1986:Table 6). (g) **Binding decisions**: Thus far, no Asian or Pacific IGOs have developed supranational capabilities. (h) **Implementation of decisions**: To measure this concept, a researcher would have to determine the percentage of resolutions for action that were actually carried out, a most Herculean research task indeed. My assessment of organizational "strength" is equivalent. (i) **Increasingly cooperative decision making**: Due to the Asian Way and Pacific Way, cooperativeness is a defining characteristic of IGOs formed in both regions. Western powers in an organization tend to insert conflictual modes of interaction. My measure "value compatibility," thus, not only operationalized what Haas had in mind but also has a statistically significant relationship with organizational survival. (j) **Centralization in decision making**: Delegating more power to a Secretariat would be an important signal of organizational success. My variable "budgets" has a positive value only for IGOs that have formal Secretariats in the Asian and Pacific regions.

7. The respective eigenvalues of the eight factors are as follows: 3.8, 2.6, 2.1, 2.1, 1.8, 1.8, 1.6, and 1.4.
8. Those who celebrate the superiority of IGOs composed of democracies note that they are more likely to trust one another and therefore agree on more organizational details, including the development of supranational capabilities (Mansfield, Milner, and Rosendorff 2002; Boehmer and Nordstrom 2008; Mansfield, Milner, and Pevehouse 2008; Kahler 2000; Pevehouse and Russett 2006).
9. Yoran Haftel (2012) provides evidence that economically oriented regional IGOs engage in conflict resolution only after they develop strong Secretariats and attract the attention of top-level leaders at summit conferences. The data presented herein indicate that the development of economically-oriented IGOs is not a precondition for effective security communities and caution that purely statistical exercises need to be supplemented with historical evidence, as he does in the case of ASEAN.
10. Donald Emmerson (2007:437–438), relying on the much criticized ratings of Freedom House, finds the ASEAN Charter to be an agreement more in principle than in practice. He refers to ASEAN as "consociational," referring to the fact that ASEAN itself conducts meetings democratically—members show respect toward one another.

References

Acharya, Amitav. 2009a. "Bangladesh: Qualified Gains." *South Asia Intelligence Review*, 8: November.

———. 2009b. *Constructing a Security Community in Southeast Asia: ASEAN and the Problem of Regional Order*, 2nd ed. London: Routledge.

Acharya, Amitav and Alastair Iain Johnston. 2007. *Crafting Cooperation: Regional International Institutions in Comparative Perspective*. New York: Cambridge University Press.

Addington, Larry H. 2000. *America's War in Vietnam: A Short Narrative History*. Bloomington: Indiana University Press.

Adler, Emanuel and Michael Barnett. 1998. "A Framework for the Study of Security Communities." In *Security Communities*, ed. Emanuel Adler and Michael Barnett, Ch. 1. Cambridge: Cambridge University Press.

Aggarwal, Vinod K. and Min Gyo Koo, eds. 2008. *Asia's New Institutional Architecture: Evolving Structures for Managing Trade, Financial, and Security Relations*. Berlin: Springer-Verlag.

Al Jazeera. 2010. "Indian Police Killed by Maoists." www.aljazeera.com. April 6.

Anand, R. P., ed. 1981. *Cultural Factors in International Relations*. New Delhi: Abhinav.

Andemicael, Berhanykun, ed. 1979. *Regionalism and the United Nations*. Dobbs Ferry, NY: Oceana.

Angell, Norman. 1910. *The Great Illusion: A Study of the Relation of Military Power in Nations to Their Economic and Social Advantage*. New York: Putnam.

Asahi Shimbun. 2012. "China Cites Japanese Wartime History to Bolster Senkakus Claim." *Asahi Shimbun*, September 27.

Asia Pacific Economic Cooperation, Eminent Persons Group. 1993. *A Vision for APEC towards an Asia-Pacific Economic Community: Report of the Eminent Persons Group to APEC Ministers*. Singapore: Alexandra Group.

AsiaViews. 2010. "Mahathir Declares Friendly Truce in Thai-Malaysian War of Words." asiaviews.org. December 21.

Awanohara, Susumu and Nayan Chanda. 1993. "Uncommon Bonds." *Far Eastern Economic Review*, November 18: 16–17.

Bailes, Alyson J. K., Pál Dunay, Pan Guang, and Mikhail Troitskiy, eds. 2007. *The Shanghai Cooperation Organization*. Stockholm: Stockholm International Peace Research Institute.

Barrera, Mario. 1969. "Reply to Philippe C. Schmitter's 'Further Notes on Operationalizing Some Variables Related to Regional Integration." *International Organization* 23 (4): 969–970.

Barrera, Mario and Ernst B. Haas. 1969. "The Operationalization of Some Variables Related to Regional Integration: A Research Note." *International Organization* 23 (1): 150–160.

BBC News. 2006a. "Japan Fisherman Killed by Russia." August 16.

———. 2006b. "Peace Deal Ends Nepal's Civil War." November 21.

———. 2011. "South China Sea: Vietnamese Hold Anti-Chinese Protest." June 5.

———. 2012a. "China Approves Military Garrison for Disputed Islands." July 22.

———. 2012b. "Philippines and Muslim Rebels Sign Key Peace Plan," October 15.

Bearce, David H. 2003. "Grasping the Commercial Institutional Peace." *International Studies Quarterly* 47 (3): 347–370.

Bearce David H. and Stacy Bondanella. 2007. "Intergovernmental Organizations, Socialization, and Member-State Interest Convergence." *International Organization* 61 (4): 703–733.

Bearce David H. and Sawa Omori. 2005. "How Do Commercial Institutions Promote Peace?" *Journal of Peace Research* 42 (4): 659–678.

Bellamy, Alex J. 2004. *Security Communities and Their Neighbors: Regional Fortresses or Global Integrators?* New York: Palgrave Macmillan.

Bergsten, C. Fred. 1997. "Open Regionalism." *Working Paper* #97-3. Washington, DC: Peterson Institute for International Economics.

Boehmer, Charles and Tim Nordstrom. 2008. "Intergovernmental Organization Membership: Examining Political Community and the Attributes of International Organizations." *International Interactions* 34 (1): 282–309.

Bordadora, Norman and T. J. Burgonio. 2008. "Lawmaker Fears RP Will Lose Out in Race for Spratlys Oil." *Philippine Daily Inquirer*, July 30.

Boswell, Bronwin M. 2010. *The Evolution of International Policing in the Pacific: A Critical Analysis*. PhD dissertation, Victoria University of Wellington, New Zealand.

Bozeman, Adda B. 1960. *Politics and Culture in International History*. Princeton, NJ: Princeton University Press.

Bradsher, Keith and Andrew Jacobs. 2012. "Protests in China after Japanese Fly Flag on Island," *Washington Post*, August 11.

Breitmeir, Belmur, Arild Underdal, and Oran R. Young. 2011. "The Effectiveness of International Environmental Regimes: Comparing and Contrasting Findings from Quantitative Research." *International Studies Review* 13 (4): 579–605.

Brown, M. Leann. 1994. *Developing Countries and Regional Economic Cooperation*. Westport. CT: Praeger.

Buzan, Barry and Ole Wæver. 2003. *Regions and Powers: The Structure of International Security*. Cambridge, UK: Cambridge University Press.

Caballero-Anthony, Melli. 1998. "Mechanisms of Dispute Settlement: The ASEAN Experience." *Contemporary Southeast Asia* 20 (1): 38–67.

Callick, Rowan. 2010. "After All These Years, the ANZUS Freeze Begins to Thaw," *The Australian*, August 9.

Cantori, Louis J. and Steven L. Spiegel. 1973. "The Analysis of Regional International Politics: The Integration Versus the Empirical System Approach." *International Organization* 27 (4): 465–494.

Caryl, Christian. 2012. "The Slow Death of 'Asian Values'." foreignpolicy.com. January 18.

Chang, Jae-Soon. 2010. "S. Korea Working on Diplomatic, Military Options Against N. Korea." english.yonhapnews.co.kr, May 20.

Chappell, David A. 2005. "New Caledonia." *Contemporary Pacific* 17 (2): 435–448.

Cheng, Tun-Jen and Hung-Mao Tien. 2000. *The Security Environment in the Asia-Pacific*. Armonk, NY: Sharpe.

China Daily. 2012. "Diaoyu Islands Belong to China," *Los Angeles Times*, September 28 (advertisement).

Choe Sang-Hun. 2012. "South Korean's Visit to Disputed Islets Angers Japan." foreignpolicy.com, August 10.

Cobden, Richard. 1835. *England, Ireland and America, by a Manchester Manufacturer*. London: Ridgeway and Sons.

Collins, Alan. 2003. *Security and Southeast Asia: Domestic, Regional, and Global Issues*. Boulder, CO: Lynne Rienner.

Conboy, Kenneth J. 1994. *War in Laos, 1954–1975*. Carrollton, TX: Squadron/Signal Publications.

Copeland, Dale C. 1996. "Economic Interdependence and War: A Theory of Trade Expectations." *International Security* 20 (1): 5–41.

Crocombe, Ronald G. 1976. *The Pacific Way*. Suva, Fiji: Lotu Pasifika Productions.

Crone, Donald. 1993. "Does Hegemony Matter? The Reorganization of the Pacific Political Economy." *World Politics* 45 (4): 501–525.

Cutler, Thomas J. 2009. *The Battle for the Paracel Islands*. Annapolis, MD: Naval Institute Press.

Dash, Kishore C. 2008. *Regionalism in South Asia: Negotiating Cooperation, Institutional Structures*. New York: Routledge.

Datta-Ray, Sunanda K. 1984. *Smash and Grab: Annexation of Sikkim*. New Delhi: Vikas.

Deck, Richard. 1999. "Foreign Policy." In *The Singapore Puzzle*, ed. Michael Haas, Ch. 7. Westport, CT: Praeger.

Deegalle, Mahinda, ed. 2006. *Buddhism, Conflict and Violence in Modern Sri Lanka*. London: Routlege.

Deutsch, Karl W. 1953. *Nationalism and Social Communication: An Inquiry into the Foundations of Nationality*. New York: Wiley.

———. 1954. *Political Community at the International Level: Problems of Definition and Measurement*. Garden City, NY: Doubleday.

Deutsch, Karl W., Sidney A. Burrell, Robert A. Kann, Maurice Lee, Jr., Martin Lichterman, Raymond E. Lindgren, Frances L. Loewenheim, and Richard W. Van Wagenen. 1957. *Political Community and the North Atlantic Area: International Organization in the Light of Historical Experience*. Princeton, NJ: Princeton University Press.

Dixit, J. N. 2002. *India-Pakistan in War and Peace*. New Delhi: Books Today.

Domke, William, K. 1988. *War and the Changing Global System*. New Haven, CT Yale University Press.
Downs, George W., David M. Rocke, and Peter M. Barsoom. 1996. "Is the Good News about Compliance Good News about Cooperation?" *International Organization* 50 (3): 379–406.
Duffield, John. 2001. "Why Is There No APTO? Why Is There No OSCAP? Asia-Pacific Security Institutions in Comparative Perspective." *Contemporary Security Policy* 22 (2): 69–95.
Duyker, Edward. 1987. *Tribal Guerrillas: The Santals of West Bengal and the Naxalite Movement*. New York: Oxford University Press.
The Economist. 1991. "Asian Trade: Bigger, Maybe Not Better." March 9: 36.
Emmerson, Donald K. 2005. "Security, Community, and Democracy in Southeast Asia: Analyzing ASEAN." *Japanese Journal of Political Science* 6 (1): 165–185.
———. 2006. "Shocks of Recognition: Leifer, Realism, and Regionalism in Southeast Asia." In *Order and Security in Southeast Asia: Essays in Memory of Michael Leifer*, eds. Joseph Chinyong Liow and Ralf Emmers, pp. 10–28. New York: Routledge.
———. 2008. "ASEAN's 'Black Swans.'" *Journal of Democracy* 19 (3): 70–84.
Etzioni, Amitai. 1965. *Political Unification*. New York: Holt, Rinehart, Winston.
Fackler, Martin. 2012. "China and Japan Say They Held Talks about Island Dispute That Has Frayed Relations," *New York Times*, October 12.
Fall, Bernard. 1963. *The Two Viet-Nams: A Political and Military Analysis*. New York: Praeger.
Far Eastern Economic Review. 1991. "US Opposes Mahathir Over East Asia Group." *Far Eastern Economic Review*, March 14: 55.
———. 1994. "No Worries." *Far Eastern Economic Review*, July 21: 12.
Fernandez, Edwin O. 2011. "Philippines: Malaysian Peace Monitors Begin Work in Mindanao's Peace Efforts." warvictims.wordpress.com. March 13.
Firth, Stewart, Jonathan Fraenkel, and Brij V. Lal, eds. 2009. *The 2006 Military Takeover in Fiji: A Coup to End All Coups?* Canberra: Australian University Press.
Fisher, William E. 1968. "An Analysis of the Deutsch Sociocausal Paradigm of Political Integration." *International Organization* 23 (2): 254–290.
Fitch. 2012. "Mindanao Accord May Herald Boost for Philippines Growth," *Reuters*, October 9.
Foroutan, Faezeh. 1998. "Does Membership in Regional Preferential Trade Arrangement Make a Country More or Less Protectionist?" *The World Economy* 21 (3): 305–335.
Fortna, Virginia P. 2004. *Peace Time: Cease-Fire Agreements and the Durability of Peace*. Princeton, NJ: Princeton University Press.
Friedrich, Carl J. 1968. *Trends of Federalism in Theory and Practice*. New York: Praeger.
Fukuyama, Francis. 1992. *The End of History and the Last Man*. New York: Free Press.
Galtung, Johan. 1973. *The European Community: A Superpower in the Making*. London: Allen & Unwin.

Garrett, Geoffrey and George Tsebelis. 1996. "An Institutional Critique of Intergovernmentalism." *International Organization* 50 (2): 269–299.

Gartze, Erik. 1998. "Kant We All Just Get Along? Motive, Opportunity, and the Origins of the Democratic Peace." *American Journal of Political Science* 42 (1): 1–27.

Gartzke, Erik, Quan Li, and Charles Boehmer. 2001. "Investing in the Peace: Economic Interdependence and International Conflict." *International Organization* 55 (2): 391–438.

Garver, John. 1992. "China's Push through the South China Sea: The Interaction of Bureaucratic and National Interests." *The China Quarterly* 132 (December): 999–1028.

Ghosn, Faten, Glenn Palmer, and Stuart A. Bremer. 2004. "The MID3 Data Set: Procedures, Coding Rules, and Description." *Conflict Management and Peace Science* 21 (1): 133–154.

Glaser, Charles L. 1994/1995. "Realists as Optimists: Cooperation as Self-Help." *International Security* 19 (1): 50–90.

Goldsmith, Benjamin. 2007. "A Liberal Peace in Asia?," *Journal of Peace Research* 44 (1): 5–27.

Gordon, Bernard K. 1966. *The Dimensions of Conflict in Southeast Asia*. Englewood Cliffs, NJ Prentice-Hall.

———. 1981. "Japan and the Pacific Basin Proposal." *Korea & World Affairs* 5 (Summer): 268–288.

Grieco, Joseph M. 1993. "Anarchy and the Limits of Cooperation: A Realist Critique of the Newest Liberal Institutionalism." In *Neorealism and Neoliberalism: The Contemporary Debate*, ed. David A. Baldwin, pp. 116–140. New York: Columbia University Press.

———. 1999. "Realism and Regionalism: American Power and German and Japanese Institutional Strategies During and After the Cold War." In *Unipolar Politics: Realism and State Strategies After the Cold War*, ed. Ethan B. Kapstein and Michael Mastanduno, pp. 107–131. New York: Columbia University Press.

Grousset, Rene. 1963. *The Rise and Splendor of the Chinese Empire*. Berkeley: University of California Press.

Haacke, Jurgen. 2003. *ASEAN's Diplomatic and Security Culture: Origins, Developments and Prospects*. New York: Routledge.

Haas, Ernst B. 1958. *The Uniting of Europe*. Stanford, CA: Stanford University Press.

———. 1974. *Beyond the Nation State*. Stanford, CA: Stanford University Press.

———. 1975. *The Obsolescence of Regional Integration Theory*. Berkeley: Institute of International Studies, University of California, *Research Series*, #25.

———. 1976. "Turbulent Fields and the Theory of Regional Integration." *International Organization* 30 (1): 173–212.

Haas, Ernst B. and Philippe Schmitter. 1964. "Economics and Differential Patterns of Political Integration: Projections about Unity in Latin America." *International Organization* 18 (4): 705–737.

Haas, Michael. 1970. "International Subsystems: Stability and Polarity." *American Political Science Review* 69 (1): 98–123.

———, comp. 1971. *International Organization: An Interdisciplinary Bibliography.* Stanford, CA: Hoover Institution.

———. 1973. "The 'Asian Way' to Peace." *Pacific Community* Tokyo, 4 (July): 498–514.

———. 1974a. "The Asian Development Bank." *International Organization* 28 (2): 281–296.

———. 1974b. "International Integration." In *International Systems,* ed. Michael Haas, pp. 204–228. New York: Intext.

———. 1986. "Comparing Regional Cooperation in Asia and the Pacific." In *Toward a World of Peace: People Create Alternatives,* ed. Jeannette P. Maas and Robert A. C. Stewart, pp. 149–182. Suva, Fiji: University of the South Pacific.

———. 1989a. *The Asian Way to Peace: A Story of Regional Cooperation.* New York: Praeger.

———. 1989b. *The Pacific Way: Regional Cooperation in the South Pacific.* New York: Praeger.

———. 1991. *Genocide by Proxy: Cambodian Pawn on a Superpower Chessboard.* New York: Praeger.

———, ed. 1999. *The Singapore Puzzle.* New York: Praeger.

———. 2008. *International Human Rights: A Comprehensive Introduction.* New York: Praeger.

———. 2011a. Barack Obama, *The Aloha Zen President: How a Son of the 50th State May Revitalize America Based on 12 Multicultural Principles.* Santa Barbara, CA: Praeger.

———. 2011b. *Modern Cambodia's Emergence from the Killing Fields: What Happened in the Critical Years?* Los Angeles, CA: Publishinghouse for Scholars.

———, ed. 2012. *Korean Reunification: Alternative Pathways,* 2nd ed. Los Angeles, CA: Publishinghouse for Scholars.

Haftel, Yoran Z. 2007. "Designing for Peace: Regional Integration Arrangement, Institutional Variations, and Militarized Interstate Disputes." *International Organization* 61 (1): 217–237.

———. 2010. "Conflict, Regional Cooperation, and Foreign Capital: Indonesian Foreign Policy and the Formation of ASEAN," *Foreign Policy Analysis* 6 (2): 87–106.

———. 2012. *Regional Economic Institutions and Conflict Mitigation: Design, Implementation, and the Promise of Peace.* Ann Arbor: University of Michigan Press.

Hansen, Roger. 1969. "Regional Integration: Reflections on a Decade of Theoretical Efforts." *World Politics* 21 (2): 242–271.

Harlan, Chris. 2012. "South Korea Underscores Its Claim to Islands Disputed with Japan." *Washington Post,* October 4.

Harvey, Rachel. 2009. "Papua's Struggle for Independence." *BBC News,* March 13.

Heo, Uk and Shale A. Horowitz, eds. 2003. *Conflict in Asia: Korea, China-Taiwan, and India-Pakistan.* Santa Barbara, CA: Praeger.

Higgot, Richard Andre Fenton Cooper, and Fenelle Bonnor. 1994. *Cooperation-Building in the Asia-Pacific Region: APEC and the New Institutionalism.* Canberra: Research Committee of the Australia-Japan Research Centre, Australian National University.

Hoffmann, Stanley. 1965. *The State of War: Essays on the Theory and Practice of International Politics.* New York: Praeger.

Hoon, Shim Jae. 1991. "Growing Pains: Formalisation of APEC Group to Loom Large at Talks." *Far Eastern Economic Review,* November 14: 27.

Huffer, Elise. 2011. "Regionalism and Cultural Identity: Putting the Pacific Back into the Plan." In *Globalization and Governance in the Pacific Islands,* ed. Stewart Firth, Ch. 3. Canberra: Australian National University. epress.anu.edu.au.

Hughes, John. 2002. *The End of Sukarno–A Coup that Misfired: A Purge That Ran Wild,* 3rd ed. Singapore: Archipelago Press.

Huntington, Samuel P. 1993. "The Clash of Civilizations?" *Foreign Affairs* 72 (3): 22–50.

Hurrell, Andrew. 1995. "Regionalism in Theoretical Perspective." In *Regionalism in World Politics: Regional Organization and International Order,* ed. L. Fawcett and Andrew Hurrell, Ch. 1. New York: Oxford University Press.

———. 2001. "The Politics of Regional Integration in Mercosur." In *Regional Integration in Latin America and the Caribbean: The Political Economy of Open Regionalism,* ed. Victor Bulmer-Thomas, pp. 194–211. London: Institute of Latin American Studies.

Hutchins, Robert Maynard. 1948. "The Constitutional Foundations for World Order." In *Federal World Government,* ed. Julia E. Johnson, pp. 108–119. New York: Wilson.

Hutt, Michael. 2004. *Himalayan People's War: Nepal's Maoist Rebellion.* London: Hurst.

Ikenberry, John G. 2001. *After Victory: Institutions, Strategic Restraint, and the Rebuilding of Order After Major Wars.* Princeton, NJ: Princeton University Press.

Ikenberry, John and Anne-Marie Slaughter. 2008. "Democracies Must Work in Concert." *Financial Times,* July 10.

Inder, Stuart. 1987. "Leaders and Their Legacies." *Pacific Islands Monthly* 58 (12): 27.

Indorf, Hans H. 1984. *Impediments to Regionalism in Southeast Asia: Bilateral Constraints among ASEAN Member States.* Singapore: Institute of Southeast Asian Studies.

International Crisis Group. 2011. "The Communist Insurgency in the Philippines: Tactics and Talks." crisisgroup.org, February 14.

Jervis, Robert. 1982. "Security Regimes." *International Organization* 36 (2): 357–378.

———. 1999. "Realism, Neoliberalism, and Cooperation." *International Security* 24 (1): 42–63.

Jeshuran, Chandran. 2007. *Malaysia: Fifty Years of Diplomacy, 1957–2007.* Petaling Jaya, Malaysia: Other Press.

Jones, Daniel M., Stuart A. Bremer, and J. David Singer. 1996. "Militarized Inter-state Disputes, 1816–1992: Rationale, Coding Rules, and Empirical Patterns." *Conflict Management and Peace Science* 15 (2): 163–213.

Jorgensen-Dahl, Arnfinn. 1982. *Regional Organization and Order in South-East Asia*. Hong Kong: Macmillan.

Kabutaulaka, Tarcisius Tara. 2005. "Australian Foreign Policy and the RAMSI Intervention in Solomon Islands." *Contemporary Pacific* 17 (2): 283–305.

Kahler, Miles. 2000. "Legalization as Strategy: The Asia-Pacific Case." *International Studies Quarterly* 54 (3): 549–571.

Kaltman, Blaine. 2007. *Under the Heel of the Dragon: Islam, Racism, Crime, and the Uighur in China*. Athens: Ohio University Press.

Kant, Immanuel. 1795. *Perpetual Peace*. New York: Liberal Arts Press, 1957.

Keohane, Robert. 1982. "The Demand for International Regimes." *International Organization* 36 (2): 141–171.

Khoman, Thanat. 1983. "Pacific Interdependence: Development of Pacific Economic Cooperation Concept." In *Pacific Economic Cooperation: The Next Phase*, ed. Hadi Soesastro and Han Sung-Joo, pp. 208–213. Jakarta: Centre for International and Strategic Studies.

Kiernan, Ben. 2003. "The Demography of Genocide in Southeast Asia: The Death Tolls in Cambodia, 1975–1979, and East Timor, 1975–1980." *Critical Asian Studies* 35 (4): 585–597.

Kim, Kiwhan and Soogil Young, eds. 2005. *The First Twenty-Five Years*. Singapore: Pacific Economic Cooperation Council International Secretariat.

Kim, Won-Ho, Heungchong Kim, and Jehoon Park. 2011. "A Comparative Analysis on Regional Integration Communities and Implications for East Asia: A Regional Index Approach." In *Regionalism, Economic Integration and Security in Asia: A Political Economy Approach*, ed. Jehoon Park, T. J. Pempel, and Heungchong Kim, Ch. 4. Northhampton, MA: Elgar.

Kindleberger, Charles. 1981. "Dominance and Leadership in the International Economy: Exploitation, Public Goods, and Free Riders." *International Studies Quarterly* 25 (2): 242–254.

Koremenos, Barbara, Charles Lipson, and Duncan Snidal. 2001. "The Rational Design of International Institutions." *International Organization* 55 (4): 761–799.

Kyodo News. 2012a. "Japan to Crank Up PR Over Senkakus Dispute With China." *Kyodo News*, September 28.

———. 2012b. "U. S. Says Senkaku Islands Fall Within Scope of Japan-U.S. Security Treaty." *Kyodo News*, July 10.

Lake, David A. 1997. "Regional Security Complexes: A Systems Approach." In *Regional Orders: Building Security in a New World*, ed. David A. Lake and Patrick M. Morgan, pp. 45–67. University Park: Pennsylvania State University Press.

Langhammer, Rolf J. and Ulrich Hiemenz. 1990. *Regional Integration among Developing Countries: Opportunities, Obstacles, and Options*. Kieler Studien, #232. Tubingen: JCB Mohr.

Lam, Willy Wo-Lap. 2003. "China Renews Taiwan Threat of War." cnn.com. November 18.

LaRocco, Tim. 2011. "ICJ Rules on Preah Vihear." the-diplomat.com. July 19.
Leadbeater, Marie. 2011. "The Bougainville Peace-Broking Experience Revisited." *Peace Researcher*, 42 (November).
Leifer, Michael. 1973. "The ASEAN States: No Common Outlook." *International Affairs* 49 (4): 600–607.
———. 1989. *ASEAN and the Security of South-East Asia*. London: Routledge.
Lemke, Douglas. 2002. *Regions of War and Peace*. Cambridge, UK: Cambridge University Press.
Lyon, Peter. 1969. *War and Peace in South-East Asia*. London: Oxford University Press.
McCargo, Duncan. 2008. *Tearing Apart the Land: Islam and Legitimacy in Southern Thailand*. Ithaca, NY: Cornell University Press.
McDonell, Stephen and Helen Brown. 2012. "China, Indonesia Wary of US Troops in Darwin." abc.net.au. November 17.
McElroy, Damien. 2012. "Burma Ends One of World's Longest Running Insurgencies After Peace Deal with Karen Rebels," telegraph.co.uk, January 12.
Mackey, Robert, 2012. "Report Says U.N. Failed in Sri Lanka," *New York Times*, November 13.
Mahathir bin Mohamad, Datuk Seri. 1992. "Look East: Proposed East Asia Economic Caucus." *New Perspectives Quarterly* 8 (Winter): 16–19.
Mak, J. N. 2009. "Sovereignty and the Problem of Maritime Cooperation in the South China Sea." In *Security and International Politics in the South China Sea: Towards a Cooperative Management Regime*, ed. Sam Bateman and Emmers Ralf, pp. 110–127. London: Routledge.
Mansfield, Edward D. 2003. "Preferential Peace: Why Preferential Trade Arrangements Inhibit Inter-State Conflict." In *Economic Interdependence and International Conflict: New Perspectives on an Enduring Debate*, ed. Edward D. Mansfield and Brian M. Pollins, pp. 222–236. Ann Arbor: University of Michigan Press.
Mansfield, Edward D. and Helen V. Milner. 1999. "The New Wave of Regionalism." *International Organization* 53 (3): 529–627.
Mansfield, Edward D., Helen V. Milner, and Jon C. Pevehouse. 2008. "Democracy, Veto Players, and the Depth of Regional Integration." *The World Economy* 31 (1): 67–96.
Mansfield, Edward D. Helen V. Milner, and B. Peter Rosendorff. 2002. "Why Democracies Cooperate More: Electoral Control and International Trade Agreements." *International Organization* 56 (3): 477–513.
Mansfield, Edward D. and Jon C. Pevehouse (2000). "Trade Blocs, Trade Flows, and International Conflict," *International Organization* 54 (4): 775–808
Mansfield, Edward D., Jon C. Pevehouse, and David H. Bearce. 1999/2000. "Preferential Trading Arrangements and Military Disputes." *Security Studies* 9 (1): 96–118.
Mansfield, Edward D. and Jack Snyder. 1995. "Democratization and the Danger of War." *International Security* 20 (1): 5–38.
———. 2002. "Democratic Transitions, Institutional Strength and War." *International Organization* 56 (2): 297–337.

Mara, Ratu Sir Kamisese. 1971. *Selected Speeches.* Suva, Fiji: Government Press.

Mearsheimer, John J. 1994/1995. "The False Promise of International Institutions." *International Security* 19 (1): 5–49.

Mitrany, David A. 1943. *A Working Peace System.* Chicago: Quadrangle, 1966.

Moravscik, Andrew. 1991. "Negotiating the Single European Act: National Interests and Conventional Statecraft in the European Community." *International Organization* 45 (1): 19–56.

Morgenthau, Hans J. 1948. *Politics Among Nations: The Struggle for Power and Peace.* New York: Knopf.

Mytelka, Lynn Krieger. 1973. "The Salience of Gains in Third-World Integrative Systems." *World Politics* 25 (2): 236–250.

News China. 2005. "China and Bhutan Agree to Equal and Amicable Talks in Order to Resolve the Border Issue Quickly." news.china.com. December 1.

Nye, Joseph S. 1971. *Peace in Parts: Integration and Conflict in Regional Organization.* Boston: Little, Brown.

Padden, Brian. 2011. "ASEAN Mediates in Cambodia, Thai Dipsute." voanews.com. February 22.

Pan, Junwu. 2009. *Toward a New Framework for Peaceful Settlement of China's Territorial and Boundary Disputes.* Leiden: Martinus Nijhoff.

Pazzibugan, Dona Z. and Jerry E. Esplanada. 2011. "US, Philippines Start War Games." globalnation.inquirer.net. October 17.

Perlez, Jane. 2012. "Beijing Exhibiting New Assertiveness in South China Sea." *New York Times*, May 31.

Pevehouse, Jon C. and Bruce Russett. 2006. "Democratic International Governmental Organizations Promote Peace." *International Organization* 60 (4): 969–1000.

Rapoport, Anatol. 1960. *Fights, Games, and Debates.* Ann Arbor: University of Michigan Press.

Ravenhill, John. 2001. *APEC and the Construction of Pacific Rim Regionalism.* New York: Cambridge University Press.

———. 2002. "A Three Bloc World? The New East Asian Regionalism." *International Relations of the Asia Pacific* 2 (2): 167–195.

Rediff. 2002. "Chronology of India-China Relations, 1962–2002." rediff.com. Accessed November 16, 2012.

Rees, Jacqueline. 1993. "Out in the Open: Keating Opts for Snap Election." *Far Eastern Economic Review*, February 18: 19.

Reuters. 2012. "Japan Protests Chinese Ships Entry into Waters Near Disputed Isles." *Reuters*, July 11.

Richburg, Keith, William Wan, and William Branigin. 2011. "China Warns U.S. in Island Dispute." *Washington Post*, June 23.

Robinson, Geoffrey. 2010. *"If You Leave Us Here, We Will Die": How Genocide Was Stopped in East Timor.* Princeton, NJ: Princeton University Press.

Russett, Bruce, John R. Oneal, and David R. Davis. 1998. "The Third Leg of the Kantian Tripod for Peace: International Organizations and Militarized Disputes, 1950–85." *International Organization* 52 (3): 441–467.

Samad, Paridah Abd. and Darusalam Abu Bakar. 1992. "Malaysia-Philippine Relations: The Issue of Sabah." *Asian Survey* 32 (6): 554–567.

Schmitter, Philippe C. 1969a. "Further Notes on Operationalizing Variables Related to Regional Integration." *International Organization* 23 (2): 327–336.

———. 1969b. "Three Neo-Functional Hypotheses about International Integration." *International Organization* 23 (1): 161–166.

———. 2005. "Ernst B. Haas and the Legacy of Neofunctionalism." *Journal of European Public Policy* 12 (2): 255–272.

Shannon, Megan, Daniel Morey, and Frederick J. Boehmke. 2011. "The Influence of International Organizations on Militarized Dispute Institution and Duration." *International Studies Quarterly* 54 (4): 1123–1141.

Siddharth, Veena. 2005. "Next Steps for Aceh After the Peace Pact." *Jakarta Post*, August 27.

Sihanouk, Norodom. 1980. *War and Hope: The Case for Cambodia*. New York: Pantheon.

Simon, Sheldon W. 1990. "ASEAN Security in the 1990s." In *ASEAN into the 1990s*, ed. Alison Broinowski, pp. 111–137. London: Macmillan.

Singer, J. David and Michael Wallace. 1970. "Intergovernmental Organizations and the Preservation of Peace, 1816–1964: Some Bivariate Relationships." *International Organization* 24 (3): 520–547.

Slaughter, Anne-Marie. 2012. "Syria Is Not a Problem from Hell." foreignpolicy.com. May 31.

Slim, Randa M. and Faredun Hodizoda. 2002. "Tajikistan: From Civil War to Peacebuilding," conflict-prevention.net.

Smith, James McCall. 2000. "The Politics of Dispute Settlement Design: Explaining Legalism in Regional Trade Pacts." *International Organization* 54 (1):137–180.

Soesastro, Hadi. 1983. "Institutional Aspects of Pacific Economic Cooperation." In *Pacific Economic Cooperation: The Next Phase*, ed. Hadi Soesastro and Han Sung-Joo, pp. 3–52. Jakarta: Centre for Strategic and International Studies.

Sohn, Louis B, comp. 1971–1972. *Basic Documents of African Regional Organizations*. Dobbs Ferry, NY: Oceana.

Solidum, Estrella D. 1974. *Towards a Southeast Asian Community*. Quezon City: University of the Philippines Press.

Solomon Times. 2012. "Pacific Plan Achievements in the Past Year." *Solomon Times* (Solomon Islands), August 17.

Sopiee, Noordin. 1983. "ASEAN and the Pacific Basin Concept: Questions and Imperatives." In *Pacific Economic Cooperation: The Next Phase*, ed. Hadi Soesastro and Han Sung-Joo, pp. 198–201. Jakarta: Centre for Strategic and International Studies.

Spear, Percival. 1960. *The Oxford History of India*, 3rd ed. New York: Oxford University Press.

Spyros, Melitsas. 2011. *Interregionalism: The Case of FEALAC*. Athens, Greece: Institute of International Economic Relations.

Stephan, John J. 1974. *The Kuril Islands: Russo-Japanese Frontier in the Pacific*. Oxford: Clarendon Press.

Streit, Clarence K. 1943. "United States Federal Union as a Model for World Organization." In *World Peace Plans*, ed. Julia E. Johnson, pp. 149–151. New York: Wilson.

Tan, Andrew. 2000. *Intra-ASEAN Tensions*. London: Royal Institute of International Affairs.

Tasker, Rodney. 1994. "Signs of Life: Japan Warms towards East Asian Caucus." *Far Eastern Economic Review*, September 15: 20–21.

Taylor, Alistair M. 1960. *Indonesian Independence and the United Nations*. London: Stevens & Sons

Thant, Myo, Min Tang, and Hiroshi Kakazu, eds. 1998. *Growth Triangles in Asia: A New Approach to Regional Economic Cooperation*, 2nd ed. New York: Oxford University Press.

Thayer, Carlyle (2007). "New Faultlines in ASEAN?," *Asia-Pacific Defence Reporter*, 33 (2): 26–28.

Tiglao, Rogoberto. 1994. "Growth Zone." *Far Eastern Economic Review*, February 10: 40–45.

Tsebelis, George and Geoffrey Garrett. 2001. "The Institutional Foundation of Intergovernmentalism and Supranationalism in the European Union." *International Organization* 55 (2): 357–390.

Tusicisny, Andrej. 2007. "Security Communities and Their Values: Taking Masses Seriously." *International Political Science Review* 28 (4): 425–449.

van der Kroef, Justus M. 1978a. "ASEAN Security and Development: Some Paradoxes and Symbols." *Asian Affairs* 6 (3): 143–160.

———. 1978b. "Irian Jaya: The Intractable Conflict." *Asian Affairs* 6 (2): 119–133.

Vatikiotis, Michael. 1991. "The Morning AFTA: Asean Takes Tentative Step towards Free-Trade Area." *Far Eastern Economic Review*, October 24: 64–65.

Väyrynen, Raimo. 2000. "Stable Peace through Security Communities? Steps towards Theory-Building." *Occasional Paper*, #18: OP: 3. Notre Dame, IN: Kroc Institute for International Peace Studies.

Wade, Francis. 2009. "ASEAN Calls for Burma Prisoner Release." intelsecuworld.com. July 23.

Wæver, Carol. 2011. "Black Sea Regional Security: Present Multipolarity and Future Possibilities." *European Security* 20 (1): 1–19.

Wallander, Celeste A. and Robert O. Keohane. 1999. "Risk, Threat, and Security Institutions." In *Imperfect Unions: Security Institutions Over Time and Space*, ed. Helga Haftendorn, Robert O. Keohane, and Celeste Wallander, pp. 21–47. Oxford, UK: Oxford University Press.

Waltz, Kenneth N. 1979. *Theory of International Politics*. Reading, MA: Addison-Wesley.

Weir, Fred. 2010. "Kyrgyzstan Riots Led to Ethnic Cleansing; Government Blames Bakiyev." *Christian Science Monitor*, June 16.

Weitz, Richard. 2008. "Russia, China End Decades-Long Border Dispute." *World Politics Review*, August 1.

West, Bing. 2011. *The Wrong War: Grit, Strategy, and the Way Out of Afghanistan*. New York: Random House.

Wilson, Edward O. 2012. *The Social Conquest of Life*. New York: Liveright.

Yamo, Henry. 2011. "Human Rights 'Fundamental' in Member Countries and Worldwide, Says UN Chief." pacific.scoop.co.nz. September 7.

Yue, Chia Siow and Mari Pangetsu. 2006. "Rise of East Asian Regionalism." In *Reshaping the Asia Pacific Economic Order*, ed. Christopher Findlay and Hadi Soesastro, Ch. 7. London: Routledge.

Zakaria, Fareed. 1994. "A Conversation with Lee Kuan Yew." *Foreign Affairs* 73 (March–April): 109–126.

Zaw, Aung. 2008. *Burma: The Censored Land*. Chiang Mai, Thailand: Irrawady Publishing Group.

Index

9781137304391